BACK IN
THE GARDEN WITH
Dulcy

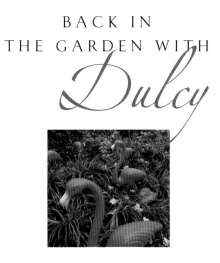

BACK IN
THE GARDEN WITH

THE BEST OF *THE OREGONIAN* GARDEN WRITER
DULCY MAHAR

Compiled and edited by TED MAHAR

Carpe Diem Books®

PORTLAND, OREGON

To Dulcy, Doug and Peggy

Introduction and Dulcy Mahar columns © 2013 Ted Mahar
Photographs and illustrations © as credited below

Carpe Diem Books®
8136 NW Skyline Boulevard
Portland, OR 97229
carpediembooks.com

First Edition

ISBN 978-0-9897104-0-4

Library of Congress Cataloging-in-Publication Data available.

Publisher: Ross Eberman
Project Director: Richard Owsiany
Acquiring Editor / Publicity: Gregory Mowery
Editor: Tricia Brown
Designer: Beth Hansen-Winter
Sales: Ken Rowe

Indexer: Cher Paul
Editorial Assistant: Jean Andrews
Prepress Consulting and Color Management:
   William Campbell, Mars Premedia
Promotional Photography: © 2013 Michael Shay,
   Polara Studio

Manufactured in China: Multicolor Media Production Limited

First Printing 2013

PHOTO CREDITS BY PAGE—Doug Beghtel: xxiiib Lower; Loree Bohl, DangerGarden.blogspot.com: xxiii Top; Marv Bondarowicz: ii, v, viii, x, xi, xii, xiv, xxii, xxiv, xxv, 2, 6, 9, 10, 14 Top left, 14 Top right, 14 Lower right, 15, 19, 21, 25, 35, 44, 45, 47, 51, 55, 59, 63, 77, 80, 84 Lower, 85, 94, 96, 105, 107, 112 ABC, 114, 116, 121, 123, 131, 136, 140, 147, 149, 154, 158, 161, 163, 165, 166, 169, 171, 174, 181, 183, 184, 186, 187, 189, 196, 198, 201, 202, 206, 212, 214, 217 Top left, 217 Top right, 217 Center right, 217 Lower right, 219, 223, 226, 228, 232, 234, 239; Ellie Daniels: 125 Top; Dreamstime Stock Photos: 204; Ross William Hamilton: i; Beth Hansen-Winter: Endpapers; Roger Jensen: 61; Dulcy Mahar: vi, 29, 39, 57, 98, 102, 128, 135, 142, 191, 194, 217 Lower left, 262; Ted Mahar: xxvi, 70, 78, 122, 125 Lower, 237, 240; Historical photos courtesy Ted Mahar: xvii, xviii, xx; James Merrell: 86; Photo Art Studio: xv, xxi; Sherrie Rieger © 2013 Sherrie Rieger, sherrierieger.com: 22, 32, 65, 68, 72, 74, 82, 84 Top, 90, 111, 120, 127, 138, 210, 230, 238, 243; Stickpen/Wikimedia Commons: 178. Loma Smith: Front cover. ILLUSTRATION CREDITS—Rene Eisenbart: 28, 41, 145, 208, 250, 251.

Cover: A tranquil moment amid flowers and friends. Page ii: Choosing plantings for height, color and texture is an art in itself. Page vi: Dulcy documented her own garden, as well as others that she visited, in pictures.

Dulcy, Ted and Orville.

Acknowledgments

Heartfelt thanks to the hundreds who sent in letters and emails over the years and in Dulcy's final days.

For your assistance in producing this book of columns and bringing it to Dulcy's readers: Tricia Brown, Greg Mowery, Ross Eberman, Dick Owsiany, Mary Volm and Beth Hansen-Winter.

My own relationship with *The Oregonian* had its occasional "Who's Afraid of Virginia Woolf?" aspect. Dulcy was far luckier in dealing with extremely sympathetic editors by email and phone, and her relationship was like something out of a fairy tale. For this, my gratitude to *The Oregonian* is unbounded.

Contents

At the end of the day . . .

FLAMINGOS, GNOMES AND THE QUEEN OF HEARTS

I N JULY OF 2011, FLOCKS OF FLAMINGOS LANDED IN PACIFIC NORTHWEST GARDENS, roosting in everything from fancy formal grounds to pots on apartment balconies. Many of the vivid plastic birds that had previously settled into neighborhood yards donned black ribbons. The kitschy icons were, alas, marking the passing of longtime garden writer Dulcy Mahar.

Or, as she was known throughout the Pacific Northwest gardening community, simply "Dulcy."

Her garden was a highlight on tours, she was a popular speaker at gardening events—and she had pretty much revolutionized readers' gardens.

Under her tutelage, gardeners tossed out the idea of mimicking the neighbors with lawn and trimmed-to-the-nth-degree hedges. Readers wrote and told her that because of her they'd embraced flamingos, gnomes, shade gardens, water features, and countless plants they had never heard of before.

More importantly, they thanked her for giving them permission to be brutal: If they accidentally killed a plant, hey, OK. Dulcy admitted she had done that. If they hated some garden gem, it didn't matter. Like the Queen of Hearts in *Alice in Wonderland*: Off with their heads! Note after note thanked Dulcy "for giving me permission to let my yard reflect me!"

Each week her lively columns—sometimes instructional, sometimes intimate, always a pleasure to read—brought readers into her 2½-story home on three-fifths of an acre in Portland's Garthwick neighborhood. When she and her husband, Ted, opened her home and garden on tours, readers loved seeing for themselves the plantings, art, pets and, most of all Dulcy.

Despite being a rock star of the Northwest gardening community, she was ever warm and gracious. Readers most often described her as "the best friend I never met."

Her passing was not a surprise. She'd been diagnosed with Stage III ovarian cancer in 2003 and had shared with readers small mentions of chemo treatments and the latest prognosis. On June 18, 2011, when the cancer spread to her brain, readers were notified her column had come to an end. Two weeks later, on July 2, 2011, Dulcy died at age 69.

There had been a column, week in and week out, for more than 22 years. Her columns started in *The Oregonian*'s "Living" section in the spring of 1989, and moved to the newspaper's "Homes & Gardens of the Northwest" when the section was started in March of 1997. In all, she wrote more than 1,200—a chunk of them still rest in readers' gardening manuals, scrapbooks, and files all over town.

When she died, readers besieged the "Homes & Gardens" section with requests to run columns they had loved and saved that, somewhere over time, had slipped away. To an overly eager husband on recycling duties. In a move from one house to another. Sent off to a friend/mother/daughter. Shared with a neighbor. *Please*, they said. *Keep running them.*

Please, they repeatedly said, *tell Ted to produce a book.* At last, here it is.

To her longtime readers, we hope you find your favorite column in here or discover a new favorite.

To those who never had a chance to meet Dulcy or read her columns before, step into her world. You're in for a treat.

Just be forewarned: Your garden—and your attitude toward it—may never be the same.

> —Peggy McMullen, Editor
> *The Oregonian*'s "Homes & Gardens of the Northwest"
> November 2009 through September 2013

Dulcy, enjoying a Virgin Mary
during one of her frequent travels.

Dulcy wrote about her garden with wit and transparency, from trying to keep her fish alive to dealing with a fallen tree just days before a Garden Tour.

When Doug turned 40, Dulcy promoted him from Doug the Wonder Boy to Doug the Wonder Guy.

Preface
CULTIVATION OF THE HEART
By Douglas Wilson (aka "Doug the Wonder Guy")

I LEFT MY BUSINESS CARD ON DULCY'S GARDEN GATE SEVERAL TIMES. I READ DULCY'S column, but didn't realize that it was *her* garden I had found while pushing my son around in his stroller. I never got a call and assumed there was already a gardener at that house, and stopped leaving cards and flyers.

Some months later, I built a reflecting pool and tiny Japanese garden for Dulcy's neighbors, Walt and Rosemary Ellis. Dulcy and Ted were invited to the little garden's unveiling.

I guess Dulcy was impressed. I was stunned when she asked if I would be interested in helping her with her garden, even more so when I realized that it was her gate I had been harassing with my flyers and business cards.

We agreed to meet early on a Thursday morning before she left for work. That misty June morning, I followed a trail of small piles of weeds and deadheads into the back garden and found Dulcy, thronged by cats and a little brown dog named Hector, dead-heading a climbing rose.

After introductions to Marian and Princess and Hector and The Perp, we began a winding walk along garden paths. As Dulcy talked about her plans, she pointed and waved her arms in great, sweeping motions as if conducting an invisible orchestra.

I began to realize that Dulcy saw a garden that wasn't there . . . yet. After an hour of walking in circles, talking excitedly, occasionally visiting the terrace to look at pictures in books and magazines, Dulcy came to rest next to a 6-foot-tall fireweed that had some-how avoided the hoe. Dulcy appeared not to notice the behemoth weed. A wry smile came to her face, she leaned forward and almost whispered, "Keep an eye out while you're working, Doug. I suspect Rosemary is transplanting weeds from her garden into mine."

That pattern would repeat for 15 years. On cold winter days and later, when she was sick from chemo, we would sit upstairs in the den by the fire. Dulcy surrounded by garden books, magazines and mystery novels, at least two cats and a little brown doggie on her lap.

We very seldom talked about politics, current events, religion or cancer, choosing instead lighter fare—flowering bulbs, French potagers, soil microorganisms, the advantages of twine over twist-ties. We laid down knot gardens, worried over late frosts and false springs, agreed on composting regimes and argued about pruning. Gradually I, too, began to see gardens that weren't there yet.

Dulcy became my dear friend, co-conspirator, and eventually my "mom away from mom," complete with occasional doses of tough love. I am blessed to still be collaborating with Dulcy on her garden. Sometimes she is the fluttering white butterfly that follows me through the garden.

Doug's Vegetable Garden, circa 1997. Doug and Dulcy engaged in many "discussions" surrounding the merits of planting veggies.

Introduction

A LOVE THAT BLOOMED

By Ted Mahar

T HERE ARE NO SECOND ACTS IN AMERICAN LIVES," WROTE F. SCOTT FITZGERALD. IT is also quoted as: "There are no second acts in the lives of American writers." Either way, Dulcy Mahar's life and career was the perfect refutation of Fitzgerald's grim dictum, derived from his own sad life. Dulcy had a dozen or so acts, and the one that defined her most publicly came five-sevenths of the way through her life: garden columnist for *The Oregonian.*

Dulcy entered the world as Dulcy Ann Marie Moran on Nov. 10, 1941, in Stockton, California. Her distinctive name came from her aunt, Dulcy Mullarkey, whose only son had drowned shortly before my Dulcy was born. Dulcy spent World War II on the Moran cattle ranch in the San Joaquin Valley. Being the only child for miles, Dulcy befriended the ranch cats, dogs and other critters. Her closest friends were a huge, battle-scarred male cat called Mary Anne and a 600-pound porker known as Hoggie Dear. Dulcy named both.

In 1989, Dulcy began a weekly column that continued for 22 years. She produced some 1,140 garden columns, never missing a deadline, never skipping a week, even for international travel, even for terminal illness. She was perfect for the job; it was perfect for her.

Readers enjoyed Dulcy's column for the encouragement to get started, wade in, give it a try. They found permission to give up and tear out dying shrubs, to move plantings around until they found a place to thrive, to break out of a gardening rut and experiment. She inspired. Her columns roved into the whimsical, the sociological, even the philosophical. Her editors requested only that she include at least one particle of garden advice per column.

Perhaps most famously, Dulcy made readers laugh, partly by parading her own mistakes ("I learn by trial and error and error and error"), her confessions of dislike for certain plants, her love for her garden companions: visitors, pets and coworkers of the

Dulcy at the University of Oregon.

soil. They came to know her heart week by week, year after year. So often, a piece of fan mail would begin or end with "I feel like I know you," words that always warmed Dulcy.

Perhaps most surprising to those who religiously followed her columns in those two decades is this: She was never trained in horticulture. Before starting her column she never took a class in garden design. Afterward her career allowed time to take no more than a half-dozen classes. She never imagined being a garden columnist until she suddenly became one. But Dulcy was an avid student. Her library of gardening books and magazines grew—into the hundreds—with her garden. She studied constantly, gleefully. She loved what she was learning, loved what she was doing, and loved sharing her excitement.

Writing was a crucial thread in both our lives. As early as age 17, Dulcy was a salaried newspaperwoman on her hometown paper in Pittsburg, California, and spent each college summer break back in the newsroom. A Navy brat, I finished most of my junior year and my senior year in Coos Bay, Ore., where I was editor of the Marshfield High School newspaper. Then, like Dulcy, I worked for a local paper upon graduation. Our psyches crossed at the University of Oregon in January 1960, where I was writing and editing for the student paper, the *Oregon Daily Emerald*.

Dulcy was slim, pretty and richly auburn-haired. While not overtly outgoing, she was lively and made friends easily. It was not love at first sight, but we saw each other almost daily on the *Emerald*. We had much in common and enjoyed each other's company. One huge factor soon preceded all else: Our senses of humor meshed. We made each other laugh.

Writing was, in fact, an essential part of our courtship. In summer 1960, while I worked on a Forest Service road crew in Oregon, Dulcy and I wrote every week. We fell in love through the mail, but didn't write love letters. We didn't have to. It was between the lines. And in time, we realized we were chatting our way into marriage. For the next 51 years, we would make each other laugh.

We graduated in a time that now seems unimaginable. Newspapers and magazines came looking for us. Recruiters visited campuses. Dulcy didn't bother meeting them, because we would simply go wherever I was hired, the common presumption in ancient times. I took *The Oregonian*'s offer because it was the best of four, plus *The O* let me start upon graduation. The others would take me only after I had served my six months' National Guard active duty at Fort Ord, Calif., which would begin on Aug. 29.

We married on June 15, 1963, in Eugene. I began pulling on the oars at *The O* on June 20. After we returned to Portland in May 1964, Dulcy found that a journalism degree, a sheaf of clippings, professional experience and bracing references got her exactly nothing. Some local papers did not like my *"Oregonian* connection." Other editors felt free to blithely tell Dulcy that she was a 22-year-old bride who would soon be pregnant and out of the work force. (In fact, we never had any human children.) Still, most said they did like her clippings.

The result was that Dulcy began her career as a part-time sales clerk in the Meier & Frank toy department at Christmas 1964. She studied the Meier & Frank employee daily news bulletin and found it not particularly newsy. She wrote a three-page memo to Jack Meier suggesting improvements. After a brief conference with Meier, Dulcy found herself

Dulcy and Ted in the Oregon Daily Emerald *office.*

editor of an expanded daily bulletin of her own devising. Three years later she became editor of the US Bank magazine, *Banknotes,* and was a US Bank officer at age 25.

After five happy years Dulcy accepted a lucrative offer to edit the company magazine at Omark Industries, but just a few years later accepted a far more challenging job as communications manager for the Oregon Education Association. She happened to enlist at a historic moment when brand new laws gave Oregon teachers the right to collective bargaining with the previously unimagined power to strike. It opened a new world to Oregon in general and Dulcy in particular.

On my 26th birthday, I became what *The Oregonian* then called Drama Editor. I reviewed all movies and plays, plus many concerts and cultural events. It required regular night work. Our schedules were rarely routine. I had two weeks' annual National Guard active duty at Fort Lewis for three years, then for 20 years in the Naval Reserve in various

Pets were a passion for us, even before we married. Here we are with Ragnel the cat in Coos Bay, 1962.

coastal locales or on ships. Dulcy traveled for her work; I traveled for mine; both of us worked odd hours at times. *The O* sent me to the San Francisco Film Festival for a week every year for 20-plus years. We were apart fairly often. But our union was solid.

We found a crucial aspect of our relationship in Khalil Gibran's *The Prophet*, a book of mystical essays that was hugely popular when we were dating. The chapter called "Marriage" contained a line that we found provocative: "Let there be spaces in your togetherness." Gibran's metaphors included the solid columns of a sturdy temple and "the strings of a lute, alone, though they quiver with the same music." We discussed this chapter from time to time with, naturally, no idea that it would be something of a blueprint for our future.

And then there was our love of animals, especially cats. This may strike some as irrational, trivial, silly, embarrassing, what-have-you. And it's easy to say that pets drew the affection we would have given to children. But we would have had as many pets as we did, kids or not.

The cliché about pets is that they give us unconditional love. My late friend Homer Groening, a skilled filmmaker whose famous son is Matt, offered my favorite metaphor

Dulcy and Ragnel.

for artistic creativity and love: "The object of painting is not to cover the wall. It's to empty the can." Our satisfaction—indeed, a profound need—is not just to get unconditional love. It is to give it. Over the years Dulcy and I had seven dogs and more than four dozen cats.

As young marrieds, Dulcy and I—and multiple pets—lived in apartments and a rental house. In 1968 we bought our first home at 3356 NE Alameda Street. Dulcy puttered, and we both did maintenance work. But the lot offered little opportunity beyond house plants, borders, small shrubs and a pair of Japanese maples.

We enjoyed being tourists in our own region. We often drove through Eastmoreland on the way to or from a drive, and one fact captivated us: We were always driving under a canopy of tree limbs. Friends in the neighborhood, Sol and Lois Maizels (operators of the Aladdin Theatre), tipped us to a bungalow for sale a block down the hill from them, on Knapp Street, across SE 27th Avenue from the Eastmoreland Golf Course. We moved in July 1976.

It was here that the love of gardening seemed to sneak up on Dulcy. Our Eastmoreland lot began to pry at Dulcy's burgeoning creativity. She was in her mid-30s when her passion began to bloom. Whenever she had to travel for her full-time job, she gave me increasingly meticulous instructions on how to babysit particular plants—always including watering the fuchsias hanging on the front porch. This new interest subtly competed with her career. Serious gardening began to demand attention and dedication that her full-time career didn't always permit. It was as if Dulcy had become a mom and juggled time to devote to her new infant.

She began reading systematically about plants and gardens. She eagerly joined the Eastmoreland Garden Club—only to be politely ejected a few months later for non-attendance of meetings, which were weekday mornings. Working women need not apply.

Opportunity knocked when Dulcy wasn't looking. After a lengthy and increasingly strenuous career as Communications Manager for the Oregon Education Association, she was head-hunted by the Northwest Power Planning Council in 1980, relieving her of a highly stressful position and launching her on a 30-year communications career in Northwest electric power, fish and wildlife conservation.

As the OEA communications manager, she got her first taste of statewide fame and found it fairly bitter. She was a spokesperson for teachers both statewide and in local communities where she went to advise teachers on how to communicate with the public and within their own systems. She was also a lobbyist in five legislative sessions, an often disillusioning adventure. She was always the only Dulcy in the news, and at social gatherings she sometimes took heat from people who didn't like unions in general and a teachers' union in particular. As an OEA representative she had to be as charming as possible. After she joined the Power Planning Council and began to describe her job to polite questioners, she was near bliss as she watched their eyes begin to glaze.

By 1985, Dulcy had gradually gardened up every reasonable space in our Eastmoreland yard. By reflex her eyes now began scanning for a larger canvas. They settled

Picnicking in our yard, about 1990.

on a two-and-a-half story house on three-fifths of an acre in Garthwick, a community whose south and west sides border the Waverly Country Club. We moved in on a chilly January 9, 1986. The flat, empty backyard could have held two croquet games. The front yard could have accommodated another, if a bit elongated.

That spring she began buying the first of the plants that would create Dulcy's Garden. This avocation became a major aspect of her waking hours, far more vital than a hobby. A lifelong art lover and student, Dulcy had tried painting and ended up burning most of her efforts (to my frequent regret). The Garthwick garden at last engaged her artistic urges as fully as she desired, and the results energized and defined her. She had finally found her way to empty the can.

In 1989, I was still happily ensconced at *The O*, writing a weekly column about upcoming TV movies, and an eight-times-weekly column about theater-run movies. My desk was near features editor Katy Muldoon. One day I overheard Katy hang up her phone and gleefully announce that she needed a new garden columnist. Instantly, I suggested Dulcy and tipped her by phone. Dulcy called Katy minutes later, they chatted, and Katy asked for three sample columns.

(Someone who worked for Dulcy at the Council tried to sandbag her. When Dulcy announced in her office that she was trying out for the sudden garden writer job, this woman scuttled into her office, closed the door and phoned Katy. She claimed to be a far better writer and gardener than Dulcy, that she should get the job, and Dulcy should not

be considered. Right after the call, Katy asked if I knew this woman. I said yes and related some painful facts. Katy decided not to complicate her own life by calling this woman back.)

In retrospect, Dulcy's bidding for the garden column seems stupendously impetuous. For decades, Dulcy had written voluminously— newsletters, press releases, news features, training manuals,

Dulcy on Kauai, 1992.

An aerial of our house, the summer before we moved in.

speeches for herself and others, editorials, and so on—and had done prodigious editing. But a column is a unique challenge. Being a good writer is barely the beginning. One becomes one's own assignment editor, a challenge that can be formidable when one first encounters it. More important, one must develop what is called "legs." Many a columnist can thrive for a while, but when one hews to the chore for a year or two, the limited number of tricks in the bag can become apparent.

Also, unpredictably, a kind of monotony can form around what was once a source of pleasure. I've known film critics who got tired of both films and criticism, as unimaginable as it seems to me. Moreover, a regular column makes demands on time and energy far beyond what a freelancer's fee could compensate. It must be done for fun. Or love.

Thus began a 22-year phenomenon. Dulcy's famous sense of whimsy sprouted tentatively but soon, and Dulcy's editors indulged her. For one, they were simply grateful. Dulcy sent in pristine copy, cleanly written, precisely edited and ready to run. For another, her editors were readers, too. They liked her work.

During the years that Dulcy wrote for the paper, she continued to work full time— more than full time, really—for first, the Northwest Power Planning Council and then the

Doug the Wonder Boy, hard at work, circa 2000.

Bonneville Power Administration. Her actual career denied her the time to do the book she wanted—this one—but enabled her to afford the lavish garden she wanted more.

Dulcy's Garden never looked the same two years in a row, and she soon learned that she needed a partner to help realize her vision. For six or seven years, Dulcy worked with Megan Torrance in the garden, until Megan married and started a family.

Next, she joined forces with a young man, Douglas Wilson, who became known as "Doug the Wonder Boy" in Dulcy's columns—gaining his own following among readers. Over the next 15 years, the relationship between Doug and Dulcy evolved into something more than partners, closer to mother and son. They fortuitously shared the same wavelength in sense of humor (rarely cited as a garden skill). On Doug's fortieth birthday, Dulcy promoted him to "Doug the Wonder Guy" in the column, feeling "Wonder Boy" was outdated.

Through the years, Dulcy and Doug had discussions, friendly disagreements, compromises and adventures, some highly successful, others requiring the application of the erasers: shears, shovels and trowels.

Despite the column's crucial importance in Dulcy's life and mine, it was more hobby than work. Her freelance income from the column was nearly invisible in our family finances. Dulcy mothered it, not for money, but for love. And she always had plenty to write about, typing in her home office, surrounded by cats and open reference books with Post-its. Dulcy virtually never set foot in *The Oregonian*, but instead sent in her columns with a few key strokes. Although she knew and liked her editors, their chats were all by email.

A unique voice emerged, and Dulcy's column became one of the paper's most popular features. It was what we call an easy read, a clear, direct style that somehow feels conversational, as if she had dashed it off quickly and easily. In fact, anyone watching her type it could also believe that. She typically wrote it on Sunday evenings in time for *Masterpiece Theatre*.

And yet, by the time Dulcy began typing, she had spent a week—in increments—

researching, planning, and pondering. The columns were filled with solid advice, warnings, lists, ideas and experiments worth trying, the latest trends, yearnings for a change of season, and more. Whatever the subject, Dulcy's wit glowed through. Pick a week, and you'd likely find a quotable quote.

In later years her whimsy leafed into a quirky fondness for plastic pink flamingos, the quintessence of kitsch. This stirred a new, steady flow of cards, letters, emails and photos from equally quirky readers about or depicting pink flamingos. But, while her pink flamingo columns amused many of Dulcy's readers, others felt that the ersatz birds were

Part of the jolly pink flock.

tacky beyond whimsy. A few wrote that they were tired of the flamingos, and even Dulcy's editor asked her to ease up on the birds.

Dulcy regularly opened her garden for charitable fund-raising causes—at least a dozen times most years—and many visitors came as much to meet Dulcy as to enjoy her garden. Some remarked that her column "sounded" just the way she spoke. The garden,

Remembering Dulcy at an open garden event at Garthwick.

Dulcy at work; Wilbur at leisure, 2009.

her column, and her steady stream of admiration came to define a major part of Dulcy's life— and at the ideal time.

Walter Cronkite famously said for years that he had retired too soon. Sadder examples are legion—singers, actors, authors and other celebrities who peaked early, faded, and then trudged through the rest of their lives in decades of obscure aftermath. But Dulcy wrote until she could write no more. She even submitted a column the week in March 2003, when she was diagnosed with Stage III ovarian cancer. She brought me the news while we were sitting at the kitchen table. We cried together and tried to settle our thoughts enough to imagine what lay ahead. It was inconceivable. Still, she didn't miss a beat at work, or with her column.

Major surgeries in March and September, with chemotherapy in between, seemed to do the trick. The day before Dulcy's September 15 operation, we surprised ourselves by getting two cats from PAWS Animal Shelter in West Linn. We kept the names PAWS had given them, Orville and Wilbur. They had been tenderly fostered and arrived at our house as affectionate kitties. They craved human contact and instantly took a liking to our dog Hector, which was great, for all three liked to pile onto Dulcy's bed.

Dulcy called Orville and Wilbur her "cancer kitties." As she recuperated from surgery at home that fall, the cats and Hector packed themselves around her, providing a comfort beyond the reach of medicine. They never let up. Words cannot convey what those cats and our other pets meant to Dulcy.

As a pitiless reminder, in the months and years following March 2003, cancer cut friends and acquaintances from our lives, among them our charming garden artist friend from the Canby area, Susan Nebeker; Vancouver landscaper and sculptor Les Bugajski; and a dear, longtime friend, Alex McPhail (he and his wife Denise had spent every Christmas Eve with us since 1975). A bitter blow to Dulcy was the loss of Jeanne Maras, sister of neighbor Maggie Jarman, who was diagnosed with the same cancer as Dulcy just a month earlier in 2003. Dulcy's cancer returned in early 2005. But Jeanne seemed to do fine for much longer. But, as those in the cancer community know: cancer learns. In 2008, Jeanne died at age 61. Her illusory success had wistfully cheered Dulcy for years.

Cancer also reached meanly into our household to take our beloved 13-year-old dog Hector in June 2008. Dulcy wrote about his passing in her column, and the next month we expanded our household with a rescue dog from a veterinarian. We named him Ernie Pie. (Few people get the Ernie Pyle reference; very few, always old.)

Bringing new pets into the family was claiming normalcy and future. By embarking on a trip to Hawaii, or buying a new "plantmobile" (a 2006 Honda CRV she named Gertie, after garden giant Gertrude Jekyll), or flying to England and Europe for garden tours, Dulcy staked her place in this living world. And she refused to stop working.

Why don't you just retire, enjoy the garden, and write that book? People often asked her that question. And she always politely replied that she was pondering it. What she did not say was that she did not want copious leisure time to think about cancer.

What is it like to know that I will die in a very finite future? I have almost no idea, despite living intimately for six years with someone in exactly that vise. It would be easy to say that the ordeal made us closer, but we had never been far apart except, occasionally, geographically. The experience just made our time together more precious.

Dulcy loved for me to read to her, and I loved doing it. We did this in our early married years, but it fell by the wayside as our careers got more complicated. After her diagnosis, we revived it. It was usually at her bedtime. My sonorous voice was as good as cocoa, better than a pill.

Just as precious was another nightly routine. Once Dulcy got into years of chemo, she suffered neuropathy in her feet, complicated by her diabetes. This produces a paradoxical mix of pins and needles and numbness. Our treatment was foot rubs. For her last six years Dulcy got a minimum 90-minute foot rub every night. It did Dulcy good in one way, me in another.

Dulcy's friends rallied and visited her at the end. But when Dulcy died in our

Dulcy and I posed with Wilbur on our veranda, 2008.

living room hospice at 2 a.m. on Saturday, July 2, only a nurse and I were in the house. Orville was asleep on the couch. Ernie was curled up on the floor by her bed. Wilbur snoozed on Dulcy's bed. It was as she pictured it for years. I was holding her hand when she gave up her last breath.

In the days that followed, those attending the three memorials to Dulcy drove along Garthwick streets spotted with pink whimsies. In tribute, more than half the front yards in Garthwick had suddenly sprouted pink flamingos, from two to six or more in each yard. Most are still there.

As I write to introduce this collection of my Dulcy's garden columns—with Orville and Wilbur snoozing on my lap—I imagine one of her favorite settings, a dinner gathering in our garden, say a mid-July evening when the slanting amber light casts a warm glow, and a soft breeze stirs the motes in the shafts of light. I am telling this tale to a circle of Dulcy's friends, cool libations in hand. Many writers of letters and emails said that they felt they knew Dulcy through her columns. I was touched by the many who used a similar phrase: "a friend I never met."

To Dulcy's last weeks she had the satisfaction of her garden, her column, and the affection of her readers. I hope that this book will help them to feel that they can still be acquainted with their friend.

Wilbur always loved shoulders, especially Dulcy's, 2009.

Part 1

PLANT LUST

❦

I started the season by buying two more clematises,

for which I have no trellis, post, frame or whatever else to grow them on.

This means I will have to find at least four trellises,

because last fall I also bought two clematises.

Hydrangea blooms display vibrant color; reason enough to plant more than one.

PHASES OF THE LOON

Obsession with gardening sneaks up on you gradually

I AM MINDFUL THAT JUST AS GARDENS HAVE seasons, gardeners have phases. For many of us, they seem to follow this pattern.

Unsuspecting new homeowners: Mow the lawn, set the sprinklers, whack back the blackberries snaking over the fence. I mean, we've got company coming, kids to raise, bicycles to ride. Who has time to garden?

The serpent in the apple tree: Saw a plant and just couldn't resist. Read some instructions and realize it needs something called compost. Whaddya know, it's blooming. Maybe I'll try more.

Before you know it: Went with friend to a nursery. She plunked a bunch of things in my wagon. No idea what they're supposed to be, but she calls them perennials. Got a "how to" book so I'll know what to do with them.

The nose under the tent: Started digging up a bit of lawn, just a tiny bit. Talked spouse into helping turn over soil and ladle this compost stuff in. (Turned him off gardening for life. Really.)

Dawning realization: Hmmm, maybe this plant would look nice next to this one. Read you should plant in drifts for effect. Maybe should pay more attention to putting things together. Bought some garden design books with fabulous pictures.

Astounding discovery: Not all shrubs are rhododendrons. They have red, gold, and variegated foliage as well as green. What fun. It's a whole new world.

The hook that gets you: Wouldn't it be swell to plant a tree or two and be able to sit under them when we're old? There's some-thing sooooo symbolic about a tree. (Now we're getting mystical.)

Obsession takes root: Hoo-hah. Spring arrives and brings with it a whole new meaning to lust. Read some catalogs over winter and must try every new cultivar (new word is evidence of growth). Even came home from work to plant by flashlight.

The root spreads: Just realized the importance of different textures, as well as colors. It's not just about flowers anymore, but foliage too. Getting sophisticated now. Even throwing out Latin names oblivious to horrendous pronunciation. *Is it CLEMatis or CleMATis?*

And now over the top: Going to plant lectures, joining plant groups, visiting open gardens, boring nongardeners at dinner parties. Coming home from a nursery with plants on every seat, the floor, and my lap.

Wake-up call: What happened? There's a jungle out there. Barely room to wedge another plant in. Where did the lawn go? Why is my back sore? Maybe the idea of a condo isn't so bad.

The fantasy: Time to relax, sit on the garden bench and read a good—no, not good, but fun—book. Life is good.

The reality: Uh-oh. Isn't that a weed I see over there?

SEPTEMBER 2, 2010

❧

TAKING IT EASY

The lazy approach to gardening

A UGUST IS A FINE MONTH TO JUST WALLOW. The dog days of summer are no time to be planting or digging, and fall, with its frenzy of cleanup, isn't far away.

So we deserve a little break, don't we? And while we're awash in indolence, it's also a great time to pass along shortcuts for the lazy gardener. Some of these will make purists break out in black spots. But, while I hold such gardeners in great esteem, I am by nature alternately energetic and loutishly lazy.

I admit it. I cheat on how far down I plant bulbs. I water roses with an overhead sprinkler. I don't dig up my dahlias for the winter; they seem to come back just fine, too. And, rather than getting rid of an old tree stump, I simply put a bowl on top and called it a birdbath.

I've learned not to get into a fight with a tough broad, Mother Nature.

I hardly ever turn the compost pile, which seems to cook despite neglect. I don't prune much, rationalizing that it's the overgrown cottage garden look I'm after. I plant too closely rather than staking, and I've been known to plop a pretty pot down to fill a hole in a flowerbed and pretend it's there for artistic effect.

Also, with the exception of roses, I simply don't fertilize. I do, however, add compost each year, and I suppose some of that breaks down into nutrients. Obviously a few heavy-feeding plants, such as delphiniums, won't do well. But most of my flowers come back year after year in relatively good health.

In perfecting a lazy approach to gardening, I've learned not to get into a fight with a tough broad, Mother Nature. If there's a perpetually wet spot in the garden, I don't work hard at getting it to drain well. I simply go with the flow, so to speak, and put in a bog garden.

There's a particularly bad sinkhole in the back of our garden where all the water pools after a rain or sprinkling. I've filled it with gravel, lined it with rocks, and stuck in a trio of pottery fish designed by Portland artist Katy McFadden. It's still a bog, but now it's an arty bog.

At the other extreme, there's a dry strip on the far side of the driveway that's unreachable by the sprinkler system and difficult to reach with a hose. It's planted with whatever happened to survive over the years with no watering. As it turns out, it's a pretty collection of plants, including yarrow, lambs' ears, euphorbia, and other drought-tolerant plants.

My ultimate coup of laziness was getting rid of some sod and creating a no-dig flowerbed in a single stroke. A few years back, I removed the sod to widen a flower border in the front garden.

At first I didn't know where to put the sod. Then I mounded it around a big plum tree in the back, laying it right over the existing grass that grew beneath the tree. About a foot of topsoil went over the top. We planted it with ferns and shade-loving ground covers.

It formed a lovely little island around the tree, and I never had to do a bit of digging. By the time the roots of the new plants had reached down to the sod below the topsoil, the sod had broken down into a nice compost-soil mixture.

You can make a no-dig planting mound right over existing grass with straight topsoil. If you use sod, as I did, under your soil, remember to lay the sod with the grass-side down so the grass doesn't continue to grow. Also, if you're forming an island bed under a true blue. The bushes were upright and compact and had long stems that bore flowers that had Olympian staying power when cut. Best of all, they bloomed non-stop from spring to late summer.

Soon, gardens everywhere had tidy rows of rose bushes. The floppy, full-figured old roses with their flat faces fell out of favor throughout most of the 20th century. But just when it seemed that romantic old roses with the sensuous names of countesses, duchesses, queens and mistresses were about to disappear, the renaissance began. It began with the return to old-fashioned flowers, spurred by the country look in interior design.

The rose was revered in Islam, too. Legend had it that the rose sprang from the drops of the Prophet's sweat during his journey to Paradise.

Roses seemed to have sprung up in nearly every part of the Northern Hemisphere except for the most inclement regions. There is no evidence that they existed naturally in the Southern Hemisphere.

The flower got its biggest boost in the early 19th century, thanks to the Empress Josephine. Bored by Napolean's long absences out conquering the world, she began creating the first world-class rose garden at the Malmaison just outside of Paris. Her goal was to include one of every kind of rose in her garden. It became so famous that the English allowed shipments of roses to the empress to pass even though France and England were at war.

Josephine's real coup was commissioning Pierre-Joseph Redoute to illustrate her roses.

It's no wonder Oregonians have a love affair with the rose.

But she died before Redoute's great three-volume work, *Les Roses*, was published. Redouté's work covered the classes of old roses. Oldest of the Western roses are the gallicas, which likely came to England from the crusades; the damasks, that date to Egypt and were imported to Greece and Rome; and the albas that go back to 100 B.C. Next came the centifolias, a product of Dutch hybridizers in the 1500s, the moss roses from the next century, followed by the Bourbons, hybrid perpetuals, and Noisette. The latter, dating to 1818, is the first hybrid rose developed in the United States.

The China and tea roses (so called because their leaves smell like tea where bruised) came to Europe in the late 18th century.

There is even a hybrid of the damasks and China teas, known as the Portland rose, named for the Duchess of Portland.

Old roses also include wild roses, such as the rugosas and sweetbriars. The sweetbriar

Black spot is the bane of the rose garden, but some roses are resistant.

is the eglantine rose mentioned by both Chaucer and Shakespeare.

JUNE 2, 1991

❦

FIELD STUDY
Another year, another harvest of lessons

I LIKE TO THINK THAT THE ADAGE THAT YOU'RE never too old to learn is true. Here are 20 things I learned this past year.

1. You can't trust the calendar to tell you when it's time to plant annuals and vegetables. In an interview in *BBC Gardeners' World*, Irish garden expert Helen Dillon says you need to sit on the ground to feel if it's warm enough to sow seeds.

2. The pond you carefully designed and built will turn out to be too small. You should decide the perfect size and then double it.

3. It's convenient to buy garden books on the Internet, but not nearly as much fun. You miss the thrill of the hunt. *Horticulture* magazine noted, "The fun is the serendipity of picking up a book that you didn't even know existed."

4. Northwest gardens are as good as private gardens anywhere. You should take advantage of any and all open gardens.

5. Every garden should have a path. That's the key difference between a garden that you just look at and a garden that you experience with all senses.

6. You need to wear thick leather gloves when you are repotting stickery plants.

7. You should use either very cheap pots or

A garden path, a resting place, a focal point—all important lessons in developing a garden.

very heavy pots on the front porch to avoid having them stolen.

8. Setting aside just one small area that will change each year can reinvigorate both you and your garden.

9. If you want to get your garden in shape, sign up to open your garden to visitors. You have no idea how it will spur you to get things done by a target date.

10. With the exception of lilies and alliums, summer-blooming bulbs may be among the most overlooked plants.

11. It helps to think of a flowerbed the way you would a vase of flowers. It works better with foliage between the spots of color. That advice comes from *Garden Life* magazine, and I like the analogy.

12. A small, boxy backyard will look more interesting if you make a circular central lawn and plant around it, rather than a square of lawn. Seems to be a no-brainer, yet so few of us do it.

13. You should always read the label about how big a plant will grow. I thought I was purchasing a Bambi, but when I got it home and looked it up, it turns out it is a King Kong. It is still sitting in its pot.

14. If you're expecting visitors and don't have much time to get the garden in shape, the most important thing you can do is edge the lawn. It will give an instant manicured look to your garden, kind of like the way a new haircut spiffs us up.

15. You should check with your utility before doing any major digging. No, I didn't pick that up from shocking experience, but I did get a news release from my friendly utility and think it's important to pass on.

16. Never gather seeds when it's damp. They'll either rot or try to germinate. I read that in *Gardens Illustrated*.

17. You should always check inside your boots before putting them on. I learned that in person, and also that boots make receptacles for fur balls.

18. You shouldn't be fooled by sunny days and take things out of the greenhouse too early. The nights are still cold. That's how I killed my third *Melianthus*.

19. It's a good idea to stagger vegetable planting, unless you are really into salads morning, noon and night.

20. You don't need to grow them all. That's another bit of advice from Helen Dillon, and I'm not sure it's a lesson I've really learned well.

DECEMBER 22, 2005

OF MYTH AND MONEY
When wives stoop to garden, husbands stoop to folly

I ATTENDED A DINNER PARTY RECENTLY. IN ALL, there were four couples, and all of the wives gardened. With a vengeance, you might say.

One couple, who live on the Clackamas River, had their garden laid out by a well-known landscape architect. After the preliminary planting, the husband arrived at the home of the second couple, who lived just down the road, and pulled the man aside. Looking out over the garden, he asked earnestly, do you have any idea what this has cost?

He was, it appeared, having the garden version of sticker shock. His wife explained to us that he thought once the garden was designed and the primary plants put in, that was the end of it.

The husbands at the table all nodded

sympathetically at how the poor man had been taken in. The wives all marveled at how anyone could be so foolish. Everyone knows, of course, that once your garden is designed and planted, it is not the end of things. In fact, it is just the beginning. That is the way of gardens.

It is even, sometimes, the point at which a previously uninvolved homeowner, who just wanted someone to come in and make the yard look "nice," discovers a latent interest in gardening. And it is not unusual for that interest to develop into full-blown plant lust.

My boss is a prime example of this. Her husband gave her a gift certificate for a garden makeover for Christmas. By late winter, the design firm had delivered a design plan and plant list.

After that, a contingent of the office gardeners spent most of our lunch hours in her office going over the plan and questioning the plant choices. My boss was asking, "What's an *Escallonia*?" and we were saying things like, "How come there are so many escallonias?"

And every one of us was insisting that she add to her plant list one or more of our favorite plants. "There's no witch hazel," I said. "You must have one." And, believe me, I wasn't the worst of the so-called advisers. The fact that we hadn't actually seen the land in question did not deter the flow of opinions on how it must be planted.

I can only imagine what the design firm thought when she returned to them with all these suggested changes. In fact, if I were a professional garden designer, I would insist on a contract clause that says, "You must

> *"Why can't you guys have a cheaper hobby?"*

never, ever share this plan with anyone you know who gardens."

I did bring in some plant books so my boss could see pictures of what the proposed plants would look like. As the weeks went by, she was tossing off Latin names with the best of us. By spring, she was itching to go to a nursery. Fortunately, or perhaps unfortunately, there is a very nice nursery within driving distance of where we work. We can just make it there and back on our lunch hour. This has led to some very expensive lunch hours.

Given how my boss is shopping, I am sure that her husband, like the husbands at the dinner party, is finding that the installed design and plants he gave her for Christmas are just the starting point. He has probably learned now that he has given the proverbial gift that keeps on giving—and costing.

You see, it is almost impossible to give someone a garden all planned and planted and expect that to be the end of it, except for routine maintenance. There is something about a garden that wakes a desire to actually pick up a trowel and poke in the dirt. There are exceptions, of course. My husband has never been moved to pick up a trowel by the sight of a spring bloom. This is as deeply mysterious to me as my gardening thrall is to him.

As for the husbands at the dinner party, once they had gotten over discussing the out-of-control gardening habits of their wives, one of them asked, "Why can't you guys have a cheaper hobby?" Another husband chimed in and said, "Yeah, Nordstrom's, like regular wives."

At which point, we four wives nearly fell off our chairs laughing. Cheaper indeed. Do they never learn?

MAY 4, 2006

❧

OBSESSED
Plant collecting . . . is it wrong?

IN THIS MONTH'S ISSUE OF *BBC GARDENERS'* *World*, a reader poses the question to the magazine's team of four writers: "Of all the thousands of garden plants, if you could collect just one group, what would you choose and why?"

One writer adores *Pulmonaria* (lungwort) for their extraordinary foliage, and another would collect climbing roses. The third admits to being a *Primula* (primrose) man, and the fourth raves about his collection of exotic edibles such as bananas, guavas, and pineapples.

Falling in love with a particular plant group is always a risk if you garden long enough, and the smaller the garden, the bigger the risk because obsessions have a way of taking over. Certain flowers always have had their enthusiasts and lend themselves to collections— roses, dahlias, chrysanthemums, hostas, primulas, and rhododendrons, to name the obvious.

> *Ken Druse groups collectors into four categories: hunters, missionaries, specialists and aesthetes.*

Some would say this is a no-brainer, since each of these plant genera has so many varieties, making them easier to collect. But the mania for collecting pushes breeders to cultivate new hybrids to meet collectors' demands. So it's one of those chicken-and-egg issues.

Not all collections focus on a particular genus. Some collections arise out of particular plant traits such as plants with variegated leaves or particular habitat such as rock garden plants.

Lately, it's become quite the thing to collect unusual, rare or new cultivars. Euphorbias are big. So are heucheras (coral bells), thanks to Portland hybridizer Dan Heims, who has gained national fame for his introductions of plants with fabulously variegated foliage—principally heucheras and pulmonarias.

Personally, I've been pretty proud of myself for resisting the urge to be a collector. When it comes to gardening, moderation is not high on my list of virtues.

This year, however, I fear I may have succumbed. As I look back, I realize, in a single year, I purchased about a dozen varieties of clematis. And, looking over my list of must-haves for next year, several varieties of clematis are near the top.

I even went so far as to swap a pretty little *Franklinia* tree for a clematis when I was walking out of a Hardy Plant Society meeting. The clematis owner and I had each won the plants as door prizes. She looked at my plant with a look that I will politely describe as healthy interest. I gazed at her plant with similarly undisguised plant lust. Our eyes met. And before you could say *Clematis integrifolia*, the swap had been made.

Ken Druse, who wrote *The Collectors'*

An obsessed gardener will never be satisfied with just one of anything.

Garden, has several theories about why people become collectors. He groups these people into four categories. Hunters are the gardeners on the prowl for anything new or different. Missionaries are driven to save threatened plants by growing them in collections. Specialists are fascinated by a particular taxonomic group or particular habitat. And aesthetes have fallen in love with the appearance of a particular plant.

When it comes to clematis, I'm in the latter group. I concede there's nothing cutting edge about my newfound fascination with this vine. Many have blazed this trail before, and I'm merely a new recruit. But I have all the signs of a collector, and so do you if you have experienced some of the symptoms.

Symptoms of obsession:

• This past year, you bought five or more plants in a particular genus.

• You gouged a small, helpless victim with your umbrella at a plant sale so you could distract her while you grabbed a plant in your selected genus.

• You have the Billy Bob syndrome. You can't say the plant name without spewing out several varietal names. As in, "I adore *Clematis texensis* 'Gravetye Beauty,' don't you?"

• When meeting someone who has an interest in the same plant group, you can sustain a conversation on said plants for 20 minutes without noticing that all your guests have quietly excused themselves.

• You are either a member of or seriously considering membership in a group dedicated to a particular plant group. That way, you won't have to politely limit yourself to only 20 minutes on the subject.

NOVEMBER 19, 1998

LUST VS. LIST
Some gardeners plan, others just fall in love

THE OTHER DAY I WAS LUNCHING WITH friends when I had the strongest urge. A single fuzzy-headed weed was sprouting up in an otherwise lovely window box outside the restaurant. I desperately wanted to lean out the window and pluck the poor thing. It would, however, have made a rather bad scene as I have zero sense of balance and it was, after all, someone else's property.

Nevertheless, the urge was strong, and I couldn't figure out why. Then it came to me. Spring is finally upon the land, bringing with it the pulsating sensations of a new growing season. I didn't expect it to hit me so hard again. I'd resolved to cut back and focus on other things besides my garden.

But there it was. I could feel the world around me percolating with the throb of little plants poking their noses skyward, the rush of leaves unfurling, the bursting of trees into pink and white ballerinas. The plants were organizing for a symphony, and soon they would burst forth into a crescendo.

It makes me want to run out to a nursery right this minute, no matter that I've misplaced all the must-have plant lists I made over the winter. Well, I didn't really make the lists; I thought about it during my winter of indolence.

I've often wondered how the results would be different if I went off to a nursery with a carefully planned list as opposed to just going off and—as so often happens—falling in love with plant after plant.

Sticking to a list, which would identify the colors, shapes, and sizes you need, would certainly make for a more refined and better-designed garden. On the other hand, there is something very freeing, very ebullient, about just going off and letting yourself succumb to the charms of every fetching plant. It may not turn out as great design, but it can make for a comforting, cosseting garden.

I'm not saying one way is better than the other. But I am saying, if you're in the list-planning category, lighten up. Allowing yourself to plant something just because you love it can be just the reinvigoration a garden needs. It will expand your horizons and allow you to discover new beauty.

If you're in the falling-tempestuously-in-love-with-every-plant group, then rid yourself of guilt. Eventually, as with a child whose unruly hair needs combing, you will pull out your garden comb and begin to neaten up, pair colors and textures, and fool all of us into believing that there was a design plan there all along.

In either case, now that the weather is thawing out, you can transplant almost anything, so long as it isn't in soggy soil. Although I wouldn't dismiss soggy soil entirely. I'm planting a hellebore garden outside my kitchen window under some rhododendrons that we limbed up last year. It is indeed soggy, but we divided a huge hosta and put it there last year, and it did splendidly. Over the years the hosta had been the gathering place for the Hells Angels Slug Convention. We divided the hosta into about 10 individual plants, and all survived their new location with nary a slug bite.

Now we are planting hellebores among

High drama: a vertical, spiky planting in a massive pot.

the hostas, which take the same conditions. You won't be able to see them from the street or even the garden path. But I'll look out my window and see them, and those little jewel-toned flowers will make my heart happy.

Then I'll go to a nursery with a cobbled-together plant list, which I will, I'm sure, all but ignore.

APRIL 7, 2011

CULTIVATE A GREEN THUMB
Basic rules for baby gardeners

IT IS AT THIS QUIVERING-IN-ANTICIPATION season that someone who has never gardened before starts to think about maybe, just perhaps, doing something with the yard. And happily, or maybe not so happily, those of us who have gardened begin to be filled with all sorts of advice. (Neither an overwaterer, nor an underwaterer be.)

> *If you can't make anything flourish, it's not your thumb, it's your hard clay soil.*

Who can resist the urge to give the new gardener advice? Certainly, as Miss Piggy would put it succinctly, not moi. Hence, here are 10 basic rules of thumb for the new gardener.

Rule 1: Compost, compost, and more compost. In the verdant Northwest, it's plain hard not to grow things. If you can't make anything flourish, it's not your thumb, it's your hard clay soil. Buy twice as much compost as you think you need. It is almost impossible to add too much organic material.

Rule 2: Raise your planting beds for good drainage. If you don't like the look of rectangular wood-bordered beds, just gently mound up your soil. Once planted, the soil will hold and look natural.

Rule 3: Be realistic. Figure out what you can manage to dig, weed and water. Better to have one perfectly wonderful flower, herb or vegetable patch rather than a whole yard of unkempt garden.

Rule 4: Don't be a perfectionist. If you wait until you have a well-worked-out plan so you know where you want to go with the whole yard, you are a rare individual indeed.

Rule 5: Treat yourself to some instant gratification. Start with some no-fail plants. There's nothing like success to spur you on. There are a lot of no-fail plants, and here are a few: day lilies, foxgloves, iris, coreopsis, asters, astilbe, lady's mantle, yarrow, Japanese anemones, purple cone flower, rudbeckia and coral bells.

Rule 6: Use nature as your design guideline. Plants grow in drifts and clumps, not straight lines. Buy at least three of each plant.

Rule 7: Don't be afraid to change things around. Use your shovel. In our enthusiasm to jump-start the garden, we all plant too closely. Not to worry. As long as the day is overcast and misty, which is about 80 percent of the time, you can move plants around with few ill effects.

Rule 8: Kick out the thugs. Don't waste energy babying a plant that is high maintenance. If you have roses that get black spot or azaleas that get mildew every year, yank them out. There are few places that can grow a wider spectrum of plants than the Pacific Northwest, so why waste your time on the few difficult specimens among our large plant family?

Rule 9: Pay attention to sun and shade. Shade is not the enemy. Shade is just a place where different kinds of plants grow. Some of the most beautiful plants grow in shade. Few of us have really dense shade, and many sun plants will do just fine in dappled shade.

Rule 10: Develop an accommodating attitude. For some mysterious reason, which scientists cannot explain, some no-fail plants will not do well in your garden. This does not mean you are a failure. For the life of me, I cannot grow hollyhocks that seem to grow just fine out of the cracks of sidewalks around town.

Your success and failure can vary from year to year. One year you will have the best stand of delphiniums in town. The next year, they will be weak and spindly. And just when you think that you've got everything going perfectly, we'll have one of those winters that wipes out a third of the garden. A good gardener will see this as an opportunity to try some new things. If that's not your attitude, stick to those potted petunias.

MARCH 4, 1994

❧

UNDERRATED FLOWERS
Invite these rare beauties into the spotlight

THEY STAND ON THE SIDELINES DECKED out in their best, but they don't get much attention. The rush is for belles with names such as rose, lily, daisy, iris and violet. You know the type: the flashy dressers with great press agents.

The wallflowers huddle hopefully in their plant trays waiting for someone to choose them. Eventually an adventurous gardener gives them a try. When the rest of us stumble across them in full bloom, we cry out to the adventurous gardener, "What is that beauty's name?"

Such is the fate of underrated flowers. Underrated flowers are those that meet all or most of the characteristics of the perfect flowers: good looks, easy growth, low maintenance, long bloom, no bad habits, and good for cutting. Yet stardom eludes them.

The No. 1 candidate for underrated flower is the meadow rue (*Thalictrum*), no relation to the herb called rue. Throughout May, the magnificent meadow rue, which sometimes reaches 6 feet, displays filmy clusters of lilac or pink flowers that will continue into June. As delightful as these flowers are, the plant is well worth growing if only for its delicate, fernlike foliage. And if these are not sufficient merits, meadow rue does very nicely in shade.

Lady's mantle (*Alchemilla mollis*) is about to break out of the underrated pack, and indeed it should. This low-growing mounding plant, so familiar in English gardens, is just being discovered by Northwest gardeners. There is perhaps no finer plant for a rainy area. Its exquisitely scalloped leaves cup just enough to hold glistening raindrops hostage. In spring, it's smothered with a froth of chartreuse flowers that continue sporadically through autumn. It too can take shade.

Don't be put off by the name. If you spot a gas plant (*Dictamnus albus*) for sale, snap it up. They're not easy to find, yet they'll give late spring flowers with no care for years. Vertical white flowers (there's a harder-to-find purple version) rise over a 2-foot clump of dark glossy leaves. Plant next to deep blue Siberian iris.

Rose campion (*Lychnis coronaria*) will bloom its heart out for you all summer. True, the vivid magenta flowers on silver foliage are hard to assimilate with summer's oranges and yellows. But if you bank rose campion with blue *Veronica* or white *Nicotiana*, it will blend into almost any scheme.

You could also bank it with another lovely plant yet to make it into the mainstream, Russian sage (*Perovskia*). Certainly the spirit of glasnost calls for trying out this subshrub with aromatic silvery leaves on arching stems. In late summer the stems are covered with a haze of blue flowers.

There are those who snub red valerian (*Centranthus ruber*) as coarse and peasanty. But therein lies its charm. Its fragrant rosy flowers and gray-green leaves look especially lovely growing amid a stand of white foxgloves. There's a white variety that would look just as well with purple foxgloves.

For late-season bloom, there's a softer alternative to the overdone chrysanthemums and kales. Try the tall and delicate Japanese anemones with pink and white flowers that resemble dogwood blossoms.

Kaffir lily (*Schizostylis*) has one special advantage. This sweet and small pinky-red flower will bloom when all the other flowers are asleep. There it will be glowing in the cold November rain. Plant it next to a doorway or where you can see it from a window.

And, yes, there is even a plant called wallflower (*Cheiranthus*), and it too is underappreciated. Plant red, violet or yellow wallflower over bulbs. It will send up fragrant

flowers in spring just in time to mask dying bulb foliage.

So consider these and other wallflowers you may have passed up for more familiar names. Isn't it time to ask some new flowers to dance in your garden?

MAY 25, 1990

GARDENING IN PARADISE
Northwesterners like to complain, but for plant lovers, there's no place better

HERE IT IS ANOTHER THANKSGIVING, AND there is much to be thankful for. We gardeners, especially, should take stock of our blessings. It is good for our little green souls to remember such things on gray, dribbly days.

We've had the very fine luck to have been plunked down in one of the most garden-friendly areas of the world, and certainly the finest in the United States. Think of a cook landing in Paris or an art historian in Florence. I am not exaggerating.

Consider our unique combination of temperate summers, moderate winters and plentiful rain. It means that the maritime Northwest is hospitable to one of the widest bands of plants in the world. How many other places can you grow towering fir trees next to an evergreen magnolia? It is a cornucopia of plant life.

That's why it's so difficult to pinpoint a Northwest style. There are so many choices. Our nurturing climate has given growth to the leading wholesale nursery industry in the nation. If you subtract the citrus crops of California and Florida, Oregon is No. 1 in ornamentals. Go ahead and drool over those

Wide, graveled paths invite the wanderer further into the garden.

slick catalogs from back East, but if you order a plant from one of them, chances are, it can be traced back to the Willamette Valley.

Which brings us to the fact that there are probably more retail nurseries, and certainly specialty nurseries, within an easy drive from your home than in any other state. Be thankful for this, at least until the Visa bill arrives. Want more proof of how much the gods have blessed us? Check out national gardening magazines. Every other story seems to feature an Oregon or Washington garden.

The length of our season is something that must make other gardeners grass-green with envy. I sometimes wonder what it must be like to invest all the work to build a garden in a climate where the last frost comes in June, the humidity drives you indoors by July and the frost is on the proverbial pumpkin by September.

Other than in California, one or more of those conditions exists just about everywhere in the nation. And what we have over California is, well, seasons.

Sure, some of those other states may have more days of sunshine come spring, but are red tomatoes all that great? What do people talk about in places where the tomatoes are dependable?

Do we really want more zucchini? Would we really trade corn as high as an elephant's eye for our roses, rhodies, and the more-than-occasional collectors' plant that is known only to grow in England, New Zealand, and the Pacific Northwest?

And, come on, let's admit it. Aren't we all secretly thankful that we really can't predict our weather? Can you imagine what it would be like if every winter were mild and everything lived? How would we come up with excuses to buy and try new plants come spring?

I am even thankful for the one worm in the apple of our gardening Eden—our clay soil. Yes, it is soggy and clammy and forms great clods, and I have been known to curse it with mild oaths. But it also is sumptuously rich and fertile, and I can't remember the last time I fertilized. Roses aside, everything seems to flourish.

The saving grace is that, for many plants, the phrase "must have well-drained soil" is like saying a person "must have fruits and vegetables rather than chocolate." If all plants needed as much drainage as experts say they do, I would have maybe two plants growing in my garden.

Finally, I am thankful to have such great gardening friends and readers who bear with me, through disasters and occasional successes, and send kind notes and affectionate advice, much of which really works and some of which (like the pasta sauce recipes) I actually follow.

NOVEMBER 23, 2000

SUMMER STUDY

A season in review

As I LOOK BACK ON THIS SUMMER, I REALIZE I've learned a number of things. First, I don't like heat. It was interesting to see how the hot weather affected me. During hot weather I am able to drive past nurseries without turning in. Usually, if I am in the vicinity of a nursery, Gertie (my plantmobile, named

for Gertrude Jekyll) just seems to home in and head in the direction of the plants.

I was convinced my plant shopping was over for the year since I had zero interest in new plants. Then I learned how ephemeral this feeling was. At the first overcast day, little tingling feelings awakened, and suddenly I just had to go to a nursery. That throbbing feeling of plant lust wasn't as strong as in spring but it was definitely there. I came home in triumph because I had found several small but bushy plants to fill in the bare spots where I had trimmed back the lady's mantle (*Alchemilla mollis*). I learned that a successful foray to a nursery can be a refreshing experience akin to what tall, thin, voluptuous babes must feel after a day at a spa. Personally, I think it is a lot better, but then I have never been a babe, so I don't know this for a fact. But I like to think it is way better.

Another thing I learned is that not all plants fall into easy categories, such as well-behaved and thugs. The truth is that many plants fall into an ambiguous area. They are fine for a few years until they see you get complacent, and then, when your back is turned, they stage a takeover.

Wisteria is an example. It is a splendid vine for covering a pergola or porch, and it will go along just fine for some time, possibly even years. But there is a point where it gets out of hand. My wisteria is at that point. It has begun gobbling up our house. I fear for the cats. It has taken over the upstairs porch. If I leave the door to the porch open, by nightfall the wisteria is poking its way into the house. If I didn't whack it back, I'm sure I'd be feeling little green tendrils curling around my toes in the middle of the night.

I also learned that once I tire of a plant and take it out, I will suddenly see it in some-

Wisteria is a beautiful, albeit aggressive, vine.

one else's garden where it is making a magnificent display. *Phlomis* is a case in point. I finally decided I didn't really like it. It is coarse, and, once it blooms, the little yellow whorls of flowers turn an ugly brown and don't have the good grace to fall off. But just as soon as I'd dispatched it, I went on garden tours where the very same plant, far from looking coarse, looked regal and exotic with its square stems and circlets of golden flowers.

Another lesson is that once you give away something, it will suddenly become a raging fad. After years of trying to find a comfortable spot for my large, cumbersome Adirondack chairs, I finally gave them to a friend. Now I see them everywhere. They are the new "in" furniture.

Still more, I have learned that plants have a perverse sense of timing. The lilies, which were gorgeous this year, broke into bloom in the only span that I didn't have an open garden. The tulip tree (*Liriodendron*), on the other hand, decided to drop its heavy and messy blooms during the height of open-garden season. I have tried to determine when my garden is at its peak, and the only thing I can come up with is that it's in the very week when there are no garden visitors.

Yet another thing I learned is that, if you have aphids, the ladybugs will come, although I must say they took their sweet time this year. But when they finally arrived, they came in droves, and we now find them everywhere, in the house, in the bathtub and on our cats. I can only imagine the battle. I picture legions of little lady beetles with tiny swords skewering the evil aphid army. Of course, this rout of the aphids occurred just after we'd had our last open garden.

And, finally, I've learned that just when you're down, and for me the low point was the suspected heatstroke death of my lovely little *Cercis canadensis* 'Forest Pansy,' your garden will do something to lift you up. I realized that the garden was at its best this year, just as it has been every previous year. Isn't that amazing, how every year can be the best?

AUGUST 24, 2006

༄

ROLLICKING INTO SPRING
Even the flamingos cut capers to welcome the season

EEK! I FIBBED WHEN I SAID I WENT TO GET one clematis and came home with five. Actually (blush) it was six. I found a little one tucked away in a box with some other plants. The overlooked clematis is *Clematis* 'Odoriba,' which is described as very feminine with pink, bell-shaped flowers.

Blame my confusion on spring. I knew it was officially here when I looked out the window the other morning and saw that Doreen and the rest of the flamingos had escaped from their dark corner and were frolicking on the lawn. I suspect that Doug the Wonder Guy might have had a hand in this.

This is not the only invasion on the block.

One year, to celebrate spring, he dragged out all my faux bunnies and put them on the lawn. In a sleep-befuddled moment, I thought we had been invaded by real bunnies. Fortunately that wasn't the case, although the other day my neighbor Rosemary did see a skunk wandering down the alley behind our houses.

Other creatures are stirring as well. The fish have risen from the depths of the pond and are mooning around happily. They appear to have multiplied. Alas, the babes won't last long because soon the dreaded bullfrogs will appear. Cats Orville and Wilbur usually dispatch the bullfrogs but not before the frogs have feasted.

Also, I have seen my first slug. Eek again! And so it begins. I am about to turn into Lizzie Borden.

Before I go any further with this prattle of spring, I must apologize for causing the spate of cold weather. Lulled by late February's warm days, we took most of the potted plants out of the greenhouse one early March day. That very night, the temperature plummeted to the low 30s, and the next day the shivering plants had to be moved back inside. How many years will I fall for false spring?

The slugs and I are not the only ones champing at the bit. Now that it really is spring, I hear conversations in the office, people talking about sowing vegetable and annual seeds outdoors. Alas, I must warn, this is a time for patience, not a trait that comes easily to many a gardener.

It is still too early to plant most annuals and vegetables or sow seeds directly into the ground. The exceptions are some leafy greens like spinach, lettuce, peas and broccoli, as well as root vegetables. The major sun lovers, usually plump plants such as tomatoes, eggplants and melons, shouldn't go in the ground until around Mother's Day.

I know it's hard to wait, but these plants just won't thrive until the ground warms up, and that takes more than warm days. The nights have to warm up too.

Patience, that irritating virtue, also comes into play when deciding if you've lost a plant or not. Some plants are very slow to leaf out. My chocolate mimosa (*Albizia julibrissin* 'Summer Chocolate'), smoke bushes (*Cotinus*), crepe myrtles (*Lagerstroemia*) and chaste tree (*Vitex*) are often tardy, but never "no-shows."

Even some normally evergreen plants die completely to the ground after a very cold spell, but do come back from the roots— hardy fuchsias and bear's breeches (*Acanthus*) are examples. I've even had plants I thought I'd lost start poking up as late as June.

But if I must practice patience, I'm not about to practice restraint. Reader Linda Neff informs me that I really should have gotten *Clematis* 'Pink Flamingo.' She says it's gorgeous. So I'm off to get it. I like to keep Doreen and the flock happy.

MARCH 25, 2010

✧

WHITHER THE WEATHER
A gardener's guide to the seasons

WE IN THE NORTHWEST ARE OBSESSED with weather. It takes up a huge hunk of our evening news, and it often is the headline story, displacing such items as drive-by shootings, bridge closures and—why this is still news, I don't know—baby born on way to hospital.

It's not that our weather is extreme. I believe the thing that makes us so obsessed with

weather is that ours is so unpredictable and changeable. Weather in western Oregon and Washington can be a lot of things, but it is never boring.

No one knows this better than gardeners. We don't need to play the lottery to take chances. There is plenty of risk in deciding when and what to plant. Just to help you understand, here is an anatomy of the Northwest seasons for the gardener.

Mid-December through February: *the turbulent season.* Or as it is sometimes called, winter. It is turbulent because it is the most unpredictable of seasons, and it has two heartbreaking features. The first is snow just before or just after Christmas, robbing us of the famous White Christmas. The second is the spate of sunshine in February known as false spring.

You can tell it's false spring by the following signs: People are all out walking their dogs. Middle-aged men are suddenly wearing shorts. Everyone is convinced this means an early spring, and only the groundhog knows better.

Gardeners spend this season worrying about what got killed during the icy weather (more likely the soggy weather), reading plant catalogs, and secretly hoping that at least a few things won't come back so they can buy more plants.

March 1 to July 4: *the wet season.* The variations are cold and gray to slightly warmer and gray. You can tell it's that season because everyone is complaining about the rain. Signs of

> *There are occasional days of sunshine during which gardeners get so frenzied that they work outside until after dark.*

the season include shivering princesses on Rose Festival floats, rusted barbecues that came out too soon, and cozying up to friends who have condos in Hawaii, Palm Springs or Arizona.

None of this moisture dampens plant lust, and there are occasional days of sunshine during which gardeners get so frenzied that they work outside until after dark. Thus the season is marked by sore muscles, idiotic smiles, and endless conversations dominated by Latin names, to the utter boredom of nongardening friends.

July 5 to mid-September: *the dry season.* It's essentially mild, although occasionally a few days spike into triple digits, in which case Northwesterners go into shock and headlines about the weather displace baby born on the way to the hospital. You can tell the season because everyone is complaining about the lack of rain. Other signs of this season are yellow lawns, garage sales in the front yard, and cozying up to friends who have swimming pools.

Mid-September to October 31: *the glorious season.* We are lost in an autumnal haze of golden weather and increasingly brilliant foliage. No one is wishing it would or wouldn't rain because we know it's coming. All we want to do is pick dahlias, take rides in the country to select pumpkins, and eat corn on the cob. A sign of the season is trying to figure out what to do with 72 tomatoes that all got ripe at the same time.

November 1 to mid-December: *the transition season.* It is marked by excessive speculation over whether it will be a hard winter or a mild winter. One scientist will say an El

Niño is headed toward us, and another will contend equally fervently that La Niña is dancing our way. The *Farmers' Almanac* will sell out, and global warming will return as the hot topic at dinner parties. We will hang on every word, and no one will agree.

So there you have it, the five seasons of the maritime Northwest. I think I'll stop here before Gov. Kulongoski accuses me of trying to assume the role of the state weatherologist.

MARCH 8, 2007

WICKED WAYS
Crafty weeds do their best to torment us

THE DEBATE OVER WHAT CONSTITUTES A weed is as old as gardening. All I know is that weeds are devious and evil plants. They lurk silently hidden under foliage until you have a visitor.

Suddenly as you are talking to your guest, you'll glance over the person's shoulder and spot a hideous weed that somehow managed to grow 6 feet tall in the past 24 hours.

This weed will have chosen a place that you can reach only after mashing some rare and delicate little plants in front of it. Then, as you stretch dangerously out of balance to pull it without trampling more plants, your weed will snap off at the top. Its roots will remain in the soil ready to fling up another monster.

Other places weeds favor are the cracks between steppingstones and bricks. These narrow spaces leave plenty of room for weeds to hurl up ugly jagged leaves but little room for you to pry out their roots.

Every gardener who has shredded fingernails knows whereof I speak. I am trying to be a responsible steward of the Earth, and I refuse to use herbicides. OK, if that sounded high and mighty, I will revise that to say that I also am too lazy to spray and have no patience with painting individual leaves with a deadly compound.

I'm told that's the only way to get rid of morning glory. Personally, I don't believe you can ever get rid of it short of a flamethrower, and maybe not even then. I've had this fantasy of finding someone who recognizes weeds, has a back in good working order, and thinks weeding is more fun than flipping burgers for summer money.

Doug the Wonder Boy is beyond weed pulling, having graduated, and rightly so, into more sophisticated ventures, such as garden designs and installations. So far neither he nor I has succeeded in getting good weeders.

Weeds seem to provoke short-term memory difficulties. If you show a helper what a weed looks like, he or she will forget within 10 minutes. You will point to a crop of weeds with very distinctive foliage

People may think all nettles are weeds; many are, but not the wonderful genus Eryngium.

and nasty-looking little flowers, and they will clear out the weeds in that patch very nicely. But once they've cleared them out, they fail to recognize the very same weeds in any other part of the garden.

The other day, I pointed directly to a weed that has annoying yellow flowers. My finger actually touched the offending weed. Then to my horror, I watched as my helper (my husband says to be clear it wasn't him) yanked out a *Corydalis lutea*.

Is this a plot, I wonder, to feign ignorance to avoid having to weed? According to my gardening friends, their spouses and children are particularly adept at feigning ignorance of weeds to the point that, if these helpers are let loose in the garden, they will pull up almost anything fragile and expensive.

They seem to have this behavior down to a science. However, I can hardly complain, I who for years have feigned ignorance of how to fill my car with gas, how to put the garbage and recyclables out on the curb, and, most ingenious of all, how to make a bed. You see, that's one thing you can never do as well as a spouse who served in the military.

There have been exceptions in getting good weeding help, especially one young woman who used to work for Doug. But the exceptions always end up either getting married and having families or going to college to become doctors or graduating to garden design and installations. Apparently, career opportunities in weeding have not been sufficiently promoted.

There are times that I think I should just

capitulate and put up a sign that says, "No weeds were harmed in the making of this garden."

JULY 24, 2008

LET'S GET DOWN AND DIRTY
When the discussion is over, dig in and get that soil improved

I DISCOVERED THE CRIME WHEN I BEGAN PLANTing bulbs. Apparently, sometime during the summer, person or persons unknown had sneaked into my yard. The villains dug up all the soft, loose soil and replaced it with hard clay.

That can be the only explanation. I swear that last spring that dirt was as crumbly as the chocolate chip cookies I just ate to console myself.

If a dark cloud hangs over this area's otherwise unlimited silver lining for gardening, it's the soil. In most parts of the Willamette Valley, the soil is made up of very fine clay particulates that clump together and ferociously bar the passage of water and roots.

If you're going to do something about your soil, this is clearly the best time— a narrow window of opportunity between the dry summer and the wintry rains. There's been enough moisture so that you can slip a shovel in, but not so much that you'll be sloshing around in mud.

I once subscribed to the theory that a gardener should simply till the existing soil and add a lot of compost. Now, I'm a convert to doing away with the existing soil and putting in a new mix. I am deeply suspicious that the existing clay somehow, via a mysterious chemical process, transforms all the fresh, crumbly topsoil into brown cement.

I'm also about to make the leap into sand. Several experts warn not to add sand to clay soil, because it will only harden to a cementlike consistency. Well, I didn't add sand, and I've still got cement. Meanwhile, people who did add sand seem to be faring pretty well.

If you're developing a new garden plot, this also is prime time to add a lot of manure. It will have the winter to enrich the soil and age so that, by the time you plant in spring, there's no danger of burning tender seedlings. But don't add manure or any heavy-duty fertilizer to existing plants. Now's not the time to stimulate growth.

The exceptions are bulbs and new plants. Sprinkle bone meal where you have existing bulbs or are planting new ones. For new shrubs and trees, add some low-nitrogen fertilizer to stimulate a little root growth before winter sets in.

It should come as no surprise that this is also the very best time to rejuvenate existing garden plots. Once, in a frenzy of gardening zeal since unequaled, I dug up an entire border in autumn, set the plants to the side under a shade tree and completely reworked the soil. The chief ingredients were tons of compost delivered by truck and two rent-a-teens, who did the shoveling and wheelbarrowing.

Yes, the job was as much work as building the Great Wall of China, but it remains

> *I swear that last spring that dirt was as crumbly as the chocolate chip cookies I just ate to console myself.*

the one area of the yard that doesn't resemble a hard-top freeway. It took three days and the rejuvenation involved digging up close to 50 perennials and small shrubs. The good news is, that after they were replanted, every single one survived. The better news is that the following spring, they filled and fluffed out in a way that eclipsed the previous year's scraggly growth.

It was a foolhardy thing to do, digging up an entire border, but it worked. And it worked thanks to a few practical precautions. First, I waited until misty overcast days to do the job. Then, I left as much soil around the roots as I could. I laid each plant gently on its side and covered the roots with damp newspapers kept constantly moist.

If all that sounds daunting, then you can do the second-best thing. If you're not willing to redig the whole area, at least you can dig extra big holes whenever you plant something new and stick a lot of compost into them. A common rule of thumb is to make the hole twice as big as the root ball. A better rule of thumb is to keep digging until you topple over with exhaustion; only then will the hole be exactly big enough.

Which brings up the next nasty surprise, for those of you who think it is time curl up with books. This is also the best time of year to start a compost pile. For one thing, you'll have plenty of materials. Just drive a lawnmower over those leaves and throw them on the pile. For another, compost really does need a winter to cook before it's applied in spring.

If you chip organic material up small enough, it will look brown and crumbly within mere weeks. But unless it's had some time for temperatures to get high enough to kill weed seeds, you could be adding a lot of trouble. Take it from someone who knows. Last spring I added too-fresh compost to a new island bed. In addition to what I actually planted, it sprouted one sunflower, three nicotiana, five tomato plants, and several thousand weeds.

So, don't wait for spring. Start the compost now, till the soil now and prepare the beds now.

The books can wait another two weeks.

OCTOBER 16, 1992

MOBBED
Thuggery runs amok in high summer

I MUST HAVE DOZED OFF FOR A BIT, BECAUSE when I awakened, my lush summer garden had turned into a tangled mass of vines running rampant, shrubs ballooning out, and perennials clumping together like street-corner gangs ready to take over the neighborhood.

I swear there were morning glories snaking up every imaginable support and blackberries dripping down like moss in the Everglades. My garden now looks like a teenager hiding blemishes with great hanks of hair hanging in his face. And blemishes there are.

The August light is so mellow that for a while one tends not to notice the black spot, weeds and slug-shredded leaves. Unfortunately, a number of small plants also are hidden, as they've been overrun by their pushy neighbors. Sigh.

With September just around the corner, I need to get up off the lounge, close my mystery novel and put the cat down. It's time to start the to-do list and begin thinking about how to make the garden better for next year.

The first thing I am going to do is get my husband to take photos around the garden now so that next spring I can remember just how big things get. That is, if I can tear him away from taking pictures of the adorable Ernie, Wilbur and Orville.

A few strategic photos will serve to remind me to move the gorgeous mahogany-red daylilies out from under a fringe flower shrub (*Loropetalum*) that has overtaken them and to move a small red barberry (*Berberis*) that is now hidden by a hydrangea. There's no telling what else I'll find as I lift up branches, pull back fronds, and uncurl vines. I even have a rose that's been swallowed up by some not-so-tender tendrils of clematis.

My to-do list also will include a great deal of editing out as well as moving plants around. You might think that you can leave these jobs until spring when the plants will

The lovely Astrantia major.

be smaller. But that can be your undoing. The coarse bracken ferns that have seeded everywhere looked charming as they unfurled in spring.

The hardy geraniums were perky in spring but later collapsed in the center and never managed to rouse themselves again. The lady's mantle, which has cropped up all over, was a welcome filler in spring. So were other spreading perennials, which have now become borderline thugs. The problem is, in spring you're smitten with these plants and can't bring yourself to dig them up. You kid yourself and think, since these plants look so lovely now, you can let them go for a while and control them later when they get out of hand.

Control them, hah! Control is not one of a gardener's strong virtues. We, who think of ourselves as nature lovers, are actually in a constant battle with nature. If you doubt this, let your garden go for a bit. You'll find it won't suddenly spring up with Doug firs carpeted by native plants. What you'll get is a tangle of blackberries, bracken fern and morning glories.

Frankly my dears, anyone who has a "natural garden" probably has done major clearing. So fall, not spring, is definitely the time to prevent a hostile takeover. It's much easier to root out things that have flopped and turned brown than to take out something fresh and green.

And keep in mind those new gardeners who will benefit from the plants you dig up. Instead of tossing the extra lady's mantle (*Alchemilla*), Japanese anemones, daylilies (*Hemerocallis*), masterwort (*Astrantia*), *Rudbeckia*, iris, crocosmia and those other spreaders on the compost pile, give them to people who still have bare spots in their gardens. They will sing your praises for the gift—at least for a while. Then they will curse you.

> *Control is not one of a gardener's strong virtues.*

You won't find a horse's head in your bed, but you may find a clump of daylilies.

AUGUST 28, 2008

✂

HIGH SUMMER MADNESS IS UPON US

Shamelessly in love with summer

I'M BEGINNING TO WEAKEN AND ACTUALLY look fondly on those florid gladiolas even if they remind me of funerals. I'm almost sorry I pulled up all the yarrow even if it does have a musty scent. I can't imagine why I didn't get around to sowing the sunflower seeds.

Are you experiencing similar symptoms? Do common hollyhocks stretching to the sky set you to dreaming about white picket fences? Is the wretched loosestrife you tried to pull out all spring suddenly exhibiting charm? Do you

The colors and scents of High Summer are upon us.

actually wish you had planted more of those big blowzy dahlias?

If such indelicate thoughts are flitting through your brain, you're under the spell of High Summer.

High Summer is the magic time when we suddenly get sappy with nostalgia. We want a garden like grandma had back in Indiana even if our real granny lived in a New York high-rise or a California ranch.

High Summer is the crescendo the whole year seems to have been building to. It is soul-satisfying mornings spent watering to beat the heat of the day. It is long afternoons lying in a hammock trying to re-read *War and Peace*. It is evenings sitting on the porch, swatting mosquitoes and smelling honeysuckle so heavy in the air that it makes your heart ache with the romance of it.

High Summer is when the dragonflies return, the crickets hop, and the raccoons bring their babies around to the side porch where you keep the kitty nibbles. High Summer is the time for spreading red-checkered tablecloths on the back lawn, making sun-tea and having the neighbors over for a barbecue.

High Summer is everything that's corny, right down to corn on the cob. It's the time of year when the act of gardening all boils down to two goals—trying to get our lawns green and our tomatoes red.

The queen of High Summer is the hollyhock, a maddening flower that succumbs to rust in well-tended gardens but flourishes beautifully in old neglected houses and cracks in the sidewalk.

It is the time when shrubs that are shameless in their extravagance—lavatera, rose-of-Sharon, butterfly bushes and hydrangeas—are made pendulous with blooms. Anything that looks like a daisy is almost always a flower of High Summer. There's sunflowers, purple coneflowers, gaillardia, black-eyed Susans and asters.

High summer is no time for good taste nor delicacy. It's a put-on-your-sunglasses time with colors bold enough to take the blazing light. Magenta campion, purple mallow, golden coreopsis, red-orange nasturtiums and neon zinnias parade like hussies. The worst of the lot are the floozies of the garden, those overblown dahlias that, lord help us, we're starting to love.

This is not the time of year to appreciate the less-is-more philosophy. The diminutive bulbs and delicate specialties of spring are a distant memory. The structured grasses and sedums of autumn have not yet caught us in their thrall. Give us big, brassy, bold, common-as-you-please flowers. Forget foliage; even plain old geraniums and petunias look better. To heck with design or what plant goes well with what. The real issue is where can we hang the hammock.

Face it; every year at about this time we become sentimental twits.

JULY 22, 1994

❧

SLEEVE-ROLLING TIME
Fall chores beckon to the protective gardener

OCTOBER WOULD BE A PERFECTLY DELIGHTful month if it didn't invoke the subject of chores. Chores are more odious than work, simply because they imply something in addition to work.

But enough whining. Planting doesn't count as a chore because it's stimulating and fun. The main chores for this time of year are cleanup and protection for the coming winter. The two may be related. Many garden experts advise against cutting back perennials in fall, opining that they offer some protective cover. Others say, do the cleanup now and clear the way for a nice blanket of compost.

I am in the former camp of putting things off, but Doug the Wonder Guy is in the neatnik camp. Personally, I don't think it matters since our climate is not extreme. But of course I will lose this particular battle with DTWG, because I am saving my energy to wage all-out war with him on pruning.

I think he overdoes it; he considers me a loose woman when it comes to garden neatness. This is our one area of disagreement, although we've managed to keep it civil all these years. I am hoping that marriage has taught him that all-important lesson of saying, "Yes, dear."

Northwest gardeners seem to have decided that not only is climate change going to happen, but it has already struck. Hence there's a proliferation of marginally hardy and even tropical plants in our gardens. I am certainly not holier than thou, with my red-leaved banana that I try to winter over every year, entirely without success.

When it comes to winterizing in-ground plants, mulch is our best friend. Mulch is any material layered over bare earth to act as an insulating blanket. The best mulches are organic material that you've either composted or bought, because they will eventually break down, which helps break up clay soil. Most of us know that and know that 2 or 3 inches will suffice.

But spot mulching is a new concept. It's about putting a deeper pile of mulch over the crowns of marginally hardy plants. We apply this technique to DTWG's favorite plant, the hemanly gunnera. First we cut off most leaves but leave a few to fold over the crown. This is then covered with perhaps a foot of mulch, not compacted but loosened with some leaves from nearby trees.

It works for the gunnera, cannas and a few other plants with delicate constitutions. But, remember, this is advice for perennials. Mulch should not touch the trunks of trees or shrubs. It can soften bark and invite insect invaders. After mulching, take a rake and clear an area of about 6 inches around woody plants.

Every year I caution gardeners to wait until after Thanksgiving to apply mulch, and every year they ignore me, as evidenced by the alpine mounds of mulch lining our streets as early as October.

Applying mulch too early will keep the ground warmer, so plants are slow to become dormant, making them more vulnerable when truly cold weather hits.

> *Every year I caution gardeners to wait until after Thanksgiving to apply mulch, and every year they ignore me.*

Last winter, we ran into another challenge. Much of the damage wasn't caused by low temperatures but rather by the weight of an unusual amount of snow. Our spoiled little shrubs and trees looked at this white stuff and cried, "Get it off me, get it off me," and promptly fainted. My neighbor's arborvitae hedge has never stood up straight again. The snow broke branches and permanently bent tall hedging. (I know, I know, it's a good argument for pruning.)

The conventional wisdom of covering a semi-hardy plant with a tarp when it's cold is a lousy idea if it's also snowing. Our fringe flower (*Loropetalum*) lived, but the snow packed down the tarp and broke so many branches that we had to take the poor thing out back and shoot it. The moral of the story here is to keep a pair of mittens handy for one more chore—brushing off that snow.

OCTOBER 15, 2009

DON'T PUT OFF A GARDEN
One New Year's resolution you really should keep

WHEN IT COMES TO MY GARDEN, I HAVE made and broken a number of New Year's resolutions. I have resolved to label my plants. I have resolved to purchase only what I can plant in one outing. I have resolved to keep a diary with weather notes, so I know what blooms when. I have resolved, sometimes even with a straight face, to limit my plants and not fall in love with every new one that comes around.

I have carried out none of these resolutions. But there is one resolution that I have tried and highly recommend. I have resolved not to be timid.

The more I think about it, the more I believe gardening is about confidence. You need confidence to try something new, and even more confidence to take things out. I have seen too many people wring their hands and do nothing because they didn't know what to plant when or where. I've seen too many people feel intimidated because they didn't know Latin names.

Very few of us have horticultural back-

Don't be shy about opening your garden to visitors.

grounds, and some of us even fell sound asleep when our post-lunch biology class covered botany. Yet we manage to have gardens. The plant knowledge, the enjoyment in research and, yes, even the Latin will come with time. But, until then, don't put off a garden. Good old trial and error can be a terrific teacher, and, with gardening, the journey is as enjoyable as the destination.

There's a wonderful passage in a book called *Consider the Lily* by Elizabeth Buchan. In it, Buchan quotes Gertrude Jekyll with advice so wise, every new gardener should pay it heed.

"For the novice, the first steps in gardening are the most difficult. There is much to learn, wrote a great gardener, Miss Gertrude Jekyll. But unlike the lessons in love or hate, even the lessons in money, they are pleasant,

oh, so pleasant, and the fallings by the wayside do not wound, only teach. The beginner, said Miss Jekyll, should be both bewildered and puzzled, for that is part of the preordained way, the road to perfection. Each step becomes lighter, less mud-clogged, until, little by little, the postulant becomes the novice, the novice the fully professed."

So, my New Year's resolution advice for any gardener, new or experienced, is to make this the year to "go for it."

Do not worry if you lack design savvy or plant experience. Don't wait to start or develop your garden until you have a finished plan or know what style you want. You're not building a cathedral that has to be structurally sound from the get-go. Some of the best gardens grow and change incrementally over time. Don't worry if you try something and it doesn't look right. Plants move amazingly well.

Don't sweat it if you haven't figured out your color scheme yet. I still haven't after all these years. Sometimes I'm in love with the idea of a misty pastel garden, sometimes with the drama of hot colors, and occasionally I flirt with the idea of a peaceful all-green garden.

Don't hesitate to try a new plant. Don't worry if you don't know the difference between compost and mulch or when and how much to fertilize or prune. Believe me, you will know in due time. A scorched yellow lawn was my great lesson in fertilizer, and over-pruned shrubs that took two years to return to their natural shapes taught me about pruning. I learned that the key is a delicate hand. And, really, both the yellow lawn and the bubble shrubs came back.

Don't hesitate to share your garden or feel self-conscious because your garden isn't trendy. I once read somewhere that one should write to express, not impress. The same can be said of why you should garden.

And above all, remember, you're not making mistakes. You're experimenting.

JANUARY 5, 2006

❧

OBSESSING ABOUT COMPULSIONS
Too much knowledge can be frustrating

IT IS FUNNY HOW AN AVOCATION OR HOBBY can take over and pervade nearly every aspect of your life. My husband, Ted, is both a WWII buff and a film freak. He used to drive me crazy when we'd be watching a war movie, and he'd get all exercised that they were using planes that hadn't even been manufactured at the time of the battle portrayed on the screen.

Of course, I was sitting there wondering if John Wayne would get the cute Army nurse, not whether he would win the war, so I couldn't understand why my husband was so fixated on this accuracy thing. It was, after all, just a movie.

But having become a gardening nut, I have begun to see his side of things. Now when we're watching a movie and I see the two lovers walking in a park full of tulips and it's supposed to be September, I'm the one who freaks out.

"Tulips don't bloom in September, you idiots, especially not in New York," I say to the screen. Fortunately, we are watching a video at home so no one comes to throw me out, although The Perp looks up from my lap and thinks, "Mom, you idiot, don't get so excited; it's not like we're talking about tuna fish."

I find that gardening has invaded my shopping, as well. Now as I wander through stores, especially antiques malls, it's as if I have finely tuned antennae that zero in on gardening accessories. I don't even see the home stuff anymore. The same is true at art shows. I am always looking for garden art. When I'm on vacation, I'm always looking for garden things to bring home.

Speaking of vacations, this year my husband and I took a late-summer trip to Europe with our neighbors, Walt and Rosemary Ellis. It was the first time in a long time I had been on an overseas trip that wasn't focused on gardening. We spent a week in Normandy visiting World War II sites and museums, then a week in Barcelona, because my husband has always had a fascination with the works of Antoni Gaudi.

In Normandy, I became increasingly frustrated that we couldn't just run off to visit Monet's garden, which I had seen only in spring. But, from where we were staying in the town of Bayeux, it was a good six-hour round trip, and I was outvoted.

Still, as we drove through Normandy in our rental car, I found myself looking at the window boxes and little front gardens in the villages we whizzed through. I became crabby. I needed a garden fix. Then one morning Walt and Rosemary were out for an early walk and discovered a lovely botanical garden in Bayeux, and the next day they took us to see it. Ah, I felt better and was ready to soldier on.

Leaving Spain, we traveled to Madrid for a stopover day between Barcelona and home, and we spent most of the time in the Prado and the Reina Sofia, magnificent national

> *Heck, I had just seen Picasso's "Guernica," and here I am getting excited about dahlias.*

museums. Even there, I dragged my poor husband in the heat of the day through the botanical garden next to the Prado.

I found myself exclaiming, "Look! There's a row of crape myrtles in bloom," or "Look here! There's a bed of dahlias." Heck, I had just seen Picasso's "Guernica," and here I am getting excited about dahlias. I don't know what this says about me. At least I don't wear print dresses with little rakes and trowels on them, but I am certain that is next. I've already got a sterling silver pin in the shape of a shovel.

OCTOBER 7, 2004

⌘

HOT AND BOTHERED
Feeling zoned out this summer?

THIS SUMMER'S HEAT WAVE TAUGHT ME something. I now grasp the limits of the plant hardiness system developed by the U.S. Department of Agriculture.

The USDA system bases plant hardiness on tolerance of cold temperatures and divides the country into 10 zones, with 10 the warmest. Except for elevated areas and areas exposed to Gorge winds, Portland is generally considered Zone 8.

But, as the *Sunset Western Garden Book*, which has developed its own zonal system, points out, a lot of factors affect plant survival, such as latitude (which determines the number of daylight hours), elevation, ocean influence, continental air influences, and mountains and hills.

Certainly we've discovered this summer that a plant's ability to withstand heat may be as important as its ability to take the cold. That news flash hit me the day I came home from work and discovered that all the leaves on my redbud (*Cercis canadensis* 'Forest Pansy') looked like potato chips. They appeared to have died all at once.

I loved that little tree with its red heart-shaped leaves. I purchased it as a stick in a gallon pot and nurtured it into a 30-foot tree. How can you not love something named 'Forest Pansy'?

According to The American Horticultural Society, help for determining heat tolerance is on the way. The society has developed a heat-zone map that divides the country into 12 areas based on the number of days over 86 degrees. That's the temperature, ac-

The 'Forest Pansy' in happier (wetter!) days.

cording to the society's literature, at which plants begin to suffer physiological damage (me too).

I'm in Zone 4 (12 is the hottest area), which means I can expect 14 to 30 days above 86 degrees based on data collected in 1997.

Of course, this isn't helpful if you don't know which plants can take heat, but the society says it is in the process of coding thousands of plants, and we can expect to see the heat-zone numbers appearing in plant catalogs and garden centers very soon.

Meanwhile, I did an inventory of my own garden to check out the heat haters. Naturally the hydrangeas were acting like prima donnas in need of a lot of pampering. "Spray me, spray me," they cried every time I walked by. For all their droop, I am confident they will survive.

I am not so confident about a number of gold-leaved plants, in particular a new golden-leaved hellebore I purchased this year. It definitely looks past resuscitation. The stems of the bear's breeches (*Acanthus mollis*) have gone all limp, and two red-leaved barberries (*Berberis*) are looking crispy.

A new little dogwood (*Cornus kousa* 'Wolf

Eyes') is also displaying scorch marks on its leaves, even though it is in the shade. And I am now resolved to move all the coral flowers (*Heuchera*) to shadier areas this fall. The heat hasn't killed them, but it has made them look pretty shabby.

Still, some plants obviously relish heat. My lilies have never grown so tall nor produced so many blooms. We had red tomatoes by mid-July, and Doug the Wonder Boy and I haven't had to fight over the cucumbers, as there are enough to go around. Even peppers, grown from seed, are producing their fruit. It makes me wish I had planted corn this year.

Some plants that I associate with moisture have stood up to the heat surprisingly well. The hostas and Japanese maples continue to look swell. My maples are all in pots because I have a soil-borne fungus that attacks them. But they remained perky, unlike that wuss of a dogwood.

Meanwhile, I'm going to take a wait-and-see approach to my redbud. I'm hoping it's just leaf drop, and next spring I'll see new leaves. If not, I may leave it in place and paint it blue. Or maybe not.

AUGUST 17, 2006

GET A CLUE
Like fortune cookies, the cryptic phrases on plant labels require interpretation

NO QUESTION THAT IT'S IMPORTANT TO read labels to get a sense of what conditions a plant will thrive in and how big it ultimately will get. Infatuated gardeners tend to ignore the latter and take Scarlett O'Hara's approach, "Tomorrow is another day."

It is equally important to know how to

translate the very minimal instructions on a plant label. Herewith, then, is a guide.

Blooms spring through fall. If it's a perennial, let me know about it, because I have never run into such a creature.

Well-drained soil. Your work is cut out for you. Order mountains of compost. Or alternately, try the plant. Many thrive in less than ideal conditions, but we're not talking about a freeway-hard surface.

Moist but well-drained soil. Unknown substance in the Willamette Valley. Keep soil evenly moist. Someone's idea of a joke after July 4.

Ground cover. Be on guard; it's a spreader and fine if you really need a ground cover. But it can be a takeover artist in other circumstances.

Tends to spread. Growers hate to admit this, so if they put it on a tag, believe it.

Prefers poor soil. This explains why hollyhocks do poorly in your garden but seem to flourish growing out of cracks in the sidewalk.

Dwarf form. Just means it's smaller than the species. It could still be 12 feet high.

Grows 8 feet in one season. Kind of scary. Do you really want a plantzilla?

Grows 5 feet by 5 feet. Woe to those of us who ignore the horizontal dimension. Pretty soon we'll have a bully in that 3-foot-wide space.

Plant 24 inches apart. Hard to do when you have bare space, and the plants are teeny tiny. But this is another one to pay attention to.

Sun or light shade. If it has yellow foliage, that generally means light shade. It also means the sun shouldn't be the hot western sun. Dappled shade is the most plant-friendly exposure, but it must belong to those mythic people who have well-drained soil.

Continuous bloom. If it's a rose, this generally means repeat bloom. It will bloom, rest, and gather strength and have other successive bursts of bloom. In other words, it will bloom in waves rather than continuously.

Acid soil. That's what most of us on the rainy side of the mountains have, and it's important for acid lovers such as rhododendrons and azaleas. But don't avoid all plants that require a chalky soil. Hydrangeas seem to do just fine here. And to all who want to change their color by adding lime, forget it. I have about 15 hydrangeas, and they've all stayed true to the color—blue, pink, rose, white—on the label.

Disease resistant. Not a guarantee. I have proof.

Hardy to 30 degrees. Not hardy.

MAY 27, 2010

LAB LESSONS
Here's what I learned in the garden this summer

EVERY SEASON HAS SOMETHING TO TEACH US, and often the best lessons are learned in the lab—not in books. In this case, the laboratory is our very own garden. In it, we experiment, we test, we go through trial and error, and sometimes the petri dish produces unexpected results.

I try to catalog the big and little discoveries of each season, and it's surprising how much turns up. Now that summer is limping into autumn, it's time to look back. And you can only imagine how heroically I will attempt not to dwell on the weather. Now, with that out of the way, here's what I learned.

Lesson 1: Drip irrigation, while great, can lull you into a false sense of security. Doug the Wonder Guy installed it last winter. Trouble is, we all forgot a very elemental thing. We have a lot of pots inserted into flowerbeds, and drip irrigation perversely does not flow up into them. It was only after we saw leaves seriously drooping that it occurred to us we had to water the pots separately. This was our big "duh" moment of the summer.

> *This was our big "duh" moment of the summer.*

Lesson 2: If you think it's dead, give it time before pulling it up. One of those pots that didn't get watered had a cute little tree that lost all of its leaves. We started watering and, after about two weeks, new leaves started emerging. It's fine.

Lesson 3: If you think it's dead, it may be. The hole in the pot of a Russian olive that we'd had for years got plugged up. We only noticed the plant was waterlogged when the leaves started drying up. We put it in an area we call the plant infirmary to dry out. It's not fine.

Lesson 4: We all know moving a plant can give it a whole new lease on life, but wonder of wonders it can also be a slug cure. We had a large old hosta on a corner back by the shed. It was a slug magnet, and by end of summer resembled a dirty lace doily. We finally decided to dig it up last autumn. But rather than toss it, my brilliant DTWG divided it into eight separate hostas and planted them under the rhodies in front of the house. They grew into healthy-sized hostas and had nary a slug bite all summer.

By the way, I planted false spirea (*Astilbe*) in the spot where we'd dug up the original hosta. This was the perfect substitution, since astilbes take the same shady and moist conditions but seem to be unappetizing to slugs.

Lesson 5: Patience really is a virtue. Boxwoods are slow growers, which is why they make good hedges. Two years ago, my boxwoods started yellowing, then dying out in their centers. We had a lot of theories: The snow had sat too long on the boxwood, there was a fungal disease, it was some kind of bug, overwatering, underwatering?

We never found the problem, but we did find the help. DTWG made a call to Boxwood Garden, a wholesale nursery west of Wilsonville. The nice people there gave him excellent advice. Cut out the deadwood in the center and do some thinning to let the light in. Today, we have substantial regrowth, and the hedges look healthy.

Lesson 6: Enjoy surprises from your garden. I was disappointed that my tall white lilies gave up the ghost just days before we and other Portland gardeners were hosting a garden tour out of Minnesota (yes, the Northwest is now officially a garden destination). But just before the group was to arrive, a lovely clematis with white flowers exploded into starry bloom. We wrapped it around the lily stakes and it gave the same tall streak of silky whiteness against a dark background that the lilies had supplied.

Lesson 7: There's a reason they call it

vegetable stew. Vegetables can be trickier to identify than you would think. Earlier in the summer I referred to Scarlett O'Hara digging up carrots. A reader gently corrected me that it was turnips.

I Googled *Scarlett* with *turnips* and got several hits confirming it was turnips. Alas, I got about the same number of hits contending it was either carrots or radishes when I Googled Scarlett's name with those vegetables. A check with the Multnomah County Library (which has a copy of the screenplay) says it's radishes, and that's what's in the book. But a look at a video clip of the scene shows long white root vegetables that don't resemble conventional radishes.

It's possible the filmmakers used another root vegetable that happened to be available. It's also possible that I wouldn't recognize a root vegetable if it bit me on the nose.

SEPTEMBER 16, 2010

✥

HURRY UP! COMPANY'S COMING!

The view from the other side of the path

DO YOU ADMIRE ALL THOSE CALM AND confident people who open their gardens to public view?

Let me give you the real lowdown on what we're like.

My own garden has been open this year for various philanthropic events. In fact, just a week after I returned from visiting fabulous English gardens, I had an open garden for the Hardy Plant Society's study weekend. People come from all over the West for this event, including British Columbia, and some even from the East Coast.

My first thought was, "What on earth had I been thinking?" How had I forgotten that this particular weekend was the exact moment the tulip tree decides to dump all of its withered blooms in the pond and all over the lawn? Or that a troop of raccoons had made mincemeat of the pond liner, and it was leaking like the proverbial sieve (a sad story for another time)?

Then there was the huge void in the middle of the main border where I'd finally yanked up those neon orange poppies. So off I went to a nursery in a panic to find a plant, any plant, mind you, to fill the bare spot left by the poppies. Fortunately and, I admit, completely by accident I found something that should do quite nicely as a permanent fixture.

I bought two Sally Holmes roses that have the palest of pink, almost white, single blossoms. They get tall, about 6 feet, but stay narrow and vase-shaped, with a width of only about 3 feet. As continuous bloomers, they should do marvelously for anchoring the center of my sunny border, unless of course they harbor a dark propensity for black spot. You never know.

But this glory is all sometime in the future. Meanwhile, this frenzied foray to the nursery all took place on a Friday night, just hours before the open garden. At the checkout stand, the cashier looked up and said, "Your neighbor was just here." I should mention that two sets of neighbors, Walt and Rosemary Ellis and Art and Lynn Knauss, also were opening their gardens.

Art had been buying bags of compost to, as his wife put it, "hide a multitude of sins." I reveal his secret only because someone on the garden tour asked me how many cats I have. When I answered six (honest), another person said, "Your neighbor Art says you have 11." One should never mess with someone who has access to the press.

On the way home from the nursery, I noticed that Rosemary and Walt had hastily borrowed a bunch of orna-

You don't have to dig to create a pond.

mental pots from a friend to fill gaps in the herb border by their front walk. Taking a cue from this ploy, I rushed home and shamelessly moved a pottery cat from the porch to cover a hole where some bulbs had died back.

The next time you visit a garden and look at the hosts and think, my, how cool these people are, you'll know better.

Then I plunked the two Sally Holmes bushes in the border, not even planted at that, hoping the surrounding foliage would hide the plastic pots. It kind of worked, but I got caught in another scam. Along with the roses, I'd also bought six or seven dahlias that were blooming in a pretty peachy-russet color and planted them where the wimpy delphiniums had gone into arrested development.

Naturally, the one question everyone asked was how I got dahlias to bloom so early. It's not cool to admit that the reason is that they just came out of someone's hothouse the day before.

The final blow was the pond pump, which decided to give up the ghost only hours before the tour was to start. Our garden helper,

Doug Wilson (or, as we call him, Doug the Wonder Boy), came to the rescue with another pump. At the last moment, we filled the pond enough so that no one noticed the leak.

The day of the open garden dawned, if not actually sunny, at least fairly dry. The Hardy Plant Society had very strict rules this year about telling people the tour was not to begin before 1 p.m. Four years ago, when I opened my garden to the same group, a man wandered in the backyard around 10 a.m. and loftily announced he wanted to avoid the crowds. You can imagine how that amused me as I stood there, a real sexy sight, coiling up hoses in my flannel nightie and fuzzy slippers.

Anyway, this year as the tour started at the correct hour, The Perp and I stationed ourselves on the back porch, one of us smugly at ease, the other praying she could remember names of plants when people asked for identities.

So the next time you visit a garden and look at the hosts and think, my, how cool these people are, you'll know better.

MARCH 5, 2007

BULBS LITE

*Get the best spring display with
the least effort*

EVERY FALL I BUY A BUNCH OF BULBS AND
then let them sit there until cold weather
stirs me into a frenzy of last-minute planting.

The thing is, it's no fun to plant bulbs.
Unlike perennials or shrubs, they don't give
immediate results. Also, it's just plain repeti-
tive because, to get a good show, you need to
plant quite a lot. Then, there's the bit about
being on your knees so long. So, every fall, I
am tempted to say, "That's enough; no more
bulbs."

But then, every spring I wish I had planted
more. There is nothing quite so joyous as
seeing those bright perky flowers emerge after a dark and drippy winter. So here I go
again. I've made some peace with the labor-
intensive duty of planting bulbs by devising
ways to get maximum show for least effort.
Here are ideas, all highly opinionated, that
work for me.

For maximum drama, concentrate on
adding tulips in just one color range. I use
varying shades of purple because purple
mixes so beautifully with the intense new yellow-green of spring foliage. Equally pretty
would be a garden with tulips all in the red
to pink range or, in a formal garden, all white.

For early-blooming bulbs, stick to small,
ground-hugging varieties, such as species tulips and miniature daffodils. They'll stand up
better to heavy rains. Most packages of bulbs
give you an approximate bloom time. Save
the big, floppy-petaled flowers for later in the
season when the rains are gentler.

Consider texture as well as color in making your selections. For example, while those
ruffled Rembrandt tulips are spectacular, I
prefer the tight-petaled varieties that have a
smooth, satiny sheen.

Remember that big isn't always better.
Miniature daffodils have a pleasant way of
clumping and naturalizing. They also seem
to return more reliably, and their dying foliage isn't nearly as unsightly as the foliage of
larger varieties. Similarly, while the giant
varieties of Allium are spectacular, they are
expensive. There are many smaller varieties
that have considerable charm.

Note also that naturalizing does not mean
invasive. Few if any bulbs are really invasive,
with the possible exception of grape hyacinths
(*Muscari*). Spanish bluebells (*Hyacinthoides
hispanica*) have naturalized in the shady parts
of my garden and make for a very romantic
look in spring. Their dying leaves don't seem
to be a problem because they stay green until
shrubs and perennials fill out. They also are
very good in clay soil. Sometimes bluebells
are sold under the name *Scilla non-scripta*, a
close relative with similar properties.

Expand your horizons beyond tulips and
daffodils. I love fritillaries, especially *Fritillaria meleagris*. Each spring I am charmed
anew by these little checkered flowers, despite their unsavory name of snake's-head.
And, if you have fritillaries, consider adding
their favorite pals, dog's-tooth violets
(*Erythronium*). Also, planting snowdrops
(*Galanthus nivalis*) is a must for me, because
they are the first flowers of the year to bloom.
They will give you an incalculable lift on a
gray January day.

Small bulbs, such as *Fritillaria*, *Galanthus*, *Leucojum* (snowflakes), *Crocus* and the
bulbous *Anemone* are smart choices for a lazy
gardener because they don't need to go deep
and are easy to plant. But plant them along a
walkway or driveway where you'll be sure to

see them in early spring. Or pool them under shrubs. Just don't stick them in with perennials, where they'll get lost.

When you plant, think clumps for small bulbs, drifts for big ones. Don't space bulbs out or line them up. Imagine what they'd look like if you discovered them naturally in a woodland. You'd find a tuft of fritillaries here and pool of anemones there.

If you still find planting a lot of bulbs too labor intensive, at least stick some in pots. The traditional bulbs survive the winter quite nicely in a container, and even just one bright spot or two can proclaim, "It's spring."

OCTOBER 6, 2005

The spectacular Allium cristophii.

❦

FUDGING IT
My top 10 (plus one) plants (for the moment)

OCCASIONALLY SOMEONE ASKS WHAT MY FAvorite plants are. There is no way I could limit myself to a top 10. Then it hit me: I could cheat. So I came up with two top 10 lists. One includes 10 perennials and bulbs—plus one irresistible grass, which makes it 11 (another bit of cheating)—and the other includes my 10 favorite shrubs and trees.

Even with two lists, it was a struggle. I kept thinking, "What about this plant or that one . . ." When I looked over my lists, I noticed a lot of my favorite plants were pretty common, which may say something about me. I was tempted to throw in some sophisticated plants, but honor won out.

Here's the first list, and next week it will be shrubs and trees. I will probably spend the week in an agony of thinking about what I "shoulda" put on this list.

1. *Acanthus mollis.* I have to wonder how an elegant foliage plant got such an inelegant name as "bear's breeches." The large sculpted leaves, often evergreen, look as if they've been polished. While the leaves are spectacular, I could do without the weird and scratchy flowers. (perennial)

2. *Alchemilla mollis.* The combination of winsome leaves and long-lasting, frothy, yellow-green flowers makes lady's mantle hard to beat. It's a quintessential cottage-garden plant but looks at home in other venues as well. And, because it's so pretty, I forgive its naughty tendency to seed around. (perennial)

3. *Allium cristophii.* Few flowers can rival the splendid display these purple balls make. *A. giganteum* is larger, but *A. cristophii* has a looser flower head that resembles a Fourth of July explosion of stars. (bulb)

4. *Dicentra spectabilis.* I am a fool for old-fashioned flowers, and none fits the bill

so well as the bleeding heart with its lacy leaves; graceful, pendulous, heart-shaped flowers; and oh-so-romantic common name. It looks fragile but is really quite hardy. There is a golden-leaved variety that has everyone swooning, but I prefer the original. (perennial)

5. *Fritillaria meleagris.* This little checkered lily looks fragile but is an easy bulb to grow in the maritime Northwest. It's not really a lily, but the diminutive flowers do have an unusual checkered veining pattern that is most exotic. (bulb)

6. *Galanthus nivalis.* There are prettier and showier bulbs but none braver. Dainty snowdrops emerge in late January and are the earliest sign that there will be a spring. It's not for nothing that they are symbols of hope. (bulb)

7. *Geranium* 'Ann Folkard.' I love the way this semi-vining hardy geranium embroiders its way through other plants without strangling them. It has saucy magenta flowers with black centers and bright apple-green leaves. It also blooms from spring to frost. (perennial)

> *I will probably spend the week in an agony of thinking about what I "shoulda" put on this list.*

8. *Hakonechloa macra* 'Aureola.' This low-growing golden grass lights up the shade. Its graceful arching habit makes it perfect for edging a path or pond, or even flowing over the edge of pot. This is one grass that doesn't spread; in fact, you'll wish it did. (grass)

9. *Heuchera* 'Chocolate Ruffles.' I am a sucker for all the coral bells, but especially the purple-leaved varieties. It's difficult to pick a favorite, but when you have the word "chocolate" in the mix, you have a winner. (perennial)

10. *Hosta sieboldiana.* The slugs and I have never met a hosta we didn't like, and the huge blue-green, puckered leaves of the sieboldiana are as gorgeous as leaves get. (perennial)

11. *Polygonatum odoratum.* Solomon's seal is an elegant and underused woodland plant that would add grace to any shade garden. Little green coils unfurl in spring, then each stem arches over and drips with dainty white, delicately scented flowers.

MARCH 23, 2006

Part 2

THE GARDENER IN YOU

⤜✦⤛

You see, it's dirt under the fingernails,

not Latin on the tongue,

that makes for a green thumb.

Think about texture in garden design, and remember: Green is a color.

CULTIVATING A GREEN THUMB

Record-keeping and reflection makes journaling worthwhile

I FOUND MY FIRST GARDEN JOURNAL THE OTHER day. First-and-only journal, actually.

I began it late in the summer of 1982, the year I began gardening in earnest. Oh, previously there had been the usual half-hearted attempts with annuals in pots on the deck. Then there was the summer when I was 12 and my father let me clear the space in back of the garage for vegetables. I raised a fine crop of radishes, and by summer's end, my family did not ever want to see a radish again.

Throughout those years, the gardening urge lay dormant, only bursting forth spottily, like the early marriage period, when houseplants dangled in front of every window. Of course, that period also coincided with the make-it-yourself-macramé-hanger craze. So the houseplants may have been an afterthought.

It's hard to say just what awakened ardor for gardening, but it seems related to a move to a new home and the need to "do something with that darn yard."

I bare my soul and confess to having come late to gardening, because of a disturbing trend among those newly come to

Botanic-speak may come later; for now, just enjoy the flower (in this case, an Icelandic poppy).

gardening. Some are an apologetic lot, who seem to think gardening expertise is something inborn, the proverbial green thumb that one either has or doesn't have. These novices are not helped by the gardening snob who baldly corrects their pronunciation the first time they have summoned the courage to use a plant's botanical name.

This novice attitude is troublesome; it breeds a sort of inferiority complex that holds that "real" gardeners are some sort of elite legion that can hardly be approached, much less joined. This complex rears up at gardening events, when newcomers get discouraged as they come up against Latin names that seem impossible to learn. It also leads people with perfectly charming little displays of country flowers to feel they are lacking because they don't have "collector's plants."

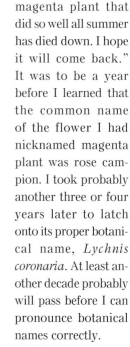

My first garden journal entry reads: "The magenta plant that did so well all summer has died down. I hope it will come back." It was to be a year before I learned that the common name of the flower I had nicknamed magenta plant was rose campion. I took probably another three or four years later to latch onto its proper botanical name, *Lychnis coronaria*. At least another decade probably will pass before I can pronounce botanical names correctly.

Even now, I

promptly forget half of the Latin names of plants over winter and gradually relearn most of them in spring. The first time I opened my garden to display, someone asked me the name of a plant. I froze, and finally said, "George."

That first-year journal records a heavy reliance on annuals, all bright colors, including the garish red salvia (so I must have liked it at one time). And while candor is the order of the day, I'll admit that one entry reads: "The daisies with lacy leaves not successful, tend to look shabby and yellow as opposed to the daisies with bigger leaves." Ah, botanical precision.

The point of these true confessions is that the only difference between a brand new gardener and an experienced one is simply time and experience, nothing more.

Another entry in that first summer is telling. It says, "A big bonus of perennials was the appearance of butterflies. But be careful of chemicals to control bugs. The butterflies disappeared, too." That was the first sign that the gardener was learning something. And it was nothing more than observation, not some inborn talent.

Gardening isn't—or shouldn't be—elitist, or even sophisticated. It's as common as sharing seeds over the back fence and as timeless as getting quite sappy overseeing the first sprouts of green in spring. You don't need to have a collector's garden of rare plants to be a bona fide gardener. There are country gardens with happy, common flowers, and other equally wonderful, sophisticated gardens with rare and exotic plants. There's no one right look.

And for every snob gardener who turns away huffily because you can't yet botanic-speak, there are half a dozen mentor gardeners who are only too happy to help you learn the language and give you a cutting as well.

As for the fabled green thumb, well, here is the three-step secret process handed down by generations of the gardening elite:

First, add compost to your soil. Second, add more compost. Third, add still more compost.

You see, it's dirt under the fingernails, not Latin on the tongue, that makes for a green thumb.

SEPTEMBER 11, 1992

UNMATCHED PAIR
Creative tension is good, but even a nongardening spouse has a way to help

LAST WEEK I HAD MY 43RD ANNIVERSARY. I am still on my first husband, which some would say shows a lack of imagination. Others wonder how we are compatible inasmuch as my husband has possibly never touched a trowel and regards gardening as a mild form of torture.

I used to envy couples who garden compatibly, and I do know a few. I also know a few who garden together, and not entirely compatibly. (*Wife*: I think some perennials would look nice there. *Husband*: Don't touch my rose bed. *Wife*: Let's put in a flowerbed over there. *Husband*: Don't touch my lawn.)

Even Doug the Wonder Boy, my garden helper, and I are not always in agreement. I love the vegetable garden for its looks. I dream of a French parterre with calendulas, nasturtiums, and sunflowers interspersed among the vegetables and herbs. He prefers to plant things that are actually edible and

Neatly trimmed boxwoods form the elegant lines of a knot garden.

healthy. My view is that until chocolate is declared a vegetable, I want room for ornamentals.

I have come to appreciate my husband's inactivity in the garden because he has one outstanding virtue when it comes to my gardening. He doesn't get in my way. Also, many years ago he learned not to ask how much something cost and, worse yet, where would I put it. He also patiently stops at nurseries when we are on weekend drives. I could hardly ask for anything more.

> *My view is that until chocolate is declared a vegetable, I want room for ornamentals.*

Still, I do enjoy company in the garden, and I think there's something to be said for the synergy that comes from two pairs of eyes regarding the garden. There is even something to be said for a degree of incompatibility in the garden.

A famous example is that of Vita Sackville-West and her husband, Harold Nicolson, who created Sissinghurst, the most famous of the grand English gardens. Nicolson was extremely disciplined and precise. He wanted everything in the garden rigidly formal, and he laid out the garden beds all in straight lines.

Sackville-West once remarked that she made it her life's work to undo his symmetry by planting everything profusely to erase the formality of the design. But she also respected her husband's work and referred to their collaboration as a creative tension. It was this creative tension, she said, that lifted the garden from merely pretty to sublime.

I see the success of that kind of creative tension in the charming garden of my neighbors Rosemary and Walt Ellis. Walt insists on a pristine space for his roses, and I suspect Rosemary has had an urge to mix plants among the roses, as I would have done. But we both have to admit that Walt's separate bed is probably why his hybrid teas look so healthy and disease-free.

The next best thing to a gardening spouse may be a gardening kid, and for me it's a surrogate kid. Doug and I do have a bit of creative tension, and I respect our differences. He has taken some of my ideas and pushed them over the top, where I would have been far more timid. When I decided to move the pond to the spot where there had been an oval herb bed, he was the one who had the idea not to fill the entire oval, but to leave room for planting around the pond.

When I decided to put a gravel path around the pond, it was his idea to bring the gravel around the entire lawn, which meant we had to reshape a flowerbed. I don't think I would have done that if he hadn't pushed me, but the resulting shape of the lawn is certainly more attractive.

When we took out the front lawn and put in a graveled path, I bought a big pot to use as a focal point. It was his idea to put rocks around the base of the pot and seed a few plants around it, giving the pot an anchored look.

And so it goes. One of us gets an idea, and the other embellishes it. And my dear, wise husband does his part as well. He stays out of our way.

JUNE 22, 2006

GOOD-NEIGHBOR GARDENING

Respect and reason add up to harmony

YEARS AGO, I HAD A NEIGHBOR WHO WOKE one morning to find that the people behind her had taken down the hedge and, along with it, all her privacy. To add insult to injury, it was her hedge. I have heard similar tales many times. It strikes me that gardens should be fertile ground for building neighborly relationships, not hurting them.

So, with a new garden season about to open, perhaps it's a good time to review the 10 Commandments of Virtuous Gardening.

1. **Thou shalt respect boundaries.** Before taking out or pruning a hedge or building a fence between your property and a neighbor's, it's mannerly to have a conversation and work out any necessary compromises. Similarly, resist the urge to lean over to prune neighbors' tree limbs or pluck their flowers if they are not actually extending into your own garden.

2. **Thou shalt give the neighbors a chance to remedy any problems first,** before calling down the wrath of God, the police or the neighborhood organization. If their precious kitty is invading your garden, pay a visit and explain the problem. If their music is too loud, talk to them, but nicely. Don't leap into counteractions, such as turning up a boom box

> *As a point of decorum, one simply should never say, "Mine are bigger" when looking at gardens or nude calendars.*

or calling the police or trapping the pet, before they've been given a chance to rectify the situation. (Flip side of this rule: Be responsive if you are the alleged offender.)

3. **Thou shalt stem the almost irresistible desire to pull a weed in another person's garden,** even though the compulsion is overwhelming in everyone's garden but thine own.

4. **Thou shalt not collect plants in the wild.** The rationalization that one is preserving the plant is, unfortunately, anything but rational. If it's rare, it probably won't survive the transplant. Go to a rare-plant breeder and buy a propagated plant if you must have it.

5. **Thou shalt do no unkindness to thy neighbor's space.** Before planting a fast-growing tree near a property line, consider the shade it will cast over a neighbor's vegetable garden. Similarly, consider the consequences before placing a scrambling vine on a fence or an invasive rooter (such as willow or bamboo) near property lines.

6. **Thou shalt limit the operation of noisy gardening equipment,** such as leaf blowers, to reasonable hours. This means avoiding early in the morning or Saturday night when your neighbors are having dinner on their terrace, even if you were not invited. In that vein, noisy devices, such as bug zappers or air-conditioning units, should not be placed near a neighbor's bedroom window. (Flip side of this rule: If you are

having an outdoor party, invite the neighbors or at the very least notify them and respect a reasonable cutoff time for the festivities.)

7. **Thou shalt not interview gardening help on a neighbor's time.** If tree trimmers, handy-persons, gardeners, etc., are doing work in the neighborhood, politely ask for their card or number. Do not engage overlong in interviewing them or invite them to look at your place while someone else is paying them hourly wages.

8. **Thou shalt not succumb to the temptation to allow one's lawn to grow overlong** in an urban setting by rationalizing that it is now a meadow.

9. **Thou shalt buy plants only from established growers, nurseries and landscapers** whose references thou hast checked. A friend of mine recently found that someone had driven up in a van, dug out a tree and some shrubs in her front yard and taken off. Nurseries are reporting record numbers of thefts. One way to deter such thievery is by refusing to be an unwitting client.

10. **Thou shalt compliment open gardens** and resist the urge to stare at the tomatoes or dahlias and say rather loudly, "Mine are bigger," as some actually did in my first open garden. It takes a lot of courage to open one's garden to public scrutiny, and one does not want to discourage such brave souls. As a point of decorum, one simply should never say, "Mine are bigger" when looking at gardens or nude calendars.

FEBRUARY 5, 2004

LOOKING RELAXED

Sometimes it's better if we close our eyes to our garden's imperfections

I HAVE NOTICED THAT WHEN GARDENERS TALK or write about their pleasure in their garden, it's often in the context of working—usually weeding and planting. They rhapsodize about the scents of soil and flowers, the music of buzzing bees and chirping birds, and the feel of soft crumbly earth. I would go on, but I've run out of clichés.

Such gardeners never seem to be sitting on one of those ubiquitous garden benches just relaxing and taking it all in. This got me thinking. I have several garden benches, and I never seem to spend time on any of them. I may sit briefly, but up I pop to snip something, pull a weed or just move on.

So now that it is June and most of the planting and moving things about is over, it's time for a resolution. My resolution is to sit back, relax and actually enjoy my garden without thinking about what needs to be done.

Do I hear the Greek chorus chanting, "Liar, liar, pants on fire?" Can I resist the urge to get up and deadhead the poppies that are losing their petals? Can I forestall grabbing a watering can for the fainting ligularia (if ever there was a voracious drinker, this is it)? Can I ignore the giant dandelion shooting up through the ground cover like a rocket ready for takeoff? I'm not sure that I can.

Even on strolls about my garden, I seem to be doing something other than just enjoying my plants. I'm usually carrying a notebook so I can jot down what needs to be done: clean water basins, put out mosquito dunks, water hanging baskets, mop shed floor, fill hole by Nora's Japanese maple and so on.

Your garden should be an expression of your personality. Bench made by Lep Bugajski.

(My friend Nora bequeathed me a couple of maples when she moved to Arizona.)

And yes, filling holes is turning out to be quite the chore, since Ernie the dog has turned out to be in the excavation business. This is despite the fact that in his application letter—petitioning for a family-dog position, that is—he claimed to be a nondigger.

It is a bitter disappointment, ranking right up there with biting into a chocolate chip cookie and finding out those brown things are raisins. But Ernie is adorable, and so all, or mostly all, is forgiven, although I'm still mourning my chewed-up loafers. But I digress.

How does one really begin to appreciate a garden, drink it in and enjoy it without having to think about chores? One way, if you're nearsighted, is to take off your glasses. Then things blur together like a lovely Impression-ist painting. (I believe that nearsightedness is also a requisite for a good marriage.) Those of you with fine eyesight will just have to squint.

But seriously, I think the answer is to be found in attitude. I once read a quote about writing that went, "Write to express, not to impress."

I'd tell you who said this, but when I looked it up on the Web, any number of people claimed to have originated this say-ing. The same guidance applies to garden-ing. We all might better appreciate our own gardens if we weren't so busy trying to make them perfect for someone else, the "someone else" being the key words.

I'm not arguing for a messy garden, but rather for a forgiving eye and for allowing oneself to relax without anxiety and guilt. It's especially hard to do this during this season of open gardens.

For many of us, our first reaction after visiting someone's garden is the urge to go home and tear up everything and start over. But don't worry, this is a temporary malaise. In a few days, you'll snap back and begin to like your own garden again.

If you can't enjoy things in June, when nature is at its peak, when can you? After all, the roses are blooming, honeysuckle scent is filling the air, the heron hasn't yet eaten all the fish, the lawn is still green and lush, the sun is shining (well, more often), and the pink flamingos are settling in. What more could you want?

Besides a nondigging doggie, that is.

JUNE 4, 2009

❧

COPING WITH GARDENING'S DARKER SIDE
When depression sets in over some gardening failure, chocolate can help

SOMEWHERE IN MID-FEBRUARY I REALIZED THE awful truth. My garden was dead, dead, dead.

It was a moonscape. Where were all those early-blooming bulbs I'd planted last fall? Surely by this time in previous years, legions of green shoots had been poking up.

Naturally, I sank into a deep depression. I immediately administered chocolate.

By early March the thrall begins. I begin dragging my poor husband out to look at everything that's popping up as if he, or I, has never seen such growth before.

I celebrate with chocolate. This disorder is known as the horticultural depressive-manic cycle. If you are going to be a gardener, you need to know that there is a dark side to gardening. The moment of truth can come unexpectedly. April is a particularly dangerous month. It's plant sale month.

One moment you'll be crowded around a table of plants, the picture of probity. Then, just as a naive soul reaches for the last variegated, spotted, lobe-leaved pot of some elusive species, your arm will snake out quick as a striking cobra and snatch that plant away.

On the other hand, you may not be aware of how despicably low you've sunk until you unload $120 worth of plants, smile sweetly at your spouse and announce: "Look what I got! For just $40."

About this time, you'll find that as you begin to describe a plant someone will correct your Latin pronunciation. "What a jerk," you'll think.

By May, panic will have set in. Little foamy dabs will be all over your perfect garden. It won't matter that everyone says spittlebugs won't do any harm. You'll be out buying chemicals with a half-life that rivals a redwood.

In June, those ecologically sound saucers of beer will be tossed out. Good grief, you'll actually reach for the salt. By July, you'll be renting flamethrowers to push down mole holes and lying awake at night devising new ideas to do in furry little critters.

Then there's plantsman's compulsive-obsessive behavior. You know you have it when you find yourself digging by flashlight. Another symptom is noticing that all the other guests at a dinner party have dozed off while you've spent the entire time talking plants to the only other guest who's into gardening.

Midsummer is a difficult time. That's when you start doing garden tours. You'll visit someone's garden and fall into deep and fickle infatuation. You'll come home and hate, hate, hate your garden.

This is the delusional phase. You'll be convinced the years you spent pouring your heart and money into building the perfect cottage garden have been misguided. What you were meant to have is a sophisticated, slightly formal green garden with clipped hedges, perfect trees, and a splendid urn placed exactly in the right spot.

Eventually, you'll get talked into opening your own garden for a tour. That's when your family will know you've gone round the bend. You will alternate between bouts of frenzied activity and deep self-loathing for what you have gotten into.

You will rob the kids of their college education money just to buy filler plants for all those bare spots you never noticed before. Your campaign to get the garden in dazzling order will put Desert Storm to shame. Your family will be booking rooms at the Depraved Gardeners Wing of the Betty Ford Clinic.

By the end of summer, you'll have reached the penultimate of corruption. You actually will correct someone else's Latin pronunciation of a plant. "What a jerk," they'll think.

Get help. I recommend chocolate.

MARCH 3, 1996

∾

CONTROL FREAKOUT

We gardeners impose order on nature, but in a good way, right?

S HORTLY AFTER THE STORY ABOUT PORTLAND Mayor Sam Adams broke, *Oregonian* col-umnist Anna Griffin wrote a piece headlined, "Sam Adams: He gardens, and he works." She wove that theme throughout the commentary, eventually declaring that gardening and working are "the twin refuges of a control freak."

When I came across that statement, I rose out of my chair, disturbing poor Orville, who, being a reader cat, was sitting on the paper in a way that I had to read around him. Reaching deep into my vocabulary of invective, I cried, "That's clapdoodle." My husband glanced up alarmed, probably most so at the fact that I had discomfited the cat.

Of course we gardeners who also work hard are not control freaks. Are we not gentle, beauty-loving folk who just want to bring beauty and order to nature? Uh-oh. There's that word "order."

I suppose we are into control. After all, we buy products for weed control, disease control and pest control. We welcome wildlife to our gardens, but by wildlife we mean butterflies and birds, not raccoons and opossums. Imagine if Noah had been so selective with the ark. Well, I think he might have been just a teensy selective. Did he really have to invite Mr. and Mrs. Slug to come aboard? But I digress.

We gardeners put up fences. We add fertilizer and compost to our gardens because we believe the earth we have is not quite good enough even though trees and grasses and other plants thrive in uncultivated areas nearby. We make a distinction between what is a weed and what is not, despite not a whit of scientific evidence for the distinction. It's as if we all got together and voted the dandelion a weed despite its perky yellow flower, but decided that violets, which are rampantly invasive, are acceptable and, in fact, sweet.

Do we not exercise control when we plant vegetables in straight rows and shape plots and lawns into squares and rectangles? Nature is not into geometry. I suppose no plant is more emblematic of man's control than the lawn. We pamper it, watering and fertilizing and mowing regularly lest our neighbors exercise lack of control over their tempers.

> *No plant is more emblematic of man's control than the lawn.*

We hybridize plants to produce what we think is bigger and better than nature's own selection—more colors, more petals, greater disease resistance, hardiness and so on. On the other hand, anyone with a nodding acquaintance with Darwin knows that nature itself is consistently adapting and evolving and crossing plants. So perhaps we are not so out of tune with nature after all.

Certainly we gardeners do tame nature, but I like to think it's in a good way, the way a parent reins in an unruly child who, left without some discipline, might be unfit for society. (Although when I was a child I thought my mother was a control freak because she would not let me pierce my ears.)

In his book *The Botany of Desire*, author Michael Pollan writes, "Partly by default, partly by design, all of nature is now in the process of being domesticated—of coming, or finding itself, under the (somewhat leaky) roof of civilization. Indeed, even the wild now depends on civilization for its survival."

So, OK, I can buy the argument that gardening is a lot about controlling. But what I can't buy is the implication that control is a pejorative as in "control freak," at least when it is applied broadly to gardeners. I like to think we are companions with nature. If Mother Nature is a goddess who tosses her wild silken hair every which way, we are the handmaidens who lovingly and carefully comb out her tangles.

Although, I have to admit the crew cut we give our lawns every week probably isn't to her liking.

FEBRUARY 12, 2009

CHEATERS ALWAYS WIN
Tips for a no-stress gardening experience

NOT ALL OF US ARE THE STOUTHEARTED gardeners we'd like to be. I am, by turns, unbelievably lazy and incredibly energetic, depending on the time of year. Lately, the moments of frenetic activity are getting shorter and shorter. That's why I feel a kinship with the truly lazy gardener.

The interesting thing about laziness is that it does not in any way diminish our zeal to have a garden. Fortunately, there are ways to have our cake and eat it, too, so to speak. All we need is a modicum of creativity, a little stretching of the rules and a gentled-down attitude. So here are some tips for lazy but clever gardeners.

1. **As the English say, sod off.** I think they mean it less politely, but let's interpret it as shrink the lawn.
2. **Take off the rose-colored glasses.** Resist hybrid tea roses. I realize this is like telling a teen-age boy to resist a peek at

We all love to push our zonal boundaries by scattering tender potted plants around the garden.

Sports Illustrated's annual swimsuit issue. But remember, most require pruning, fertilizing, spraying and a lot of watering to reach perfection. The roses, that is.

3. **Let annuals go to pot.** If you want flowers, plant perennials and leave annuals for containers.

4. **Remember, green is a color.** If you really want to save time, limit flowers and opt for shrubs and ground covers. A lush green garden can be gorgeous as well as relaxing.

5. **Raise your beds and your spirits.** Save your back and don't double-dig clay soil, a form of torture devised by English authors to get back at the colonists. Turn over just one spade depth and add compost, then haul in some rich, friable topsoil and pile a foot of it on top.

6. **Write a new script.** If there's a messy, overgrown section you haven't gotten to, put up a sign that says "wildlife garden," and everyone will think it's a charming area. Just make sure it's not your front yard.

7. **Go with the flow.** Be sensitive to your garden's varying conditions and don't fight them. Make a pond or bog garden out of places that collect water. Have a rock garden in a dry area. If flowers lean over, move them to where they'll get more sun.

8. **Make a clean break.** Edge flowerbeds by digging a furrow below the root depth of grass. It also helps to put in a barrier. Otherwise, you'll be fighting grass creeping into your flowerbeds forever.

9. **Don't hedge your bets.** Avoid fast-growing hedges because they almost always turn out to be high-maintenance in terms of pruning once they're mature. Consider a natural border of varied shrubs. Or, if you need instant privacy, put up a fence.

10. **Use a cover-up strategy.** Mulch bare ground in spring and late fall. It will suppress weeds and help soil retain water. If it's organic, it also will add nutrients as it breaks down.

11. **Relax the rules.** Don't fertilize if plants look healthy. If you have clay soil, it's probably rich in nutrients. Watch that trigger finger on pruning. If a plant looks healthy and shapely, leave it alone. Don't do things just because a book says it's time.

12. **Eject the miscreants.** If a plant needs continual hacking to keep it to the right size, it's in the wrong spot. Move it. If a plant continues to look sickly, toss it.

13. **Be nice to Mother Earth.** Can the intensive spraying and learn to live with a few bug bites.

14. **Don't sweat failures.** We all have them. I'm lousy with roses and delphiniums. We can grow more plants here than anywhere else in the United States, so move on to something that works for you.

15. **Don't try to keep up with the Joneses.** You only have to satisfy yourself. I've said it before, and I'll say it again: Gardening is not a competitive sport.

APRIL 11, 2002

> *I've said it before, and I'll say it again: Gardening is not a competitive sport.*

WISE ACRE

Expectations exceeded realities of maturity

THOSE OF YOU WHO ARE NEW GARDENERS probably think that those of us with mature gardens have it made. Well, let me tell you, that is not true at all.

When I was younger, I dreamed of having a garden where plants had reached their maturity and everything was filled in and lush. To some extent that happened. But other dreams proved unrealistic.

Somehow, I imagined that a mature garden would have done much to satiate my plant lust. This didn't happen. I turn giddy as a teenager in the throes of first love at the sight of a spring plant sale.

I imagined that a mature garden would bring the leisure to sit and enjoy it. After all, isn't that why they make garden benches? Apparently not. I don't seem to be able to sit on a bench for more than five minutes without jumping up to pluck an errant weed or snip a swooning flower.

I imagined that a mature garden would be full and lush. What I didn't imagine is that the lushness would overdo itself and that I'd be slashing through the jungle like Tarzan on his way to meet Jane. All those little self-sowers that brought me joy in my early garden years are now on the thug list.

I imagined that a mature garden would finally have achieved soil perfection and that the backbreaking work of digging in compost would be over. I did not take into account the tendency of clay soil to fall off the wagon and return to its original consistency of concrete.

I imagined that plants that flourished when my garden was new would continue to flourish. That did not happen. I have watched some formerly robust plants turn wimpy or not return at all. I now have an appreciation for crop rotation and the need to amend tired soil.

I imagined that I would finally wrest control from irksome weeds, slimy slugs and awful aphids. I had read about the Hundred Years' War in school, and now realize this is the battle they were describing.

I imagined that one could do almost anything that needed doing in a garden with the right tools—good shovels, spading forks,

Your novice garden will bear little resemblance to the one you create as a mature gardener.

sharp clippers and a solid wheelbarrow. I did not realize then that good tools also included a strong back and knees that worked.

I imagined that I would achieve a point at which there was nothing left to do, no room for any more projects. But there always seems to be some patch that needs a tune-up, especially because trees have matured to cast shade where once there was sun, while other trees have expired, sometimes crashingly, to create new sun spots.

I even imagined, foolish me, that after several years I'd get a handle on Northwest weather and know what I could leave in the ground and what I had to move into shelter. Well, last winter certainly reminded me that no one should count on the predictability of our climate.

Finally, I imagined that when my garden matured, all would be perfection and contentment. All I can say is, thank goodness perfection didn't happen. I can't think of anything that would make me less content than not having something new to plant, prune, divide, fix, redo, take out, pull up, nurse or otherwise putter with.

SEPTEMBER 9, 2004

❧

ACTING THE PART
Appearance, actions brand the longtime gardener

I AM HERE TO TELL YOU THAT GARDENING CAN change a person, and not necessarily for the better.

For example, the other day I came in from a couple of hours in the garden and looked in the mirror. I was wearing a floppy hat that had lost both its shape and color. My hair was matted down from a fine rain. A swipe of mud ran along one cheek.

I had on a shapeless old sweater with holes in the elbows, baggy pants and a T-shirt commemorating Earth Day '96. Bits of leaves and other debris were clinging to me like ornaments on a chubby Christmas tree. My knees were caked with mud.

"Good grief," I thought. "I look like one of those crazy old ladies I used to see out in the garden when I was a kid." A nanosecond later, it hit me. I am one of those crazy old ladies. When did this all happen, I wondered, this drift into contented slobhood?

Gardening can change one. Not only have some of us embraced slobbery, but we also have become gifted at duplicity and rationalization, if not downright deceit.

As a case in point, I recently spent an afternoon plant shopping with a friend. When we arrived at her house, she said to hold off unloading the car until her husband left. She didn't want him to see how many plants tumbled out. This made me wonder if there is a spouse anywhere who fully grasps just what his or her gardening half spends. It happened that my friend's husband never left and ended up helping us unload the car, with the good grace not to ask, "How much?"

Once when my husband was doing our income taxes he foolishly added up all our vet bills for the year. It turned out we could have gone on a Mediterranean cruise for the price of our pets. I have since forbidden him ever to add up either vet bills or garden bills. Ignorance, I feel, makes for a happier relationship.

Then there's a gardener's skill with rationalization. I was at a fancy specialty nursery with another friend who fell in love with a rare and expensive plant. She decided she

If you live with a nongardener, you may enlist other help, like Doug the Wonder Guy.

couldn't afford it. But then she came up with a creative solution. "Hey," she said. "It's almost Father's Day. I'll give it to him for Father's Day."

I have been known to do that with some art I've wanted, but given that my husband has zip interest in gardening, I have never been able to pull off giving him a plant as an actual gift. I am working on it, though.

Gardening also changes you physically. You become capable of feats of strength. Those of us who can barely push a vacuum find that we can carry an inordinate number of plants and garden ornaments.

I had a friend who bought and dragged an antique iron garden ornament all over England. On the way back, she and I hauled it from one end of O'Hare International Airport to another. Now that she's home, neither of us can lift it.

Then there's that bit about defying the laws of physics. Some of us have honed the art of loading an ordinary automobile far beyond its actual carrying capacity. I have personally driven down the freeway with six people and more than 100 plants stuffed in the vehicle. We were a force to behold.

In addition to slobhood, deceit, rationalization and improbability, one can also add another item to the gardeners' list of vices. We almost never feel penitent.

MAY 20, 2004

IT'S OFFICIAL: THE SEASON'S ON
Getting in shape for your own private Olympics

LET THE GAMES BEGIN. OR SUBSTITUTE WHATever exhortation that officially opens the gardening season at your house. Sure, a rambunctious rhodie or cheeky cherry have jumped the starter's gun here and there. But this is the real thing.

The rosy haze of nodules about to pop like corn into full-fledged blossoms on the trees is one sign. The music of mowers—yes, lawn mowers in February—is another. But for Portlanders the tried, true, traditional event that lights the torch to start the season is that most time-honored of all season openers—the Official Rose Pruning Heats.

All over town, gardeners are donning the official garb: rubber shoes, baggy swats, cheap gloves and expensive clippers. Their hearts are beating faster, their breath coming in quick gasps, their eyes glazing over as they line up at the starting gate. Nongardening spouses and household pets had better step aside or prepare to get trampled as the nation's greatest amateur sport gets underway.

They're going for the green.

And as with all great sports, the players who will emerge champions are the ones who live by the following rules:

- **Get off to a fast start:** Unless you take the time to condition soil, none of your subsequent efforts will count for much. And, in our land of hard clay, that means adding compost, compost and more compost to get the crumbly texture that underlies champion-class gardens.

- **Pace yourself:** Don't take on so much that you'll exhaust yourself before the end of the season. The best gardens emerge over several seasons. Start small and know your limits. If you're carving up areas of lawn for flowerbeds, for example, don't just consider your capacity to plant. Consider also what you can maintain over the long term, and that means ongoing weeding and watering.

- **Get good training:** There are wonderful opportunities to learn more about gardening, especially at the start of the season. Myriad plant workshops and classes are readily available in this area. Join a garden club, plant society or botanical garden, such as Portland's Leach and Berry gardens. All offer excellent seminars at low prices.

- **Stay in condition:** The back is the first to go. Then the knees. In the first thrall of the season, it's easy to stay hunched over in a planting frenzy for hours. The result is stiffness and soreness on Monday. Use common sense. Change positions frequently. Protect yourself from sun exposure with a good sunscreen and a silly hat. Don't lift more than you can handle. Don't spray insecticides and fungicides on windy days.

- **Keep a track record:** Without a garden journal, it's difficult to remember from year to year how late frosts can come, which periods are down-times for flowering, which plants fizzled early and which ones went on to sizzle.

- **Invest in good equipment:** The essential items are spade, pitchfork, trowel, long- and short-handled pruning clippers, wheelbarrow, and lawn rake. For tools that last, look for tempered steel and fewest seams. Biggest and heaviest aren't always best. Choose the weight that you can handle most efficiently.

- **Don't let the competition psych you:** Avoid being intimidated because you don't know all the Latin names of plants. Plants grow just fine if you call them George and Alice. After a while, those mysterious botanical names will come naturally.

- **Take risks:** Winning performances have drama. Introduce some with taller prairie plants, big-foliaged beauties or bolder colors—or just add something you haven't tried before.

- **Keep a good attitude:** In any sport, state of mind is as important as physical condition. Perfection is no fun. Live with a few weeds. Accept that the dog has big feet. Grin when the kids' ball lands on your prize roses. Don't worry if the neighbor's grass is greener. It always will be.

- **Stay with your amateur status:** Gardening is supposed to be fun. When it's more work or guilt than pleasure, it's time to cut back.

FEBRUARY 21, 1992

REBEL IN THE GARDEN

*Some rules deserve to be broken, or why
I fell for a gnome*

L ORD HELP ME, I'VE GONE AND DONE IT. I'VE
bought a gnome. I can't explain it. It just
looked at me in an appealing way, and I
couldn't resist. For reasons inexplicable even
to myself, I've always had a soft spot in my
heart for gnomes.

I realize that any tenuous claims to sophistication I might have entertained are out
the window. I can hear the sirens of the Taste
Police coming to get me. My politically in-
correct comments about plastic flamingos are
exposed for the hypocrisy they are.

Worse yet, it seems everything I read this
spring counsels restraint. One must not
overdo the ornaments. One must pick a style
and stick to it. Discipline, spareness, tasteful
discretion, all are encouraged.

I am ready to revolt. If you can't be exuberant or even outrageous in your own garden, where can you be? What better place to
indulge your whims? Where else to practice
self-expression? At least I don't express myself by going around in low-cut dresses and
hats with giant flowers. Well, I might, if I
had any cleavage, but that's another story.

I realize these are the defensive statements
of a woman caught with a gnome in her yard.
All I can say in my defense is that it was a
pricey gnome, and it seems to have more expression than most. It is ceramic, not plastic,
and, yes, I can hear some of you murmuring,
"like that matters." He is going to live in the

At home with gnomes. What's the big deal anyway?

shady area of the garden we call the Blue Mushroom Woods because it is filled with clumps of blue ceramic mushrooms. I think they are charming, although my friend Carlene never fails to tell me they are exceedingly tacky.

Which brings me to something I have learned recently about style. It's a great lesson. You don't have to have it. Style, that is. This realization is very freeing. I remember when I was younger trying to decide what style my garden should be.

First, I fell in love with the cottage garden look. Then I migrated to the more woodland look of shrubs and small ornamental trees. I've even flirted with the tropical look, but soon realized that an occasional clump of cannas and a single trumpet flower do not a jungle make.

For years I was filled with mild angst thinking I could never pick a style and get it down just right. So, now it is very restful not to worry about style any more. Any person of a certain age who has long said goodbye to his or her waistline will know the feeling.

I am not advocating throwing out all the rules. I do not, after all, preach garden anarchy. I am simply saying that rigid adherence to design rules may not be the best way to foster creativity. And, I am advocating, if you love something, even if it is a gnome for gosh sakes, go for it. But you need to learn to carry it off. That requires honing the fine skill of rationalization.

One way is to learn to think of your garden in the correct terms. It is not messy or kitsch; it is "eclectic." It does not lack style; it simply has personal style (which you should

> *Just keep in mind, "The woman has a gnome; what does she know?"*

always insist is the "in" thing). You should also disregard garden writers who scorn your pink flamingos or cutouts of ladies bending over with their bloomers showing.

Believe me, we will continue to heap insults, but you can let them roll off your back now. You know we have our own dirty little secrets. Just keep in mind, "The woman has a gnome; what does she know?"

Finally—and buckle your seat belt because here comes the single most important advice for gardening contentment ever—realize that your garden is a place to express, not impress.

APRIL 10, 2003

THE ROAD TO CONTENTMENT
Infatuations lose sway as a new emotion surfaces

I HAD BEEN WORRYING THAT I HAD LOST THE "fire in my belly" for gardening. This past year, I added relatively few new plants. I admired the early catalogs, but they failed to stir much plant lust. I didn't even make my customary list of must-have plants.

I visited other gardens, loved them but wasn't compelled to come home and do my garden over. I saw terrific new trends in garden magazines but for once was immune to new fads. I didn't really have a serious infatuation this year. (The flamingo fling doesn't count.)

I worried that I was losing my zeal, getting too old, dropping out. But on reflection,

I don't think that's the case. Now I recognize that there's a new overriding emotion in my gardening life. It's contentment. But it's been a long journey getting there. Some of you may recognize the stages.

The age of innocence: We were young. It was our first house, and we wanted to be good neighbors, which meant mowing and edging the lawn. I dutifully planted a few annuals each spring, mostly in pots on a deck. We never used the term garden. It was the backyard. Inside the house, it was a different scene. Ferns hung in the bathroom, begonias bloomed in the kitchen, and small plants sat on windowsills gathering a rim of something icky and white just above the soil.

The voyage of discovery: I discovered perennials. That's when the first twinges of plant lust hit like a jolt. I bought how-to garden books and started a garden diary. Unfortunately, a little knowledge proved dangerous. My poor husband helped me double-dig a garden plot because I had read that this was the way to prepare soil. But I neglected to put in compost. My husband never gardened again. The lawn started to shrink while my Latin vocabulary grew. I started to go to garden shows and joined a plant society and helped form a garden club (The Dirty Ladies). Meanwhile, the indoor plants shriveled up for lack of care and interest.

The era of thrall: I finally discovered woody plants. What a surprise to realize there were actually shrubs that weren't rhododendrons or azaleas. We discovered not all roses are hybrid teas. My plant lust went into hyperdrive, and I thought I might have been the first person in the world to notice foliage. We made pilgrimages to English gardens. My friends and I tossed around Latin names with aplomb. We even read catalogs that didn't have pictures. I'm afraid we were somewhat smug.

The thrill of the chase: My gardening friends and I yearned for the rare and unusual. We worshipped at the shrine of Northwest plantsman Dan Hinkley. Not just any nursery would do; we sought out "destination" nurseries. We pushed the zonal envelope with plants from New Zealand, South Africa, South America and the Mediterranean. We planted things in gravel. Now we got the Latin pronunciations right. We knew a CLEM-a-tis from a cle-MAT-tis. We dropped names of garden greats. We had gone from smug to insufferable.

The age of consent, or is it content: I began to appreciate that the benches and chairs in my garden weren't merely decorative. I admitted to myself that, while

Fronds of a fern unfurl almost before your eyes.

those elegant and stylized gardens are fun to visit, I am most comfortable in my unsophisticated little Eden, even if it's more like a cottage garden. I still welcome visitors but have stopped saying, "You should have been here last week."

I continue to buy plants, but they're just as likely to be vegetables and a few annuals. I have taken a new perspective about those semi-tropical plants. I think of them as annuals. If they live over, great; if not, no biggie.

If you also have reached this stage, you will recognize it by your ability to rationalize. We haven't lost our zeal. Age hasn't tempered our energy. I like to think we have just evolved to a new enlightened state.

NOVEMBER 19, 2009

STARTING THE PLOT
16 tips for a new garden

THERE IS A THEORY THAT YOU SHOULD LIVE in a place for a year and get to know it before plotting out a garden. That makes a lot of sense. But sometimes gardening is about fun and passion, not about good sense. Here are 16 tips for starting a garden in a new home; some are sensible, and some feed that passion.

1. **Plant a few things right away** to make the space your own and give you a sense of your soil's fertility. Put in some flowers or small shrubs near the front door or driveway, where you can see them as you come and go. You can always move them later if you have a change of heart.

2. **Check out the light patterns** throughout the day. Morning sun is the growing sun, so this is prime territory for ornamental shrubs and flowers. If you want a rose bed or vegetable patch, it'll need a place that gets at least six hours of sun. And if you have a deeply shady area where not much will grow, that's a good spot for a terrace or garden shed.

3. **Determine what kind of soil you have.** While soil test kits are available, you can pretty much tell on sight. If you stick a shovel in and there are big hard chunks of dirt, you have clay. If the shovel slides in easily and you see a lot of grit, your soil is sandy. If the soil is nice and crumbly, lucky you. Most new homeowners aren't so lucky. If you live west of the Cascades in the interior valley, you probably have heavy clay soil, and if it's a newly built house, the soil may be badly compacted by heavy equipment.

4. **Once you have a general idea** of where plants will go, bring in topsoil and/or lots of organic compost. This is the remedy for both clay and sandy soil. It helps to find a teenager who would rather earn college money hauling compost than flipping hamburgers.

5. **Consider raising your planting beds.** Raised beds don't need to be formally framed with bricks or railroad ties. Mounding them up a foot or so works well and gives them a natural look. Raised beds create much better drainage and will help your plants thrive.

6. **Some new homeowners** know exactly what they want. Some will want to hire a landscape designer or a landscape architect. But which one? If all you need is a good eye to help you pick and place plants, a designer will do just fine. But if you have significant challenges, such as

grade changes and drainage problems, or are going to install large expanses of expensive hardscape or structures, call in a landscape architect.

7. **Make a list of priorities** for what you want from your garden: flowers, vegetables, entertaining space, children's play area, pool, outdoor kitchen and so on. Keep these priorities in mind as you or your landscaper lays out your garden.

8. **Think outside the box** in deciding where things go. A terrace does not need to go right off the back of the house. If that's the sunniest spot, it might work better as an herb or vegetable garden, easily accessible from the kitchen. Drag a chair around your yard and sit in it awhile. Take a book. Eat a sandwich. Pretty soon you can figure out where you are most comfortable sitting. That's the place for the terrace.

9. **Go inside your new home** and look out windows. Deciding what kind of view you'd like will help you place plants and hardscape.

10. **If you're going to put in** a major feature, such as a deck, terrace or pond, decide what size you want, and then think about making it twice as big. Most people eventually regret that they were too timid in sizing a feature. Remember that paths should be wide enough for a wheelbarrow, and ponds should not be under trees.

11. **Consider installing** an in-ground sprinkler system before you start planting. A good

The "before" of a new bed.

system will put water where it does the most good and will cut down on waste.

12. **If you inherited** a pre-owned garden, steel yourself to take some things out. It is likely to be overgrown or possibly too shady. Sometimes, merely limbing up trees and shrubs can let in light without drastic surgery.

13. **As you buy plants**, know what your climate zone is because plants will be labeled with the zone they are hardy to. If you look at the U.S. Department of Agriculture maps in most garden books, it appears Portland is Zone 8. (Personally, I consider it Zone 7.) But there will be wide variations within the same area. Just a few feet of elevation will mean colder temperatures. A garden in a depression will collect frost. Some exposed windy sites can be protected with plant screens, but if you live in the path of the Columbia Gorge winds, assume you are in a colder zone. Your overall hardiness can also vary by whether you are on a slope facing southwest or northeast.

14. **Visit other gardens** in your neighborhood and take advantage of open gardens. In the thrall of design ideas, don't forget to look at individual plants. Look for visual clues such as messiness, length of flowering period, growth habits, and mature size, signs of disease or mildew, and appearance when not in bloom. These will help you decide what to plant and what not to plant. If you see something all over your neighborhood, be wary. It may be invasive.

15. **One of the most rewarding things** you can do with a new garden is plant a tree. It gives you a connection with your own piece of earth. Years later, you will sit under the mature tree, and it will bring you enormous pleasure and contentment to think you planted it.

16. **And, finally, remember** to take "before" photos.

JUNE 15, 2006

GREEN THUMBS OR ALL THUMBS
In the garden, or in the kitchen, humility awaits

THIS YEAR, I HAVE RENEWED COMPASSION for the inexperienced gardener, the person who tells me they can't grow a thing. I used to think, how is that possible? How could you live in such verdant surroundings and not be able to grow things? But a recent humbling experience has been a revelation.

You see, I'm the anti-Martha Stewart in the kitchen, a klutz from the get-go. But in the grip of some latent and misguided culinary urge, I decided to cook something that did not come in a microwave box.

By the time I arrived at our local market, the only roast left was something called bottom round. I opened some cookbooks, which informed me that one did not stick this sort of roast in the oven because it was too tough for dry roasting. The illustrations of little cows divided into sections indicated that I had acquired the cow's bottom, and I should braise it. Unfortunately, I couldn't find a recipe for "braised" roast.

Finally, one cookbook helpfully explained that braising and pot roasting were one and the same. The pot roast called for red wine, and the only bottle we had was something very cobwebby in the basement. When my husband opened it, he said he thought it had gone to vinegar.

By this time I had the darned meat browned on the top of the stove and didn't have time for niceties, so I just said "gimme that" and grabbed for the wine/vinegar. Already, I had given up on Julia Child's herb bouquet, which was beginning to sound too complicated (does everyone else know what allspice berries are?).

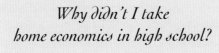

Why didn't I take home economics in high school?

Over the course of the next few hours, I managed to spill the rest of the wine, drop flour on the floor and dirty just about every pot in the house. When we sat down to eat, I was exhausted, smeared with pan drippings and not very hungry. That was just as well since the carrots were overdone, the celery was stringy and the gravy full of odd little lumps, although the wine/vinegar-soaked roast was passable.

After this awful experience, I marveled at how men and women manage to cook real homemade meals every day, some even more than once a day and some for several people. How is it they don't go mad? How do they intrinsically know things such as what braise means and where to get allspice berries? And why didn't I take home economics in high school?

And then it hit me. This is what people mean when they say they don't have a green thumb. This is how it feels to be wondering what to plant and when and how deep and whether to fertilize. This is what it's like to wonder what the heck the difference is between mulch and compost. This is what it feels like to be stumped about when and what to prune.

Suddenly I am filled with compassion. I can relate to you who think you can't grow anything. After all, you can't get flowers in little microwaveable packages.

So I'd like to start off the new gardening season—in my book, it starts officially this week because this is when the first bulbs (snowdrops) bloom—by giving novice gardeners and those of you who think you have black thumbs a list of some great starter books. (See page 248.)

And next time you come up to me or someone like me and feel a bit intimidated because you don't think you can grow something, just smile and say, "I can cook a pot roast with allspice berries." That'll put me in my place.

JANUARY 24, 2002

DIRT THERAPY
Gardening nurtures the spirit, too

THERE HAVE BEEN TIMES WHEN I'VE JOKED about never needing a psychiatrist as long as I have my old-fashioned deep bathtub and my garden.

I realize there are people with serious illnesses, and I don't want to belittle the good that they get from medical help. But I have become increasingly aware of the therapeutic effect gardening can have on us. Just recently, I ran into two women who without realizing it drove home that point.

One woman was a veterinarian technical assistant at the Oregon Zoo, but hasn't been able to work lately due to health problems. She spoke of her garden as a lifesaver. And,

More varieties—even tropical plants—thrive in the Northwest than anywhere else in the country.

as she said, "If something dies in the garden, it's not like a giraffe died."

Another gardener, recuperating from cancer treatment, spoke of her garden as real therapy. "I just get in and dig around, and every time I yank a weed, I imagine I'm yanking a cancer cell out."

> *The point really is, when it starts being more work than joy, you've got to ask, "Is it worth doing?"*

There are books about gardening as therapy, and I don't pretend to know about it from a medical standpoint. But from an intuitive perspective, there does seem to be a calming, healing quality about gardening.

I don't know why gardening has this effect on people. I just know it does, and maybe that's enough. I remember my father coming home from work and going out to water in the warm California evenings. Of course, it looked to me like he was watering the sidewalk as much as the roses, but adults did a lot of silly things so I didn't pay too much attention.

Now I can relate to why my father went straight to the garden as soon as he got off work. It wasn't a chore. I love to come home and water. There's something restful about doing something mindless. The tensions of the day seem to drain out that hose and ebb away.

Sometimes, when I'm in the right frame

of mind, weeding can provide release, too. I make a game of it, telling myself I have to fill up one bucket with weeds each night. There's a sense of accomplishment when I meet the quota. I suppose by now that you are thinking, what a simpleton this woman is. But it is healthier than dosing oneself with chocolate.

However, you have to work to keep your garden at the therapy level. It's easy to slip over to the other side, where the garden becomes real work and a tension additive rather than a balm for the spirit.

You can get into a tailspin trying to have the perfect garden. You know you've gone over the edge when you think in terms of, I have to get home and water, I have to do such and such, I'll never be in shape for company. . . . Sure, at times we all get a little bit like that, especially when there is company coming. But when it reaches a consistently frantic pitch, you know you've got too much garden to handle for the kind of lifestyle you want and need.

To be therapeutic, a garden should be a quest for pleasure, not a quest for perfection. A lot is attitude. For example, I used to feel guilty because none of my plants are labeled, and I've even forgotten what some of the cultivars are. Feeling I had to find the time to work on labels just increased my guilt.

Then one day I decided, heck, this isn't a display garden. I love having people in, but that's not why I garden. I have a garden for me, not for show. So, now I accept that I'll never get around to labeling my plants. Truthfully, I don't really care if I remember the names of some plants. For me, it's enough that they are pretty or interesting.

I certainly admire people who label their plants, and for some that's as calming as watering is for me. The point really is, when it starts being more work than joy, you've got to ask, "Is it worth doing?"

After all, as the lady said, if something dies in the garden, it's not like a giraffe died.

AUGUST 19, 1999

❧

GARDEN GLEE
Happiness becomes a habit in spring

I LOVE SPRING GARDENING, NOT JUST BECAUSE of the plants, but also because of the rituals that come with it. Among my favorite rituals are the shared visits with my neighbor Rosemary. Either she will drop by and we'll talk plants over a cup of tea and walk around my garden, or I will drop by and wander through her garden.

We never tire of admiring each other's garden, talking plants, and sharing seeds and seedlings. Her garden always looks ahead of mine, although she says the same about mine. There is no question, though, that of the two of us, she is by far the better plantswoman. She grows plants from seed, and I am often the lucky beneficiary.

On occasion when I find a new plant, I'll get one for both Rosemary and myself. It's a small repayment for the many meals she's cooked us. The last plant I bought for the two of us was a *Corydalis solida* 'Beth Evans,' which has pink flowers. But Rosemary always gives more than she takes. After I delivered the plant, she sent me home with a half-dozen plants she'd grown from seed, including two *Clematis recta* grown from Hampton Court seeds.

There are other happy rituals going on in the neighborhood. Everyone is taking walks, with and without dogs. It is as if we've all been in hibernation and are now coming out of our caves with big stretches and happy yawns. The neighbors are saying hi over the hedge and peeking into the garden, all the while ignoring Hector's barking because the whole neighborhood knows a wuss of a dog when they see one.

At times like this I can almost imagine we're back to simpler times in an idyllic village where everyone knows each other and trades plants, casseroles and gossip over the back fence. There is something about spring gardening that makes people happier.

I see it every Monday morning when I come to work. As we're riding up the elevator someone invariably says, "I worked in my garden all weekend, and, boy, am I sore." But it's always said with this big sappy grin, and everyone smiles back, knowingly. Bodies may be sore, but souls are restored.

I suspect that, despite the grousing about sore knees, too many weeds, and the plant that didn't make it, we gardeners are generally a contented lot. I've seldom met a truly

Pet therapy is on par with garden therapy.

crabby gardener. That isn't to say we don't do our share of crabbing, but it is a sort of companionable grousing, not a mean-spirited thing.

Sure, we'll complain about clay soil, the weather, plants we don't like, the weather, tomatoes that don't ripen, the weather, our aging bodies that don't bend as well, and did I say the weather? But that's all part of the sport.

We might criticize gnomes and pink flamingos, but some of us have our deep, dark secrets (yes, I had a fling with gnomes). We announce we can't stand dahlias and gladioluses and bearded irises because they are old-lady plants, and then suddenly we are "older ladies" ourselves and love them again (well, maybe not the gladioluses).

We go off to other people's gardens and come back in feigned despair, wanting to tear up our own patch and start anew. But then it's Sunday morning, the sun is shining, the trees are leafing out, a hummingbird is flitting around the honeysuckle, the cats are sunning on the terrace, and we look out at our own garden and think it's wonderful.

When you're an adult, there are just a few things that can bring back that childlike glee. For many of us, it's a garden. And maybe a scoop of chocolate ice cream just to seal the deal.

APRIL 12, 2007

ARE YOU OBSESSED?
Let's count all the ways

MY FRIEND CHERI IS A SQUEALER. SHE literally squeals with joy when she spots a plant or ornament that she loves. I can hear her clear on the other side of the nursery.

I have another friend who has a winter home in Arizona but flies back for a week in February to do her pruning. And still another friend keeps a journal of every plant she's ever purchased.

Obviously, these are passionate gardeners. It's gotten me to thinking, what sets the passionate gardener apart from the dilettantes? So, I've devised this little test.

If you answer the majority of these 25 questions in the affirmative, then you are somewhat obsessed . . . or should we say possessed? Anyway, we've got lots of company.

1. **You think** the finest perfume can't compete with the scent of fresh-dug earth and well-cooked compost.
2. **There are** certain plants you can't have just one of, and you find yourself trying to acquire all of the cultivars of (lilies, heucheras, hostas, you name it).
3. **You read** plant catalogs even when they don't have photos.
4. **You can pronounce** Latin plant names that end in "ii."
5. **You know** there's no plant called a cotton Easter.
6. **You know** what a dibble is. You also know that a trowel works just as well.
7. **You take** at least one gardening magazine and you own a plant reference book, such as *Flora* or the *American Horticultural Society A-Z Encyclopedia of Garden Plants*.
8. **You have been** on a garden tour in England, or it remains one of the great lusts of your life.
9. **You'd rather be gifted** with fine garden tools than something from Victoria's Secret.

10. **You have gardened** after dark with a flashlight.
11. **You recognize** at least half of these names: Piet Oudolf, Tony Avent, Dan Hinkley, Sean Hogan, Tracy DiSabato-Aust, Ken Druse, Helen Dillon and Roger Gossler.
12. **You have attended** gardening conferences and/or classes and belong to a garden club or society.

We gardeners are generally a contented lot. I've seldom met a truly crabby gardener.

13. **You fall** into an animated discussion of plants with friends at a dinner party and are oblivious to the fact that the non-gardening attendees are suddenly and indulgently quiet.
14. **You consider** the term no-maintenance gardening an oxymoron (rightly so, I might add).
15. **You have had** the grit to actually remove a healthy plant that wasn't working.
16. **When you purchased** a vehicle, your choice was influenced by how well it could transport plants.
17. **You have** a compost pile.
18. **There are days** when you call up a friend and say you've just got to visit a nursery. You get points here only if you don't actually need something.
19. **You have fibbed** about what you actually paid for a plant.
20. **You know** what an *Arisaema* is.
21. **A great deal** of your shower or bath time is spent dreaming about what you'd like to do in the garden.

Happiness is a fulsome clematis.

22. **When you are away** from Oregon, you call home to see whether it's raining or, if not, to make sure that someone is watering your garden.

23. **You regard** those specially designed cute garden clothes as something for "dude" gardeners. You garden in old comfortable jeans with holes and a large shapeless shirt.

24. **Your lawn has been** steadily shrinking.

25. **While intellectually you endorse** the focus on native plants, more and more tender exotics have been creeping into your garden.

MARCH 6, 2008

THE SHABBY GARDENER
Stow the stylish togs, ditch the white shoes

SPRING BRINGS THE INEVITABLE PROMOTION in garden magazines of what the well-dressed gardener should wear. They've got it all wrong.

So-called gardening clothes, at least for women, include denim overalls, adorable flowered jackets, straw hats and fancy clogs. They are spiffy, well creased and stylish. In other words, they're not something most of us would wear to work in the garden.

If you want to know what gardeners wear, it's clothes that are loose (OK, baggy), not stiff, and that won't break your heart when the knees and bottoms become permanently mud-stained despite faithful washings. In short, it's all about comfort.

Elastic waistbands are a favorite since they are easy to maneuver with muddy hands for potty stops. The same can't be said of those cute but cumbersome overalls. Flowered jackets are lovely, but sweatshirts, oversized men's shirts and T-shirts are what we really wear, the softer and looser the better.

Straw hats may work for garden parties, but unless they are remarkably smooth, they can be scratchy, and it's hard to scratch your noggin with muddy gloves. Soft cotton brimmed hats or your kids' visor caps are the thing. As for footwear, it's got to be something that can withstand water and mud and still be comfortable, even if shapeless. Thick socks, which will never be white again despite multiple washings, are a must.

Years ago, I recall seeing a gardening book by Martha Stewart. She was on the cover posed with a hoe or rake and wearing garden gloves and shoes that were so white you practically had to wear sunglasses. It was obvious these items had never touched actual soil. This image of Miss Perfect was so unrealistic that I couldn't bring myself to buy the book.

I have, however, come to respect Martha over the years for her creativity, marketing skills, and the fact that she was nice to fellow prisoners. So all is forgiven. But I digress. The point is that what is touted in magazines as gardening wear is actually garden-visit and garden-party wear, not actual work-in-the-dirt togs.

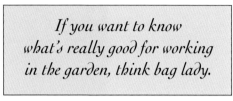

If you want to know what's really good for working in the garden, think bag lady.

If you want to know what's really good for working in the garden, think bag lady. But this comes with a warning: It's probably unwise to end your gardening day with a little stroll before cleaning up. Years ago, after working in the garden all day, I was full of kinks and decided to take a walk before I went in for a bath.

As I rounded a corner, some neighbors—long since gone—were unloading groceries. As I started to pass their house, they purposely left their gate open and out bounded their SUV-sized dog, which began snarling furiously. His name was Rommel, which should give you an idea of his ferocious looks.

Fortunately, I had talked to them over the fence many times and had even been to dinner at their house, so I knew Rommel wouldn't hurt me. I looked down the driveway at the neighbors. They looked up but made no move to call their by-now-frothing beast.

Indeed, I did look like a bum, caked in mud, wearing old sagging clothes, with a floppy hat shading my face. Nevertheless, I considered their attempted intimidation unforgivable. Later, lolling in a bathtub, I dreamed up multiple revenge stratagems, none of which of course would be carried out.

One thought was to stroll by again with a shopping cart filled with a ratty sleeping bag. But my favorite idea was to go by and fall over in a faint as if I'd had been frightened into a heart attack by the dog. Of course, knowing that dog, had I fallen to the ground, he probably would have just licked my face. That would have gotten me giggling, ruining the whole effect.

APRIL 9, 2009

TIME FOR TUCKING IN
Putting the garden—and the tools—to bed . . . for a while

A GARDENER WHO HAS EARNED HIS OR HER green thumb knows which holidays mark significant gardening events. For example, Presidents' Day in February is really "Rose Pruning Day." And, of course, the whole idea for taking the Friday off after Thanksgiving is that it's the official day to tuck the garden in for the winter.

Thanksgiving is the best way to remember when it's time to mulch. The nights have cooled the ground sufficiently so that mulching won't keep plants too warm (and prevent their dormancy). Mulch should be about 4 inches thick, but you can pile it up higher around the crowns of tender woody-stemmed plants such as roses.

Use any material that insulates the ground, but organic materials such as shredded leaves, grass, bark chips, straw, compost, and sawdust are best because they eventually will break down and enrich the soil.

The exception to overall use of organic mulches at this time of year is manure. On one hand, it's the best of times to apply manure; on the other, it's the worst of times. The difference is where you add it.

This time of year, don't use it as mulch around plants. It's still warm enough that a heavy dose of fertilizer will spur some quick growth, and that's the last thing you want. A growing plant is most susceptible to cold damage.

But it's a great time to apply raw fertilizer to bare areas that will be planted next spring, such as vegetable and annual beds and new lawns.

Manures that are ladled on now will have the winter to break down and work into the soil, so they won't burn tender new seedlings that are set out in spring. In some respects, straight manures are superior to composts. They are weed-free.

There's another considerable advantage to applying manure now: It will have time to lose its distinctive aroma. There's nothing like applying a fresh batch of manure and having the neighbors over for a barbecue.

Late November is also the right time to take the lazy way to prepare a new planting area in existing lawn. You can cover the area you want carved out of the lawn with newspapers, black plastic or anything that won't let in light and can be anchored down with bricks or rocks. By next spring, the grass will be dead and you can just till up the ground.

The same trick works for areas where you've lost the battle with weeds and don't want to use heavy herbicides. Just be sure you aren't also covering up desirable plants.

A clever way to repurpose a fountain.

If the tarp or papers look too unsightly, cover them with a layer of organic mulch.

One of the perennial questions at this time of the year is what to do with leaves. Yes, they do make good compost, but they really should be shredded or else they form a dense mat and won't decompose thoroughly. If you don't have a shredder, run over them with a lawn mower.

Then clean off the mower and put it away. While you're at it, wash off all of the garden implements and drain the hoses and store them. A good pair of clippers costs between $40 and $60; so it's smart to bring them in to a warm dry area where they won't rust.

Take in silvered garden balls, pottery and delicate statuary, stained-glass windows, banners, pillows and other garden ornamentation that can get cracked, tattered, sodden, moldy and otherwise disgusting left out over winter.

And if you haven't topped tall roses and tied down climbers to prevent wind damage, now's your last chance.

If all this dismantling makes you blue, there is one thing you can set up. Putting up a bird feeder within sight of a window is a great antidote for winter blahs. It's a way to stay in tune with nature even in the coldest weather.

NOVEMBER 22, 1991

❧

THE SUPPORT CREW
Now let us thank our better halves

THE OTHER DAY I WAS ATTENDING THE Gardeners' Faire, a benefit for the Oregon Symphony, when I was accosted by a gentleman. Well, accosted may be too strong a term because the encounter was both benign and polite. Nevertheless, the gentleman had very pointed words for me.

"What about us," he asked, wagging his finger at me. "We're the wonder boys. Why don't you write about us? We're the real wonder boys." It took me a few seconds to grasp what he was talking about. First, he was referring to my description of my garden helper as "Doug the Wonder Boy." And, second, he was speaking for spouses the world over, or at least the gardening world over.

I took the point. It is time to applaud those spouses and significant others who do not share their partners' zeal for gardening but who, nevertheless, are good sports and don't get in our way.

The perfect spouse, of course, is one who enjoys driving around to nurseries, gets just as excited about plants as we do, relishes working in the yard, doesn't go nuts when you start to dig up more of the lawn and looks like Harrison Ford. Or, fill in the blank for the last qualification.

I have several friends whose spouses meet most of these requirements, although the last two are what we will politely term "stretch goals." But many of us, myself included, do not have a spouse or partner who shares the giddy feeling one gets at the sight of the first green shoot of the year and does not consider a seed catalog truly exciting bedtime reading.

Nevertheless, such spouses and partners should indeed get their due. So here's to all the wonder boys and wonder girls. They're the ones who know these 10 commandments of good garden partnering:

1. **Does not regard lawn** as a sacred object that can never be reduced in size.
2. **Cheerfully unloads plants** from the car without noticing the dirt that spilled on the floor.
3. **Never, ever asks how much** those plants cost.
4. **No longer asks,** "But where will you put it?"
5. **Is willing to help out during** commercials (in broadcasts of sports events for most, John Wayne movies at our house).
6. **Allows extra time** when going places in case you pass a nursery.
7. **Under no circumstances has ardent opinions** about what to do in the garden (unless he or she actually is willing to take up gardening).
8. **Manages to get own dinner** during spring planting season.

9. (For females) Leaves roses alone. Does not try to stick them in with other flowers.

10. (For males) Does not say things like, "I admire Pamela Anderson's long, clean fingernails."

MAY 17, 2001

❧

GOOD INTENTIONS
So begins the annual cycle of resolution and remorse

AS A TRADITIONALIST, I ALWAYS START THE new year with a list of resolutions. They're pretty much the same every year, and if the coming year is like every other year, I will regrettably ignore most of them. But I like to think I might keep one or more.

I resolve to keep plant labels when I buy new plants and to record where I put the plant. Because I have failed to do this in the past, my garden is filled with plants whose specific variety eludes me. This is unfortunate because my garden is often open, and people ask me about plants. I think they are beginning to catch on when I say a certain plant is *Hydrangea mysteriosii*.

I resolve to weed a bit each day as soon as it is spring, when those horrid little green things with white flowers spread all over. Keeping this resolution will depend not only on my discipline, but also on my continuing ability to rise up off the ground. Knees, I am learning, are not to be trusted past a certain age.

I resolve not to buy more plants than I can put in within two weeks. I can hear Doug

> *Knees, I am learning, are not to be trusted past a certain age.*

the Wonder Boy chortling over this resolution. But honestly, since I have no more room for plants, surely I will keep this resolution this year. Or will I?

I resolve not to get carried away by some exotic specimen that I have no hope of successfully nourishing. I adore those fancy woodland plants, but, unfortunately, my shade is not moist. It is very dry thanks to some large and rude trees that suck up every bit of moisture. So, alas, unlike Ingrid and Humphrey, I will not always have Paris (the plant).

I resolve to finally eradicate invasive plants. In my case, the monsters are ribbon grass (*Phalaris*) and an ugly orange *Crocosmia* (not one of the exciting cultivars). Doug the Wonder Boy and I have been working away for years on these miscreants, but then we get tired and let up. As soon as we do, they're back with renewed vigor.

I resolve to plant more bulbs. Every fall, it is a strain to put in more bulbs, because this must be done in a kneeling position. Every spring I rue that I didn't try harder. This is an annual cycle of remorse.

I resolve to do a little (emphasis on little) stretching and exercising so that the feat of ascending from said kneeling position isn't quite like Godzilla rising out of the sea.

I resolve to put away my tools when I am finished for the day. Someday, someone will buy this property and find hundreds of rusted trowels and clippers buried in hedges, lost under shrubs and stuck in the mud in remote spots.

I resolve that on those occasions when it has been raining for 40 days and nights, I will not betray my hard-won Northwest roots. I think of former President Carter's famous confession of lust in his heart. In my case, it is occasional lust for a little plot in, say, Santa Barbara.

I resolve to do something that almost every gardener resolves to do, and that's to spend more time sitting and enjoying my garden rather than just working in it. For some reason, we gardeners are very bad at using our benches.

Finally, *I resolve* to master Latin pronunciation. Personally, I don't care if someone says clem-MAH-tis instead of the correct CLEM-ah-tis, but it is embarrassing when you're asked to speak in public and someone in the audience shouts out a correction. I also resolve to be polite when this happens and

Chairs are made for sitting. Try it sometime.

not shout back, "May a thousand slugs descend on your garden."

JANUARY 11, 2007

❧

TRACKING THE SEASONS
Impulses can overwhelm reason

THERE IS SOMETHING ABOUT AUTUMN THAT makes me want to do cutesy, craftsy things. I want to stack pumpkins and dried corn and little tufts of straw around my door. I want to run out in the yard and gather seeds and dried flowers and colored leaves, and make wreaths.

It's not that I have a scintilla of talent for these things. Once, I was invited to decorate a small Christmas tree for an auction of celebrity trees. I went for a garden theme using cones and assorted debris from my garden, but I had not mastered the art of the glue gun, and the so-called natural ornaments kept falling off. The backers of this fund-raising scheme very wisely did not call on me the next year.

Nevertheless, there's this little throbbing urge at this time of year that makes me want to gather moss and twigs and try to make something of them. I think maybe it's a primitive urge to harvest.

I, for one, believe that once you become a gardener, the seasons resonate in new, nobler ways. You find you have these little urges to reap and make homespun things in the fall, just as you have an awakening of energy and need to sow in the spring. All you have to do is look at people at a spring plant sale to realize they are in the grip of some gigantic primeval urge.

In my pre-gardening days, the advent of seasons seemed to bring only different cloth-

Winter inspires us to evaluate our garden and plan the next project.

ing urges. I could tell when it was autumn because I had an urge to buy my annual pair of loafers. Winter was an annoying period when I had to decide if it was time to buy a new raincoat, and spring was when I put away all my woolens and got out those clothes that needed ironing. Summer was when I went through the ordeal of trying on swimsuits.

> *If anything, the four seasons seemed to be marked by a cycle of footwear: loafers, fuzzy slippers, tennies and flip-flops.*

If anything, the four seasons seemed to be marked by a cycle of footwear: loafers, fuzzy slippers, tennies and flip-flops.

Now that I am a gardener, the seasons bring about other moods and urges. In fall, filled with creativity, I hit the pre-holiday bazaars and see things like mosaic stepping-stones and think, "I could do that." It rarely means follow-through.

Winter is a time of wild dreaming of new garden projects and the devouring of catalogs and magazines. Spring, of course, is the frenzy of plant sales and planting so driven that otherwise normal people have been known to work by flashlight.

You'd think summer would be a gardener's finest moment, a time to relax and enjoy one's creation. And I suppose some gardeners do find it a season of fulfillment. Then there are those of us who find that summer is the most frustrating of seasons. The time to plant has passed and, gosh, the garden isn't perfect after all.

We seek solace by visiting each other's gardens to find that not only is the grass greener, but also the flowers are taller and the tomatoes are redder on the other side of the fence. As we are watering our drooping plants, we begin to wonder if it's all worth it. This is the "maybe a condo in the Pearl isn't such a bad idea" phase.

Finally, the freshening rains of autumn sweep in, bringing this bundle of hunting, gathering and creating instincts. I find myself reduced to gathering bits of lichen in the yard, thinking I'll do something with them.

The only thing standing between my friends and my stupid homemade Christmas gifts is, lucky for them, the fact that a stronger urge is overtaking me: to shop. After all, my old loafers are looking pretty ratty.

OCTOBER 21, 2004

✂

RISK FACTORS
Danger lurks in the shrubbery

Now THAT GARDENING SEASON IS TAKING off, it's time to talk safety. Yeah, I know it's a boring subject. But very necessary.

I have broken a bone twice in my life. Both times were in a garden. The first time I stepped back from a step that was no more than 6 inches high. I landed hard on my heel and sustained a hairline fracture.

The second time was in my mother's garden, where I slipped on mossy stone steps and ended up in the emergency room with multiple fractures of my wrist. I remember looking up the stairs and seeing my mother looking off into the distance as if nothing happened. Fortunately my husband was there to help me up and take me to emergency.

Strangely, my mother never mentioned the event—even though I wore a cast from my wrist to above my elbow for several weeks. My mother had this amazing way of blocking out anything unpleasant. I guess having your daughter break her wrist in front of you qualified as unpleasant—like her first husband (or possibly second if family gossip is to be believed).

But I digress.

A garden poses numerous dangers. It's like a cuddly cat just waiting to spring. There are two reasons to be aware of these dangers. The first is you don't want anyone to get hurt, yourself included. The second is that nasty word "litigation."

Here are things to watch for:

Small changes in level. We can see major changes such as a step, but it's the small changes such as a depression in a path or lawn that trip us up. If possible, level them out with gravel or soil.

Trippers. Leave tools lying around, and for sure someone will fall over them.

Steep and often slippery steps. Handrails, handrails, handrails.

Low branches. I had one over a path that sometimes would conk unwary tall people. The problem ended when I hung a carved wooden duck from the branch.

Don't plant thorny plants along your walking paths. When they fill out, you'll feel the sting.

Thorny shrubs. Don't plant thorny shrubs next to the edge of a path. I used to have a large rose that leaned over into a path. If someone got too close, it sucked them in with a scratchy embrace, then whooshed them out with such force that they landed in Gresham.

Ladders. Who doesn't have an old, rickety ladder? Make sure your ladder is in good shape and the right height for pruning. If you have to reach out too far, the next sound you'll hear is "splat" just like Humpty Dumpty.

Mowing. Pick all twigs and debris off the lawn first. Use goggles to prevent chips flying into an eye, and never mow with bare feet or flip-flops. Toes are nice to have.

Using gas. If you're refilling a gas mower, let the engine cool first and refill it outside.

Electric tools. Watch that cords are out of the way of pruning and mowing activities and never prune near electrical wires. Leave that to professionals. Wear ear protection when operating loud equipment.

Handling chemicals. If you must use chemicals, don't do it on a windy day. Wear goggles and gloves and wash your hands afterward.

Storage. Store chemicals in a locked cabinet and keep sharp tools away from kids and that "Chain Saw Massacre" guy.

There's more. I haven't even gotten to the 800-pound slug.

APRIL 21, 2011

SEASONED TO PERFECTION

As garden improves with age, so too does the gardener

LATE AUGUST AND EARLY SEPTEMBER FINDS Northwest gardeners in the eye of the hurricane. The main season has wound down, but it's still too early for fall planting and cleanup. So there's a little hiatus, and even time to sit on one of those ubiquitous garden benches we all have that rarely get sat on.

And when you do finally sit down and gaze around your plot, it's easy to get in a reflective mood. That's what happened to me the other day. Sitting on one of my little benches, I got to thinking about how much my approach to gardening has changed since I began this garden some 15 years ago.

In those years, I have become both ruthless and pragmatic. I have fallen in and out of love, and sometimes back in love, with any number of plants. I have gotten ruthless about yanking things out that either don't work or are labor-intensive. Plants that need deadheading, staking or otherwise pampering have pretty much been exiled.

For the most part, I don't miss them, with the exception of roses. I do admit to nursing a broken heart over my late roses. There are few left, and I do mightily envy those gardeners who have the deft touch with roses. As for me, I'm just great at cultivating black spot.

When I started this garden, I thought anything that was "self-sowing" was a miracle plant. Now, even my beloved lady's mantle can be irritating as I dig up more and more of the seeders. Given enough time, certain plants transition from "filler" to "invader."

Early on, I gravitated to flowers, both perennials and annuals. Now, I am a foliage fanatic and much more likely to plant a shrub

Most experienced gardeners are happy to share advice on what to plant and where.

or even a small tree. When I go to a nursery, I tend to be taken with a plant's structure and texture rather than with its blossoms, although I do have my weak moments. I recently did come home with another toad lily just because of the fabulous rosy flowers.

I used to think the ideal plot was one that had full sun, and I fantasized that the neighbor's tall trees behind our yard would topple in a storm. Now, my favorite parts of the garden are shady, and if I didn't have trees, I would plant them.

At the beginning, I focused on a spring garden, then once spring was over, I tried to play catch-up, stuffing in annuals to keep some interest going. Now I'm much more careful about selecting multi-season plants as well as late bloomers because late summer and autumn are the best times in Northwest gardens.

I suppose in many ways I've gotten more sophisticated, but I can't really say gardening is more fun. It is still enormously satisfying, but there was something about those early days of testing and trying things out and coming away surprised and delighted when something worked. Sometimes I even envy young people who are just beginning to garden. They've got all this ahead of them.

But enough of this rumination. It's time to get off the bench. I'm looking around at some of the holes and tatty areas and now that I think about it, I've got another 15 years of work ahead to get this place in shape. Maybe I'll even figure out how to have roses by then.

AUGUST 30, 2001

CALENDAR WHIRL

What's my favorite season? Depends when you ask

OCCASIONALLY I DREAM ABOUT WHAT IT would be like to live in a place like Santa Barbara, where you can have a year-round garden without temperature extremes. I think of things like this when I am out on a freezing night throwing a blanket over my tender shrubs and on triple-digit days when I am up early to soak everything.

But these are fleeting thoughts because I know in my heart that I couldn't give up the seasons. And, while others are addressing world problems or contemplating scientific breakthroughs, I am wrestling with myself trying to figure out whether spring or fall is my favorite season.

You would think late June into summer would be a gardener's favorite time because June always gets top billing in poems and songs. Maybe because it rhymes with moon. Certainly, it's the month when all the buildup reaches its crescendo.

But most gardeners seem to favor the seasons of transition. Some of us find that getting there is much of the fun. In the Northwest we are very lucky because the garden starts to awaken as early as February. By March, little surprises are poking up and leaves are unfurling. One must have ferns, for this reason alone, because there is nothing quite so amazing as seeing their fronds coiled up one morning and unrolled by afternoon. (We gardeners are easily amazed.)

April is a particularly good month be-cause you can stop holding your breath that there will be a freeze. It's also when you can start looking up because it's the month the ballerinas arrive. At least that's the way I think of all the trees decorated in a puffery of blossoms like so much pink and white tulle.

May is always hard for me to remember because by then I am in the throes of plant lust. And, well, you know June. That's when we're visiting all the open gardens and swooning over the latest, newest, most exotic, brightest and biggest. Some of us also are feeling slightly envious because "our banana" did not survive the winter.

On the one hand, July can be a bit of a letdown because much of the flower power is on the wane. On the other hand, we can finally expect a run of dry and sunny days, while things are still looking fresh. Those insidious yellow patches have not yet begun to take over the lawn.

August is a different matter. The lawn may now be more yellow than green. August has taught me that it makes sense to focus on different parts of the garden in different seasons. The shady woodland is best in early spring when it is bursting with hellebores and bulbs. In early summer, the borders are at their best. By August, the focus is on the vegetable garden, where the dahlias and nasturtiums are snuggling against bright red tomatoes and big green zucchinis in a display every bit as dazzling as spring bulbs.

I actually find September the most restful month even though August is supposed to be hammock time. The thing is, by September, I

> *When you look at those gold and scarlet trees, can't you just hear the cannons going off?*

Resist the urge to "jam and cram." Those plantings will fluff out in due season.

don't mind my shabby garden. September is supposed to look a bit ragged, like an over-the-hill actress who still has "it." I always think of someone with a wonderful non-plasticized face like Jeanne Moreau, someone who isn't ashamed to show her wrinkles.

October, of course, is the fiercest month, ushering out the end of gardening season with a blaze of glorious color. It reminds me of when all the gongs and cymbals clang at the close of the *1812 Overture*. It's the end, but what

The lovely late-winter flowers of Cornus mas, *the Cornelian cherry, become bright red, edible fruits by late summer.*

an end. When you look at those gold and scarlet trees, can't you just hear the cannons going off?

So, as far as favorite seasons go, I'm still trying to decide. Spring has an advantage by the mere fact that winter doesn't follow and that there's so much more to come. Autumn, on the other hand, has an advantage that, for a while at least, there's not a lot to come. It will be nice to come home from work and not have to water everything. It will be even nicer to catch up on the latest gardening books. So for now, I'll vote for fall. By next spring, I reserve my right to change my mind. All it probably will take is seeing one little fern uncoil.

OCTOBER 19, 2006

WHAT'S IN A NAME?
Snobbery often duels with stubbornness over botanical Latin

ONE OF THE ODD DIVIDES IN GARDENING circles concerns botanical Latin. There are those who say that, for the life of them, they can't learn Latin plant names. On the other end of the spectrum, there are people who wouldn't be caught dead—or *mortuum*—uttering a common name.

The oddity is how botanical Latin affects people. I have seen people who simply do not want to associate with those who use common names and, when writing about plants, refuse to include the common names. I wonder if they've ever heard of the principle of mentoring.

I also have heard gardeners say dismissively that plants grow just as well whether you call them Salvia or Sally. That

The giant grass Arundo donax.

may be so, but there can be quite a difference in your salvias or sallies, about five feet between tall, shrubby *Salvia elegans* and the more diminutive *Salvia lavandulifolia*. You'll get scarlet flowers with *Salvia splendens* and brilliant blue with *Salvia patens*.

I could go on. There are salvias with tiny, scented, green leaves and salvias with big, silver, woolly leaves. Some are hardy; many are not. In other words, a plant called Salvia is entirely unpredictable if you don't take a closer look at its botanical lineage.

That's the practical side of learning botanical Latin. There's also the sensual side. Latin names have music in them—and history, geography and more—but let's stay with the music. Rolling out names such as *Cercis canadensis* 'Forest Pansy' or *Cornus controversa* 'Variegata' can be a delicious experience.

I have been among groups of gardeners who pronounce plant names lovingly, simply savoring their sound. There is magic in the words. They bond you to the plants. You feel you know them intimately. The sound of *Arundo donax* is so he-manly, much like the huge grass itself, while *Primula rosea* is as perky as the little primrose it describes.

But the code of a good gardener is never to use botanical Latin to exclude others or exude superiority, and I have seen it wielded as such a weapon. A novice gardener is to be nurtured and treasured like a fledgling chick, not someone to be left out of the "in" group. We are not, after all, in high school. It is quite appropriate to gently offer a Latin name or correct a pronun-

No garden is ever finished, but gradually polished to a personal Eden. Sissinghurst, England.

ciation, but it must be given as a gift, like a bride tossing a bouquet, not lobbed at the unfortunate novice like a grenade.

The novice, on the other hand, must be prepared to receive the gift graciously. The fledgling must not be obstinate or overly fearful about learning Latin. It is not so frightening if you allow yourself to go at your own speed.

Ralph the plant will continue to grow. But eventually, it will be nice to know that Ralph is a *Ranunculus asiaticus*, and he has a cousin, *Ranunculus flammula*, that is not at all like Ralph, but possibly equally pleasing.

I myself am no Latin expert, although I had three years of Latin in school. The nuns maintained that learning Latin was an excellent basis for learning another language. I always wondered how three years of Latin was a better basis for learning French than three years of French, but I did not have the courage to opine that in front of the awesome Sister Reginalda.

> ## *"Ugh, I'd rather have scurvy than Agapanthus."*

Naturally, I promptly forgot all the Latin I'd learned once I left school. It was only years later when I became interested in gardening that I began to learn and delight in the music of Latin plant names. But I too have much to learn. All I have to do is read one of the Hardy Plant Society bulletins to realize how many plant names I don't know. Oh well, a humbling experience is good for one.

Still, there will be some people who are hopeless cases when it comes to Latin. Take my co-worker Scott Simms. I was in a meet-

ing the other day when the woman sitting next to me said, "I have *Agapanthus*, would you like some, too?" Immediately, Scott piped up, "Ugh, I'd rather have scurvy than *Agapanthus*."

AUGUST 9, 2007

HEAVEN WITH A TROWEL
I'd rather make a garden than have one

WHEN I WAS IN THE FIFTH GRADE, ONE OF my classmates asked our teacher the inevitable question, "What is heaven like?" As some of you know, nuns are never at a loss for answers, and Sister Mary Emily did not fail us.

She told us to close our eyes and imagine the best possible place. As we squeezed our little eyes shut and let our imaginations run, we heard her say, "What you're now imagining, that's what heaven will be like."

So, for several years, I thought heaven was in Sherwood Forest (I had just seen a movie about Robin Hood and thought it the idyllic setting). All the pets I'd ever had were there, and large trestle tables were set under spreading oaks. These were laden with all my favorite foods. There were bowls of spaghetti, popcorn and ice cream. At age 10, carbs figured heavily in my desires. I had not yet discovered boys.

Now, decades later, if I close my eyes and imagine the perfect place, it is quite different, and it is distinguished by what isn't there rather than what is. I am in my garden, and there are no slugs, no snails, no aphids, no debris-hurling trees, no moles, no raccoons, no spider webs, no weeds and no grass where it shouldn't be.

That would be, if not heaven, at least my personal Garden of Eden.

But perhaps heaven would be boring if there were no challenges and everything was already done for you. Certainly, there is a long-standing debate over what gardeners enjoy most—having a garden or making a garden. I ran into someone the other day who said she had just bought her first house and was making her first garden. She said she envied my mature garden.

But the fact of the matter is that I was never so sublimely happy as when I made my first garden and didn't know quite what I was doing. Everything that survived in those heady days was a happy surprise and much treasured. Oddly, back then I didn't feel nearly as insecure about my garden as I do now when I know people are going to visit. I think that's because I worry now that people will have high expectations and, I'm ashamed to admit, I fear I won't live up to them.

Here it is late summer, for example, and I have not removed some plants that I meant to because there is still one group that plans to visit my garden as a result of a charity auction. I don't want to have bare spots.

But I am itching to take out some of the ferns and weed trees that have seeded themselves and more of the rampant perennials that have marched beyond their allotted space. If the urge in spring was to plant, the urge in late summer is to edit, which is a civil term for yank, chop and rip out.

Isn't it strange how when we start out gardening we can hardly wait until the plants close ranks? The gardener's credo is "No earth must show." But now I am desperate to open up spaces so I can just fill them up again with new plants.

> *Now I'm starting to revise my concept of heaven.*

I guess that answers the question. I am one of those who would rather make a garden than have a garden, a completed garden, that is.

So now I'm starting to revise my concept of heaven. It isn't a finished garden. It is a garden that holds much promise but needs work, and I am there with a trowel in hand. This heavenly garden, however, would be a bit different from my earthly garden. The soil would be rich and crumbly. The weather would be mild and sunny during the day, and it would rain only at night.

And, while we're at it, it would be nice if there were a few angels who were good at pulling weeds.

AUGUST 30, 2007

Part 3

GARDEN DESIGN:
MORE THAN RHODIES AND ROSES

❧

My helpers are rolling their eyes, and I can see

thought balloons over their heads that say things like,

"Just make up your (bad word) mind, lady."

The charm of garden ornaments will reflect your whimsical side.

STYLIN'

A little bit of soul does a garden good

FOR SOME TIME, I LABORED UNDER THE mistaken impression that to reach perfection, a garden had to have a specific style.

Garden books will tell you that you must decide whether you want your garden to be formal, cottage, woodsy, country or Asian, to name a few choices. Trouble was, I was a little bit in love with all of these styles, and my garden, a hodgepodge of design (if the word design can even be used), certainly reflected this indecision.

That's why I was thrilled to attend a lecture a couple of years ago by Ann Lovejoy, a Northwest gardening author. She exhorted us to follow our own hearts. She said personal style was what it was all about. And who am I to argue with a goddess? I felt vindicated and freed.

I went home and told all my mismatched ornamental garden critters that they could stay. I looked at the mishmash of stone and terracotta pots with new eyes and appreciation for their diversity. I decided that I didn't have to feel guilty because I had a bilious-green gazing ball.

This new insight got me to thinking about what really constitutes garden perfection.

I put a lot of energy into the research: buying the latest spring garden magazines, nobly giving up weeding my own garden to explore others and, for an added dose of brain power, having another helping of my mom's German chocolate cake.

It occurred to me that if perfection doesn't depend on a specific style, neither does it depend on wealth. Sure, I adore great big mansions with elegant formal gardens for the vicarious thrill of imagining what it's like to live in lady-of-the-manor style.

Although I've been privileged to see some of the world's great gardens, I love best the teensy little homemade gardens for their personality and charm. I may swoon at the thought of going back to England, but truth be told, I also get a thrill when I amble through Old Sellwood near my home and check out the clever little gardens fronting tiny Victorian homes.

Big or small, what's essential is evidence of the garden owner's soul. Even if the owner hired a designer and landscaper, there should be personal quirks, eccentricities or individual expressions that show the resident's guiding hand. A good professional designer understands this.

The gardens I love most, and thus find most perfect, are those that change regularly as their owners decide to add a trellis, move the roses, dig up more lawn, put in another pond, terrace the hill, tear up the old border and redesign it, widen or curve the paths, and on and on to other projects.

> *In gardening, as in much of life, we don't really want to find the Holy Grail. We just spend our lives thinking we do.*

The garden that remains static may be lovely, but to me it's merely a botanical museum. I take the view that a garden is a place where actual gardening goes on.

Similarly, I think finding room to tuck in yet another plant discovery should take precedence over eschewing new plants because they upset some so-called perfection of balance.

In my book, a perfect garden also is a forgiving space that allows you one year to fall for the latest fad and the next year to remove the fad you tried that really didn't work out. In short, it's a canvas where you can try out ideas, make mistakes and, more often than not, have accidental triumphs. Some of my best plant combinations were completely accidental.

Given all this, it's odd that for years I dreamed of having a finished garden, thinking somehow that would be perfection.

I imagined what all the paths would look like if I could afford to pave them with stone. I longed for the day when the *Davidia* tree would be sufficiently mature so I could cut down the clumsy laurel next to it without leaving a bare spot. I imagined what the little garden shed out back would look like if it were fixed up as a summerhouse.

Then it hit me. If my garden were finished, I'd probably want to move and start a new one. So, for me, the perfect garden is an unfinished garden. Just as some enjoy the thrill of the hunt, many gardeners live for the titillation of the dig.

In gardening, as in much of life, we don't really want to find the Holy Grail. We just spend our lives thinking we do.

JUNE 5, 1997

❧

ONE GLASS CEILING WE LIKE
Our neighbors' covered patio proves bigger is better

WHEN MY NEIGHBORS THE ELLISES WERE expanding their terrace and adding a glass cover earlier in the year, Rosemary worried that it would be too big. Now, with sum-

> *Once you've tasted blood, so to speak, you become a monster.*

mer nearly over, that worry has been put to rest. Not only is it not too big, it may actually be too small, to gauge by its popularity.

Since spring, the glass-topped terrace has been party central—the site of anniversary fetes, birthday celebrations, potlucks for departing neighbors, and a potluck to welcome neighbors returning from a year in France.

There's plenty of room for a big table laden with goodies and lots of chairs for our aging neighborhood denizens. There's even space—but just barely—for all of us to go around Dakota the dog, who, like big dogs everywhere, prefers to sprawl full length in the middle of the party. And nobody has opined that the space is too big.

Oddly enough, a common mistake people make in planning garden features is not making them big enough. Sooner or later, you will wish your terrace, your pond, your greenhouse, your gazebo or your garden shed were twice its size. You'll regret that your paths, now overgrown by encroaching plants, aren't wider, and you'll wonder why your flower borders or islands don't look like the pictures in garden books. It could be that they're simply too skimpy.

I know whereof I speak, since I made nearly everything too small at first. The flower borders, now about 12 feet deep, started out 4 feet deep. Each year, I'd timidly dig another foot or so out of the lawn to extend the borders, until one day they suddenly looked "right." It's hard to believe that in the early days of my garden it made me nervous to take out lawn. But once you've tasted blood, so to speak, you become a monster.

The ultimate folly, of course, was our first pond. We made it too shallow, and raccoons, who don't like to swim, were able to wade in. We stocked it with expensive koi and made the mistake of naming them as if they were pets. Raccoons and blue herons quickly gobbled up "the fleet"—my husband, an ex-Navy guy, insisted on naming them after battleships. (He just corrected me: It was Japanese aircraft carriers.)

Eventually, the raccoons' toenails dug through the liner, so we had to make a new pond. It was just as well. The old pond was too small and looked dinky.

When we installed a new pond in another spot, we made it twice as wide and about three times deeper than the old pond. There are times, however, that I look at it and wish it were bigger. Instead of floating gently on the surface, the water lilies are crowded and tend to pile up so the leaves hide any flowers.

I know there are designers who lecture about the importance of proportion. But for every designer who declares you should put small furniture in a small room and use wall-papers with diminutive patterns, there is another designer who tells you to be brave and use oversize furniture and bold graphics to make a small room look, if not bigger, at least more important.

Out in the garden, I am in the latter group. If you love the idea of a terrace, pond, ga-zebo, greenhouse, etc., decide where you will put it and how big it should be. Then make it twice as big. Next, triple the contractor's estimate. But you'd have to do that anyway, regardless of the size.

SEPTEMBER 11, 2008

◦✃◦

20 WAYS TO GLAM UP YOUR YARD

Great ideas I've borrowed (ahem, stolen) over the years

I'VE COME UP WITH MY OWN TWIST ON WHAT makes a garden a grand place to visit: Not only does it have to hold my attention, but also it must provide at least a couple of new ideas to take home. You see, I am an inveterate horticultural plagiarist. And unrepentant about it, too.

Here are 20 super ideas I've picked up visiting gardens:

1. **Ornaments** such as carved animals atop fence posts.
2. **Wicker baskets and empty ornamental urns** placed strategically around the garden so that the gardener can pull weeds and toss them in.
3. **Stained-glass panels** hanging from a tree.
4. **Huge terra-cotta pots** planted with hostas and used to frame a garden entrance.
5. **Different-colored pebbles** embedded in paths to make a design.
6. **Flexible rebar arbors.** They're wrapped in twigs and bits of vine tied with twine to give a natural look and disguise the metal.
7. **A double row of tuteurs** (wooden tepees) clothed in clematis. It's a great way to create an instant French allée without waiting for trees to mature.
8. **Strips of bamboo** used as girdles around flowerbeds edging a lawn. That way you can mow the lawn without cutting the flowers.
9. **Fun with mulches in potted plants**—such

Climbers, floral and vegetable, fill out a row of elegant tuteurs.

as river rock or a thick carpet of Scotch moss.

10. A great, arching water plant on the top tier of a fountain. The water drizzles down the leaves.

11. A wooden trough to feed water into a pond. It's not as labor-intensive as a waterfall but creates the same musical effect.

12. Color-coordinated pots and plant colors; for example, red canna edged with red begonias in a wine-red glazed pot.

13. Bright banners to lighten dark corners of the garden, especially the shady areas.

14. Rocks stacked up for instant sculptures. A grouping of three stacks is particularly effective.

15. A forest of birdhouses set in a cluster on poles of different heights. They look best in natural wood and stone in a sunny area, but a shady area could take a collection of brightly colored birdhouses.

16. Ornamental animals in herds. In one garden, the owners had a row of elephants roaming through the garden.

17. Bits of colored pottery and glass embedded in concrete to cover an otherwise unremarkable birdbath bowl or any water bowl.

18. Vines that completely cover a bed frame or bench. I've seen pictures of bedsteads filled in with flowers, too. Talk about a flowerbed!

19. A children's tree house transformed into an adult retreat. It was draped with mosquito netting and outfitted with soft futons and ornamental lanterns.

20. **Standard arbors lined up to make a long vine-filled tunnel.** It's cheaper than a custom-built pergola, and when the plants cover it, you won't be able to tell it's not one long connected arbor.

AUGUST 6, 1998

EXERT YOUR INFLUENCE
How people use a garden can depend on its design

I HAVE ALWAYS LIKED TO THINK OF MYSELF AS a "natural" gardener. But lately I have been reading that a garden is anything but natural.

When you think about it, gardening is an attempt to control, discipline or, heavens, even manipulate nature. That sounds distasteful because words such as "manipulative" have unpleasant connotations.

But if we weren't somewhat manipulative, most of us would probably live in a blackberry patch. Certainly every time we prune, weed, or mow we are manipulating plants. If we put mosquito repellent in our water basins and spray our roses for black spot, we are manipulating nature.

So, what we gardeners may really be after isn't natural but rather an idealized version of nature. This is an idea that has been in and out of vogue. The most famous proponent of idealized nature was 18th-century landscape designer Lancelot Brown, who created romantic landscapes. He picked up the name Capability Brown because he was always telling his clients that their garden had "capabilities."

At one time he was an icon of landscape design, but lately he has fallen out of favor. In creating his so-called natural landscapes, he obliterated gardens that now are considered of historical importance.

Recently I have become aware of the fact that not only can we manipulate nature, but by the way we design our garden we can also manipulate—or, to use a nicer word, influence—how the garden is used.

This summer I noticed some interesting dynamics in my own garden that seem to bear this out. None of this was intentional, mind you. But ever since we put a path around the pond and extended the pathway all around the lawn, it has changed the way people move through our garden. People are not walking on the grass.

Lord knows, it is not because we have great grass, and we certainly don't ask visitors to stay off the grass. It's just that now that we have a pathway girdling the entire lawn, people instinctively stay on the pathway rather than cutting across the lawn.

We've also noticed that as visitors move through the garden and come to the fire pit surrounded by chairs, they plop down. The gazebo used to be in the same spot, but few, if any, people sat in it. It was enclosed and somewhat elevated and, therefore, apparently not as inviting.

On the other hand, although I love my little sheltered "bus stop," no one sits in it. Maybe it doesn't work. Well, it does work as a folly of sorts, a picturesque garden structure, but not particularly as a sitting area, although Hector the dog and I have found it's a swell place to take a nap.

But if we think about it, there are a number of simple ways we influence how people interact with a garden. Chairs in a circle invite people to sit down. Chairs spaced far apart don't. Paths that wind and disappear around a corner draw people in. Straight paths are less likely to. Arbors and gates make you want to pass through and see what's on the other side. Narrow openings are tempting to peek through because they suggest a secret garden.

Benches by a pond make us want to sit down, much more than a bench simply placed along a path. Ponds, like fire, invite meditation. A garden that can't be taken in all in one viewing invites you to explore. Sunken terraces make you feel cozy. Hammocks tucked in a hideaway are more likely to be used than hammocks out in the open.

If you think about it, understanding how people can be manipulated is an interesting way to arrange one's garden. At the very least, the idea has "capabilities."

SEPTEMBER 7, 2006

FANTASY GARDENING
Dream big, but design small

I HAVE BEEN THINKING A LOT ABOUT GARDEN style lately. The reason is that I've been poring over last year's garden magazines, giving them one last look before passing them on to friends. The old favorites—they often have the word "country" in the title—still show a lot of romantic gardens, although even they are influenced by the tropical look.

The posh new magazines—the word "design" is often in the title—are touting a new style, which for lack of a better term I'll call the "modern garden." It is characterized by an architectural look and a certain sparse-

The firepit in a rare, unoccupied moment.

ness. Most of these gardens would be quite at home in Los Angeles with their pink stucco walls, abstract sculptures and designer plants.

I can't say that I'm crazy about the modern style. Of course, anyone who has seen my home knows that the word minimalist is one of those foreign terms, like "health food" and "exercise." Still, I like the idea that people are exploring a variety of styles whether I like them or not.

I myself have several fantasy gardens. One is a big English country garden with lots of space for flower borders, arbors, vegetables, herbs and vistas. Oh, and a quaint little woods would do nicely, too. And, while we're fantasizing, let's throw in a babbling brook at the bottom of the garden.

> *I do dream of things besides Harrison Ford and chocolate.*

On the other hand, I love the charm of those small courtyard gardens, such as the ones you see in San Francisco and New Orleans. They're tiny spaces encased in walls—preferably brick—with access through a charming antique wrought-iron gate. Inside this cozy space, paved in cobbles, of course, a tiered fountain and some antique benches.

There are other fantasies. (I do dream of things besides Harrison Ford and chocolate.) One is an Asian-influenced woodland garden with meandering paths, bridges over placid ponds, hillocks covered in velvety mosses, and lots of small, perfectly pruned ornamental trees.

Unfortunately, most of us don't have the layout for the gardens of our dreams, neither wide-open country acreage nor little enclosed courtyards. In fact, most of us have city- or suburban-lot-sized gardens of boringly rectangular dimensions. And, often, the front yard is dominated by that slab of concrete called a driveway.

Plenty of books feature designs for "small" city gardens, but most emphasize plans for long, narrow lots, such as what you find in row houses back East or in England. Someday, someone is going to make a fortune publishing a book of garden designs for the short wide lot, with a big driveway out front (in other words, the typical suburban lot).

Until then, we have to be creative in dealing with the challenge of our city lots. I have risen to the challenge by creating a total mishmash of styles and then decreeing—I believe it was last year—that the "personal" garden is the "in" style. This conveniently covers a multitude of my sins.

Here are some tips to add style to the conventional city or suburban lot:

• **Invest in a tree or two.** There are small trees for small spaces. It's the quickest way to cure the flat look of the square surrounded by a fence.

• **Use plants as camouflage.** In small gardens, the typical 6-foot fence can be the dominating feature. Create a green wall by covering it with vines.

• **Break convention.** For example, plant a flower and shrub border in the front yard up next to the sidewalk instead of against the house.

• **Move your seat.** Sitting areas don't need to be slabs of concrete or decking off the family room. Site a terrace under a tree, perhaps in a cozy corner.

• **Invent mystery.** Create spaces that you can't see all at once. Hedges and arbors can be walls and doors to more intimate spaces.

• **Soften angles, add height.** For a soft, lush look, avoid square lawns and straight bor-

Nestle in a pot for a quick fix, or a deliberate design choice.

ders. Create islands of plantings or lawns with meandering paths. Mounding some island beds can add interest to a flat space.

• **Bring in drama.** Even a small space can be made more interesting with a focal point such as a fountain, large urn, tiered plant holder, sculpture, or ornamental found object.

• **De-emphasize the driveway.** A broad curving front walk with interesting paving that leads to attractive plantings around the front door can direct attention away from a featureless driveway.

JANUARY 10, 2002

✧

DRESSED IN THEIR BEST
Tricks and trimmings give houseplants a holiday lift

MY MIND HAS TURNED TO HOUSEPLANTS. Perhaps that's because there's a huge in-your-face flowering cactus in my office that belongs to our office manager, Karol-Jo, who doesn't have a window. So she's put a couple of her potted plants on my windowsill. I let her do it, and I'll continue to, because she puts bags of M&Ms in my in-basket on occasion.

Unfortunately, this Christmas cactus has burst into florid bloom. Its flowers are a lurid flamingo pink. I am sure they glow in the dark. If Pamela Anderson were suddenly turned into a plant, she would be this plant. Obviously, I am out of step, because everyone who comes into my office admires it enormously. Perhaps it's because it's actually flowering when it's supposed to be. It never would if it were mine. I have little talent or patience with houseplants, although I have had one poor little *peperomia* going on 30 years. I never fertilize it and only water when I think of it, which is not often.

The trouble with houseplants is they don't have the decency to die when they aren't flourishing. They just sit there looking pitiful and making you feel guilty so you don't have the heart to put them down.

Despite this rocky history with house-plants, I have a few to get me through the winter. During the holidays I add some because, frankly, they're cheaper than cut flowers. I've also discovered—or perhaps stolen is the appropriate word—some great tricks to dress them up. Here are some ideas I've spotted at arty friends' homes to make wimpy plants look passable and any plant look more festive.

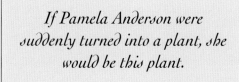

If Pamela Anderson were suddenly turned into a plant, she would be this plant.

• The easiest way to dress up a houseplant is to tuck fluffy moss around its base so no soil shows. The trick is not to be skimpy. For the holidays, nestle little ornamental birds and/or pinecones in the moss.

• Many garden centers now carry polished rocks and glass to mulch around the base of houseplants. These have a practical as well as ornamental effect because, just like mulch outside, they help keep the plant from drying out.

• Make a skimpy plant look grand by sticking in branches of evergreens or berries. Poke them into the soil, and they'll stay fresh for a few weeks if the soil is kept slightly moist. Good choices are laurel, holly, nandina and boxwood. Make a large plant magnificent by surrounding it with boughs of evergreen magnolia.

• Give small plants more presence by grouping them in a large bowl, then tucking greenery in around them. This works well with small pots of cyclamen and poinset-tias. You can get the impact of an expensive big plant this way.

• Scavenge your garden for pretty twigs to stick in with plants. Shiny red and golden dogwood, mossy or lichen-covered twigs and curly willow are especially ornamental. For a festive look, dangle a carved bird or other charming object from one or more of the twigs.

• Some houseplants need a trellis, particularly amaryllis, which tends to get top heavy and fall over. Natural twigs set in a loose triangle around the stalk are a lot more attractive than plastic or metal supports. To jazz it up, encircle the twigs and plant with a pretty silk ribbon or raffia.

• Take an idea from the latest rage in outdoor pots: Instead of a single large plant in one pot, jam in a variety of plants of varying textures and heights. It's most effective when you use a large glamorous pot.

• Lift ordinary plants to new heights with staging. Stick trailing plants such as asparagus fern and pencil cactus in pretty birdcages. Tuck a tiny jewel-like plant in a partially open drawer of a small tabletop cabinet. Look for creative pedestals to set plants on.

• Get creative with containers. Go elegant with Chinese blue and white pots (dazzling with red flowers or berries) or go rustic with twig baskets. Other ideas: painted sand pails, wooden boxes, Italian terra cotta, wooden Chinese buckets, drawers from old apothecary cabinets, ceramic umbrella stands (perfect for a big fern). Protect wood with a waterproof container or liner.

• **For a party look, dress up** larger plants as you would a Christmas tree. Lace tiny sparkling lights or shimmering ribbons through the leaves. Or hang delicate ornaments or foil-wrapped sweets from the branches. Tie on dried flowers for a fanciful look. Turn plants into charming lamps by sticking votive candles around the base, only this time forgo the dry moss.

• **Make a ficus** or other large plant sensational by mounding lemons, tangerines, lady apples or pomegranates around the base. Or hang a single golden pear from a branch, and hope for a partridge to fly by.

DECEMBER 5, 2002

❧

WEEDING OUT OUR MINOR SINS

Most gardening transgressions are annoying, not deadly

WE ARE QUITE FAMILIAR AT OUR HOUSE with at least some of the seven deadly sins. We have had cats and dogs that were distinctly guilty of both gluttony and sloth. If plant lust counts, then I am drenched in guilt. And, on occasion, I've had a touch of envy when visiting someone else's garden.

If there is a subset of deadly sins for gardeners, I suggest these seven:

1. **Failing** to improve heavy clay soil before planting.

2. **Not digging** a planting hole big enough to allow for root growth.

3. **Pruning maliciously** (giving trees flattops and rounding rhodies into balls).

4. **Waging** chemical warfare.

5. **Planting** invasive plants and noxious weeds.

6. **Including** poisonous plants in gardens that children frequent.

7. **Not mowing** your lawn.

Number 7, of course, is a transgression that can set the neighbors after you with torches and pitchforks, like they did in the old Frankenstein movies.

But most of us aren't guilty of seriously deadly garden sins. Instead, we tend to trip up in little ways. I thought about this the other day when I drove by a home with a single line of tulips all in a row like little soldiers. So I submit the following list as seven motley misdemeanors:

1. **Lining plants up in a straight row.** If you want a straight planting—against a walkway, for example—at least stagger the plants. But for the most part, set out plants of the same kind in drifts or pools, the way they grow in nature.

2. **Not following the rule of right plant, right place.** Think lighting and moisture conditions. That golden shrub will look glorious in the sun—until it burns. Pay heed to those "needs good drainage" labels. Even the best garden design won't triumph if plants don't look healthy.

3. **Not taking into account how big and fast shrubs and trees will grow.** The result is that you are left always hacking back and, for all that effort, losing the graceful shape of your plant.

4. Pruning all plants exactly the same way. It's worth doing a little research. Some plants won't come back if you cut back to stumps. Some won't flower if you cut back last year's wood. Pruning at the wrong time may mean losing the current year's flowers (spring bloomers should be pruned only after they bloom). And some plants don't need pruning at all. Why cut back a little spirea that only grows to 3 feet?

5. Taking shortcuts and skimping on hygiene. If you are removing diseased leaves, such as those on black-spot-infected roses (oh, how I know thee), don't put the leaves in the compost pile, because they can infect other plants. Most of us don't let our homemade compost cook enough to rid it of all diseases. Bag up sickly leaves and toss them in the garbage. Clean your cutting tools before using them again.

6. Putting warm-weather vegetables, annuals, and tropicals out too early. Spring days may be warm enough, but the soil isn't. Mother's Day is the key date to start putting sun lovers out, so feel free to haul out those tomato plants now.

7. Fearing that lightning will strike you if you dare to remove a plant. If it's overgrown, casts too much shade or is on the sickly side, take it out. But do try to find a home for healthy plants.

Notice that, among these depredations, I did not include buying more plants than you have room for. As my husband always says, "Knowing better doesn't help."

MAY 14, 2009

COLOR ME CLEVER
Add paint to your list of tools

COLOR IN THE GARDEN IS A POPULAR SUBject these days, but it usually refers to flower or foliage color. Furniture and structures in a garden also can be wonderful opportunities for color grace notes or, as in the following example, gruesome notes.

> *The paint job did wonders. The chairs look splendid against the green grass.*

About a dozen or so years ago, I bought four unpainted Adirondack-style chairs. In one of those moments that becomes frozen in time with the phrase, "What was I thinking," I painted them red. Not a soft cream-of-tomato-soup red or burnished-brick red, but fire-engine red.

It wasn't long before the flagrancy of my offense became even more than I could bear. The chairs were consigned to storage in the back shed, where they stayed for a number of years.

Finally, after reading *Martha Stewart* magazine surreptitiously at the supermarket checkout counter, I decided to deal with the chairs before the taste police raided the shed. Recently I had the chairs painted a pale robin's egg blue.

The paint job did wonders. The chairs look splendid against the green grass.

So I went a step further and painted the gazebo, which had been innocuous white, the same color as the chairs. Now it positively shimmers in the leafy shade. Oddly, it no longer looks quite like a kit-assembled

The gazebo clothed in its new color, shimmering in the shade.

gazebo, which it is. The new color makes it look more tailored to the garden.

From this simple experiment (such a better way of looking at it than calling it a mistake), I have come to appreciate the instant impact paint can have on a garden.

English gardeners discovered this long before us, but I suspect they were motivated by the fact that most of their homes are brick or stone. So painting a door, gate, arbor or outbuilding becomes more of a necessity to liven up the gray stone.

My parable of the red chairs is not meant to warn people off vivid color. I have seen wonderful purple Adirondack chairs. I have friends who have a mustard-yellow gate in their garden.

The color of one's house, the predominant color of the garden and just plain personal comfort will dictate how far to push the paint envelope. Sometimes it's a matter of choosing the right hue or tint. I think red on my chairs would have worked if I'd chosen a more brick-colored red.

One place to start with paint is on otherwise ordinary objects. Wooden arbors, birdhouses, sheds, posts, planting boxes and furniture all can be blank canvases waiting for your paint brushes.

Just go easy on the bright red.

JUNE 8, 2000

❧

UNITED FRONT

Making front yards more hospitable brings neighbors together

I THOUGHT SPRING WAS SUPPOSED TO BE THE season of renewal. In our neighborhood, the season seems to be late summer, and the whole renewal thing appears to be contagious.

Lately, driving through our streets has resembled a slalom run, what with the assorted Dumpsters, trucks, and earth-moving equipment. In particular, a lot of the work involves front yards. Certainly there are a number of sprinkler systems going in, but it's more than a utilitarian push.

All of a sudden, bland concrete driveways are being transformed with cobblestones, bricks and stamped concrete. Hedges and fences, particularly cast iron, are springing up to frame front yards. They are low enough to give a sense of enclosure without presenting formidable fortress-like barriers. People can still say "howdy" over the hedge or fence.

Homeowners are beginning to see the front yard as a place to be, not just as a stage for the front of the house. Low rock and brick walls have gone up to frame little terraces. Spaces for tables, chairs and benches have been carved out. It is almost as if we are having a renaissance in the front garden.

I always felt it was too bad that front porches had all but disappeared, because they are such sociable appendages to houses. People used to sit out on their porch or front steps on warm summer evenings and greet the neighbors as they promenaded by.

I rediscovered the joys of the front yard a few years back when I replaced my narrow and rather ordinary concrete front walk with a much wider, stamped-concrete terrace. I never used to spend time in the front unless it was for maintenance. But now, because the terrace has room for a chair and bench, I like to go out there in the evening and just sit and relax with a book, while watching and moving sprinklers.

My dog Hector announces every passerby by sticking his nose through the fence and barking maniacally. The other night four sets of neighbors came by, walking their much-better-behaved dogs, and stopped to chat. An elderly couple drove up, rolled down the car window and said they used to live in my house. I invited them to come see the garden when it was light.

Then a little girl came by with her father and brother. She was carrying a tree frog in a jar, which she said must have escaped from my pond. She had discovered it in the family swimming pool. So we all trooped to the back and solemnly launched the frog into the pond.

All this socialization is more than merely pleasant. You pick up all the neighborhood gossip—who's selling their house and for how much, who has a new puppy and who recently had a break-in. This is an important part of being a neighborhood. Front garden spaces, whether a porch or a little terrace, encourage this kind of neighborliness. You make connections and learn to watch out for one another.

But maybe it's not necessary to have a porch, but more important to maintain the hospitable spirit of the front porch. My neighbor Kay Holman is a good example of someone who does just that. She has a little white chair in front of her house where she often sits. I wave when I come and go, or sometimes one of us wanders across the street just to say hi.

Just seeing each other is an excuse to communicate, and intrinsically it reinforces that we are neighbors and we're there for each other.

AUGUST 23, 2007

SERENDIPITOUS SOLUTION

Fixing a practical problem gives the pond an attractive new look

WHAT WAS I THINKING WHEN I SAID THERE would be no major new garden projects this year? What was I thinking when I declared, after years of digging out lawn, that the remaining lawn would get no smaller?

I must have lost my head for a bit and thought I'd turned into a disciplined person. Unfortunately, such statements, at least from earnest gardeners, must be taken with a big bag of salt.

It is amazing how otherwise fairly reasonable people can delude themselves when it comes to gardening. On many occasions I have announced I am not going to buy any more plants, because there's no room left. And meant it quite sincerely at that moment. No wonder my friends roll their eyes in ever the most subtle way, just short of actually being rude.

So now that I have declared my perfidy, I can hardly wait to describe my new project. But first, let me set the context. Our back lawn has been the shape of a large amoeba, with the nucleus being the pond.

Unfortunately, the area behind the pond and to one side has exceedingly poor drainage. After this winter's deluge, it resembles a swamp. In the past, every time we had an open garden, it got very muddy and bare from all the foot traffic, and we had to reseed the grass.

I decided enough was enough. In the past few weeks, we have reshaped our lawn. It is now the ubiquitous kidney shape, which I'm sorry to admit since it so lacks originality. The area around the pond, which was formerly grass, is now gravel.

Gravel is a lovely material that is just

catching on in this country. You see it all over the place in European gardens, where even patios and driveways are more likely to be graveled than paved or tarred when one cannot afford real stone paving.

Of course, the Europeans have that lovely pinky-brown gravel that is so much warmer than our gray. I think someone could make quite a fortune by importing European gravel for upscale gardens. Since my garden has no pretensions of being upscale, I'm quite content with Northwest gray.

Years ago, I graveled all my paths when it became clear that the bark dust that had covered them quickly became a perfect medium for weeds, not to mention splinters. I even graveled a long, cracked concrete path in the back, and no one's the wiser. It was a lot cheaper than breaking up and removing the concrete.

We have set paving stones right into the gravel in some places where the accent is appropriate. But for the most part, it's just gravel. Years back, when we first did the paths, we used gravel that came in the quarter-inch size. But now we use quarter-minus, which means it is basically a quarter-inch plus some finer pieces. Because the finer pieces make it pack down better, it is easier to walk on.

Before we add gravel anywhere, we always lay down landscape cloth (available at garden centers) to block weeds and allow drainage. One

> *Now that the pond is framed by gravel, it stands out more. I will claim, of course, that this was my plan all along.*

should really put down a couple of inches of sand before the gravel goes on. But, to be perfectly candid, we have been too lazy, and the lack of sand has never been a problem.

At first, we lined the paths with some old bricks left on the property to keep the gravel from migrating into the flowerbeds. When we ran out of bricks, we found the quarter-minus doesn't really migrate much. Also, since we heap com-

A tidy gravel path now leads to the koi pond.

post on the flowerbeds in spring and late autumn, they are generally slightly raised, so this keeps the gravel out.

And while we did this new project for practical reasons, there's been an aesthetic benefit as well. Now that the pond is framed by gravel, it stands out more. I will claim, of course, that this was my plan all along.

APRIL 27, 2006

NO MOW
A comeback to 'garden rules'

MAKE THIS THE YEAR YOU BLAST SOME stereotypes, have some fun, loosen up, take chances and live on the cutting edge. And the pruning edge. And mowing edge. It's time to break or bend a few rules, and here's an even dozen to smash to smithereens.

Rule No. 1: *You have to have lawn.* This isn't an anti-lawn campaign, but merely a suggestion that lawns are not required for citizenship (green cards aside). If you don't need a play area and hate maintenance, consider a luxuriant ground cover. At first your neighbors will think you're weird, but they will come around when they see you lounging in your hammock while they're pushing a mower.

Rule No. 2: *A deck or terrace has to be adjacent to the house.* Come on now, you can carry that corn on the cob an extra 30 feet. You might find that a little terrace nestled under a shade tree in a corner works better than an open space smack against the house. Move a couple of chairs around to different parts of your yard and try them out for views. You may be surprised at how the mood changes in different spots.

Rule No. 3: *You have to work around existing trees.* Let me count the times that I've heard homeowners fret about finding something that will grow under a huge fir tree that rains needles and casts a shadow the size of a solar eclipse. It is not yet a capital offense to take a tree down, so long as you do it selectively. No clear-cutting please.

Rule No. 4: *There's a front yard and a backyard and never the twain shall meet.* Who says all the flowers belong in the back, while the front is supposed to look like a golf course? The loveliest gardens frame their houses, wrapping cozily around them in a continuous flow. When planning a garden, think in terms of boundary area, not two separate pieces.

Rule No. 5: *You can't do much with that narrow side yard.* Set stepping stones in a gently meandering path in that narrow space between fence and side wall. Slap some vines on both sides, pack in lots of leafy plants to hug the path, then go play George of the Jungle. For extra fun, make your leafy bower a gallery, with a bronze frog here, a water dish there and other discoveries along the way.

Rule No. 6: *Flowers belong in borders.* Borders are great, but there's more than one way to showcase artistic endeavors with plants. Consider island beds, especially where you have sweeping lawns. With an island bed, you can view flowers from all sides. Anchor it with a nice focal point: a small ornamental tree, a bird bath or that chain saw sculpture Uncle Elwood gave you for Christmas (you can always grow vines over it).

A romantic table for two is tucked into one corner.

Rule No. 7: *Vegetables should have their own space.* A well-planned vegetable garden is a thing of beauty, but not every city lot has room for a separate plot. That shouldn't deter you from growing veggies. Artichokes, rhubarb and asparagus are fine foliage plants to accent flowers. Chard, lettuce and cabbages make swell border edgers. In fact, most any veggie works, save, perhaps, a stalk of corn. Now that does look funny among flowers.

Rule No. 8: *Roses should not mix with other flowers.* That's what purists say, and if you're growing hybrid teas, you really do need good air circulation around them to ward off dreaded black spot and mildew. But lovely shrubby roses look oh so romantic fraternizing with flower pals. Look for old-fashioned, shrub, and English-style (sometimes called David Austin) roses.

Rule No. 9: *It's vital to prune.* Pruning is entirely overrated. There's nothing wrong with letting a plant grow into its lovely natural shape so long as it's healthy. Conversely, there's nothing wrong with closely pruned topiary. The problem is when big-leaved plants that aren't suited to close cropping start to look like gumdrops.

Rule No. 10: *Small spaces call for small plants.* That would seem to make sense, but sometimes a gutsy challenge to the rules produces dramatic results. Go ahead and take a chance with a heroic stand of ornamental grass or some extravagantly big-leaved plants in a small area. They might provide an extra jolt of excitement.

Rule No. 11: *The shortest flowers belong in the front.* This is a rule best practiced halfway. Unless you're taking the class picture, you don't need rigid stair-stepping. Live dangerously and pull the occasional stately plant out toward the front where it can flaunt its stuff. You'll have a more natural-looking border.

Rule No. 12: *It's easiest to design a garden on a flat, well-proportioned rectangle.* I wish. Often it takes a challenge to spark creativity. The way you deal with such oddities as a slope, an odd-shaped lot or a change in levels is what makes a garden unique. Problem lots push you to exciting solutions. But the perfect blank canvas tries to seduce you into boring clichés. Very dangerous indeed.

FEBRUARY 11, 1999

TURNING OVER A NEW STONE

Witness the rebirth of a garden-obsessed woman

SO FAR, THIS SPRING HAS PASSED IN A BLUR. I've been in a thrall. I haven't had such a magnificent obsession since junior high school when I had a crush on Chuck Carnduff. This time the infatuation is renewed interest in my garden. Like El Niño, these things must come in cycles.

My current garden is now in its 12th year. In the early years, I came out of hibernation each winter armed with crude drawings, magazine pictures, lists of must-have plants and a zest for doing everything at once. In those days, there was always a project: putting in flower borders, planting a rose garden, adding an herb garden, developing the shade walk along the back and adding the gazebo, arbors, and of course, the pond, which took two tries to get right.

But in the last few years, I'd run out of steam. There was plenty of maintenance to keep me occupied, but I thought, gee, things are kind of done. Earlier this year, when Ketzel Levine wrote about her new garden and asked for ideas, I was spring green with jealousy.

I envied Ketzel her clean slate. Wouldn't it be swell, I thought, to start over. Get the bones right in the first shot, put in the structural shrubs and trees, and then, only then, allow myself to drift off into flowerland.

Silly me, I thought I simply could not fit one more project into my now fairly mature garden. Wow, was I wrong.

> *I haven't had such a magnificent obsession since junior high school . . .*

Something happened. I don't know how it happened; it just did, and that's how most gardens are transformed. After a time, they tell you what they need, and if you're smart, you'll just go with the proverbial flow and not think too hard.

It started with the paths. We decided to gravel them because the barkdust had gone all mushy and by now was too high to add a fresh layer. The "we" is Doug Wilson, my once-a-week gardener, and myself.

Doug started playing around in the back making the path look like a dry streambed with some larger rock groupings. From there, we dug two more miniature ponds to go with the tiny one we put in last summer where the dogwood had fallen over because the whole area is a bog. The three little ponds, now known as the Minor Lakes, are being linked up with stonework.

That stonework led to terracing around the little shed in back and then to some steppingstones through another boggy area that will be carpeted with a golden form of creeping Jenny (*Lysimachia nummularia* 'Goldilocks'). Around the pond (which sadly sprang another leak this year), we've added small boulders in what we hope is an artful way to take away the flatness.

All of this, it turns out, was only the opening act. Picture this. The back lawn is bordered by what can loosely be described as a horseshoe of mixed borders. The top of the horseshoe, the flat part, butts up against the broad porch that runs across the back of the house.

There's always been something that bothered me about this straight line of lawn against the porch in an otherwise gently curving garden. Well, we took care of that. We draped a hose around the lawn to make a broad curve and started digging up turf between the hose line and porch.

What we will end up with is a large green amoeba of lawn, with the oval herb bed as the nucleus, not that any scientific connection was intended here. It may be that since Chuck Carnduff, my first crush, and I were in biology class together, this imagery just naturally leaps to mind.

The evacuated lawn will become stone terracing, loosely fitted so that little rock garden plants can be tucked in among the stones. That's the fantasy, anyway.

There's more. We had a copper arbor at the end of a small path, and we're connecting it with more arbors to make a tunnel along the entire path. In my mind's eye at least, it will be swathed in fragrant roses, jasmine and clematis.

The white garden, which I reported earlier was "The Project" for the year, now pales (no pun intended) before the other projects. Still, it has begun to take shape. We've planted two ornamental trees (*Stewartia pseudocamellia*), which blossom white and will frame the arbor, as well as hide the world's most ill-pruned apple tree in the neighbors' yard. (The pruning atrocity was committed by a previous owner.)

Almost all the bold-colored plants have been moved out, except for two decidedly orange rose bushes, the last thing you'd want in a white garden. But wouldn't you know it, they are the two healthiest rose bushes here at what I fondly think of as Blackspot Manor.

Suffice it to say, I am reborn. It is as if the renaissance has arrived after the Dark Ages. I am living proof that you can teach an old garden new tricks.

MAY 28, 1998

❧

OUTSIDE THE BOX
A small garden plot by the shed generates big plans

I HAVE NO BIG PROJECT PLANNED FOR MY garden this year, just a few little ones. The most pressing is doing something with the space in front of our back shed, which really looks more like a small cottage.

We'd carved out what we called our "Zen" garden there under the shade of a lovely old Japanese maple. Alas, the tree has succumbed to verticillium wilt, a fungal disease that is especially vicious on maples. Now that the area will get full sun, we've moved the ferns and mosses to a shadier spot, and I suppose the little Japanese lantern will have to migrate too.

I haven't figured out exactly what I want to do with the spot, but I'm playing with several ideas. It's a small rectangular space in front of the shed, framed by boxwood with an arbor entry. Given its tiny size, it may be a good spot for a collection of jewel-like rock-garden plants.

Or this newly sunny space could become a home for a collection of succulent plants, which are all the fashion now. If I go in this direction, it would probably need to be a container garden so that I could move the plants into the greenhouse for winter.

Then there's the idea of playing up the cottage look. I could make a small, old-fashioned garden of billowing flowers within the boxwood frame. It would be fun to have more flowers for cutting, since much of my garden has become a collection of shrubs and foliage plants and I have fewer flowers.

Or (and isn't there always an "or"?), we could be practical and decide we have enough plants and pave the

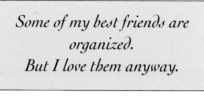

Some of my best friends are organized.

But I love them anyway.

space to make a peaceful courtyard with a small table and a pair of chairs. Perhaps, since it will now be a sunny space, we could set up an ornamental parasol to shade us as we sip our lemonade.

So there you have my "organized" planning process. I rummage through garden ideas in much the way Madonna rummages through new images.

But the point is, as much as I mourn the loss of my Japanese maple, it's fun to have a new space to try out ideas on. And even a small garden area can have many possibilities. It may even be a shady place again someday when the chocolate mimosa I planted last summer grows up.

February is a good time of year to figure out what you want to do in your own little garden areas designated for development or renewal. Once you settle on a look, you can begin your plant research. Make a list so that you can get exactly what you need when you hit the nurseries and plant sales.

Oh, I could hardly say that with a straight face. I am practically rolling on the floor, and the cats and Hector the dog are looking askance. Of course, it is excellent advice. But can I follow that advice? Hardly.

I will probably decide at the last moment what "look" I want and even make a mental list of plants I will need. But I will hit the plant sales and be seduced by whatever is out there, throw plants willy-nilly into the back of my new plantmobile and drive home, leaving the plants to sit in their boxes while I wander around and wonder what I have gotten and where I will put them.

Fortunately, the broad appeal of gardening is that it is an activity you can enjoy wherever you fall on the spectrum of organizational skills—from the systematic, plan-ahead, stick-to-your-list gardener to the muddled and befuddled gardener easily seduced by whatever some wily nursery manager has put on display. I appear to be the personification of the latter end of that spectrum.

All I can say is, some of my best friends are organized. But I love them anyway.

FEBRUARY 23, 2006

SPRING RITE MAY BE WRONG
Will this be the year when I finally come to my senses?

A GREENHOUSE MAY BE THE FOCUS OF MANY gardeners' lust, but it also can be a dangerous thing. With seed-germination season in full swing, some of my friends have said they envy me my greenhouse.

While I do have a fair-sized greenhouse, it really doesn't work for propagation. Instead, it has mutated into a winter storage locker for tender plants, and by seed-starting time it is still chock-full of plants.

We winter over so many plants that some have spilled into the garage, which hasn't seen an actual car in a number of years. We even had a handyman put a skylight in the garage a few years back to accommodate the plants. This will seem over the top to some people, but gardeners will understand.

My greenhouse seems to have given me license to overdo it on tender plants. It's quite a chore to haul them into the greenhouse in late fall and back out in spring, not that I do the actual hauling. Instead, I stand there saying, "Put the pot there, or, no, maybe it looks better back there."

Meanwhile, my helpers are rolling their eyes, and I can see thought balloons over their heads that say things like, "Just make up your (bad word) mind, lady."

Usually about two-thirds of the plants I winter over survive. Of those two-thirds, about half are so ratty that I shouldn't bother saving them. But I do, and out they'll go in their little pots when the weather gets clement. And there they'll sit looking bare and sickly. I always have hopes that a bit of sun and fertilizer will be just the face-lift they need. Sometimes it works, but most times it doesn't.

I am not good at horticide. It took me four years of wintering over a poor little ginger plant that clung to life but always looked spindly with brown edges to its leaves. Finally, I tossed it on the compost pile and ran off before I could hear its last whimper.

The thing is, I've had dreams of those big round platters of succulents such as you see in Thomas Hobbs' book *Shocking Beauty*. Someone dubbed them plant pizzas. They are always so plump and juicy-looking with interesting shades of rose and green and infinite variations of leaves ranging from old-fashioned hens and chickens to tiny-leaved trailers.

Finding just the right spot for your pots takes time.

By winter's end, when I drag my "pizzas" out, they look as if the dog has gotten into them and chewed off all the pepperoni and licked the cheese. There are bare spots, some shriveled succulents, some entirely too leggy succulents and a few that are passable. I end up having to replant the healthy survivors with a good dose of new plants.

This isn't easy since I have to dig into compact soil full of the thready roots of the deceased succulents. It would be easier to just start fresh with new soil and new plants and clean pots. So I am rethinking how to make the annual rite of getting the garden back in shape easier. Sometimes it takes weeks to drag everything out of the greenhouse/garage, clean it up and figure out where the various pots should go.

Maybe this is the winter of coming to my senses and making life

I am not good at horticide.

simpler. I don't have to have a collection of succulent platters. I don't have to have so many tender babies just because they are the latest thing. I don't have to have a bunch of little pots that require excessive watering. I don't have to have semi-tropical plants (except, of course, for a red-leaved banana).

Anyway, lest I forget, I must be sure to write on the blackboard 100 times those words that never fail to choke up a gardener, "I don't need it."

FEBRUARY 26, 2009

~✕~

BED FELLOWS
Unveil vegetables in the flower garden

CONSIDER A TALL, STATELY PLANT WITH silver foliage, deeply sculpted leaves and giant purple flowers. Or how about one that forms a small mounding bush with heroic-sized glossy green leaves and scarlet stems. They sound like perfect addi-

tions to the flower garden. And they should be. But the plants in question, an artichoke and rhubarb, are, ahem, vegetables.

Until recently, the idea of putting anything edible, other than an herb, in with ornamental plants was considered horticultural heresy. Perpetrators were thought to deserve the harshest of punishments—a plague of slugs followed by seven years of clay soil.

It's time to break that inane rule.

For one thing, not many urban gardens have neat little back-of-the-garage spaces where they can hide vegetables. For another, vegetables grow perfectly well mixed in with flowers. And the most potent argument for a change of vegetable venue may simply be that there are a lot of vegetables that look great.

George Washington and Thomas Jefferson were on to that. Vegetables weren't hidden away at Mount Vernon and Monticello like nasty children to be cleaned up for company. And in Europe, the Chateau Villandry in the Loire Valley is one of the

Chard and other veggies can be every bit as ornamental as roses and dahlias.

top tourist attractions even though it's basically a vegetable garden. The French call their vegetable patches potagers, which seems to give them instant elegance, making it OK to have vegetables in plain sight.

If you're still not convinced and don't want to make the trek to Villandry, you can simply cross the river and visit Fort Vancouver's historic garden to see how attractively vegetables and flowers mix.

The French call their vegetable patches potagers, which seems to give them instant elegance.

Just about any vegetable can be grown among flowers, but some actually will add to the design. Leaf lettuces with their deep green, apple green and burgundy red leaves make rich edges to flower borders. Asparagus and carrots add ferny foliage. Carrots are especially pretty when mixed with annuals.

Several vegetables have a sculptural effect: The artichoke is without peer. If the head is allowed to open, it will have spectacular purple flowers. A stalk of Brussels sprouts being what appear to be mini-cabbages can be a conversation piece. And the florets of broccoli, which come in burgundy and white as well as green, are as striking as a flower. Some vegetables have notable flowers. Scarlet runner beans are among the prettiest. With their red, pink, or white blossoms, they can be used as a vine. Okra and eggplant are blossoms, too.

But vegetables add most in terms of foliage. Rhubarb is one of the finest foliage plants around. Cabbages sport some of the fanciest colored leaves in the garden world. They are also one of the first vegetables to be accepted for their purely ornamental value. Then there are the blues of leeks. The reds of Swiss chard and beets and the yellow-green of celery.

What about vegetables that have neither significant flowers nor colorful foliage? For them, it's a case of beauty in the eye of the beholder. Some gardeners love the sight of a pyramid of tomatoes with fat ripening red fruit and leaves, or the deep purple eggplant growing rounder by the day. The towers of beans, peas and cucumbers strung up on pretty lattice supports can give important vertical interest to a flowerbed.

And there's nothing like a stand of corn as high as an elephant's eye to prove your gardening prowess to the neighborhood. Petunias could never do that.

MAY 29, 1992

YES, IT'S LOVE
Hot and heavy over hostas

I AM A FICKLE LOVER, AT LEAST WHEN IT COMES to plants. Well, it's not that I toss over old loves, but I definitely have room in my heart for new fancies. I am afraid there is nothing monogamous about my plant relationships.

A few years back, I discovered lady's mantle and overnight transformed every sharp edge into billowing waves of chartreuse-yellow lace. I was quite convinced that I was the only one this side of the ocean who had discovered this charming plant (that is, until I began to spot it in everyone else's garden and in every corner of my own, since it is not at all discreet about spreading).

The lush foliage of hostas, such as 'Great Expectations,' shown in the foreground, beautifully fills out shady areas.

Since then, I have dallied with a number of flowers, promoting each in turn to Favorite Plant status for as long as the romance burned hot.

This year I have a new passion. It's an old familiar face that went unnoticed like the boy next door, then suddenly appeared, like the heroes in teen movies, in a new light.

My heart, I blush to say, has been captured by, of all things, a plant that is known for its foliage rather than its flower. It is the fair hosta. Give me giant hostas with great quilted fans of bluish leaves (*Hosta sieboldiana*), lime- or frost-rimmed green leaves of *H. fortunei* 'Albomarginata' or the golden fronds of *H. fortunei* 'Aurea.'

But it's a mistake to even mention some by name, because that implies that one is the best. With the exception of *H. sieboldiana*—an absolute necessity—it is hard to pick wrong. Having only one kind of hosta is like having only one kind of rose.

Hostas truly live up to the term hardy in the category of hardy plants (the English name for perennials). They are virtually indestructible. You can dig up a clump almost anytime between spring and fall and divide it. Before long, you'll have two or more full-sized plants. On the other hand, they are polite as can be, staying in neat but lush clumps without straying out of bounds.

The hosta always has had the virtue of turning in a virtuoso performance in heavy clay soil and fairly dense shade, which makes it a natural for those all-too-frequent dark, wet corners. But I have seen it performing perfectly well in sunshine, and—if last summer is any indication—it is surprisingly drought-resistant.

But convenience alone isn't sufficient recommendation for people who are basically madly impractical. Let's face it. We spend our weekends weeding while others are cruising to the coast.

No, practicality is simply a bonus. Hostas are winners for their looks, particularly for the manner in which they bracket the garden season.

In spring, they send up furled, purple-tinged shoots that rise exquisitely until they gradually unfurl into sumptuous fans. You can almost see them grow day by day. (So, too, can the slugs who regard hosta shoots as the caviar of the garden.) In autumn, hostas are among the few perennials that show fall color, lingering on in rich gold rather than turning shabby brown like most other perennials.

Between those extremes, hostas perform nonstop with near-perfection. That's because they don't depend on a short-term flowering season for show. Nevertheless, although hosta flowers are dismissed as insignificant, some are worthy in their own right. The midsummer blooming *H. plantaginea* even offers fragrance.

Having only one kind of hosta is like having only one kind of rose.

APRIL 16, 1993

10 RULES TO BREAK
Don't let advice stifle your creativity

THERE ARE PLENTY OF "HOW-TO" TOMES that spout a number of serviceable gar-

No need to totally eliminate lawn; but shrinking it allows room for more creative ideas.

den rules. Undeniably, rules are useful to give direction and discipline, especially when one is starting out.

But after a while, experience becomes the great teacher, and one of the things it can teach us is that too much rigidity in following rules is not necessarily a good thing. After all, departing from the norm and trying new things is one of the definitions of creativity.

Here, for example, are 10 rules ripe for the breaking.

1. **Get rid of the lawn.** This has been the mantra for the past few years as we strive to save water and reduce labor. But the truth is, a little bit of green is a beautiful foil for plants, and one shouldn't be made to feel overly guilty about enjoying some turf. My advice is that if you like lawn, just downsize and water smartly.

2. **Focus on native plants.** I'm all for native plants, but living as we do in an area that is hospitable to such a wide array of plants, I can't see the point of rigidly limiting oneself to natives. Besides, it's tough these days to figure out just what is a real native. Just avoid invasive and demanding plants, and you can still have a clear conscience.

3. **Double-dig to get good soil.** And, I might add, a bad back. This is the English school of thought, and double-digging—that is, going down two spade depths and working in compost—is a good thing. But frankly, you can get robust perennials by tilling a spade's depth, and digging a good hole will do fine for trees and shrubs. And you can

get great results by building up your soil with spring and fall covers of organic mulch.

4. **Lose the roses if you don't want black spot.** Not all roses are hybrid teas, and even some of these are fairly trouble-free. But if you love clean roses, diversify into some of the old-fashioned roses, especially the trouble-free rugosas. Sure, some of them bloom only once, but that's never stopped us from enjoying rhododendrons.

5. **Be sure to step your border.** While it makes sense to put tall plants in back and short ones in front, if you follow this rule too scrupulously, you'll get an artificial stair-step look, quite unlike anything you'd see in nature. It relaxes a border to pull a taller plant out front here and there, especially if it's a delicate plant that you can see through.

6. **Buy plants in threes or fives.** Here's a rule that I both followed and expounded in my early garden days, believing that I had to do things in sweeps and clusters. But that's before I realized that many plants are sufficiently dramatic and shouldn't be mashed together.

7. **Stick to plants for your climate zone.** Increasingly, we are finding that, with judicious siting, we can grow some things that were once considered tender. This, of course, seems to work best if it's in someone else's garden, not mine. But I can't argue with the success of some of my friends. And who doesn't like a little living on the edge, even if it's just the edge of a climate zone.

8. **Fertilize and prune on a regular schedule.** Surely you need to prune deadwood or unshapely plants, and you need to fertilize if your plants look sickly. But the clay soil in much of the Willamette Val-

ley is enormously rich in nutrients, and if you have been putting a carpet of organic mulch on top of your soil regularly, it may be sufficiently fertile for years. And, when it comes to pruning, there's a tendency to way overdo it. So go by your eyes, not by the rulebooks.

9. **Little plants are a better buy.** As long as a plant is healthy and shapely, not root-bound or leggy, it should do fine, and sometimes, especially in the case of shrubs, a larger plant is a better buy because of the head start you'll get. Also, some plants, such as wisteria, should be bought in bloom because they can take years to bloom if they're not ready.

10. **Have a plan before you start.** Oh my, this is a great rule, but if I'd followed it, I would never have started a garden. Hurray for the organized people who have a plan before they start a garden, but for the rest of us, a lack of an overall plan (or in some of our cases, too many plans and ideas) shouldn't deter us. Plants in these parts are easy to move, and some of the most delightful gardens are those that have grown a bit on the willy-nilly side.

JANUARY 19, 2006

COLORS RUN WILD
Where I envisioned tasteful schemes, a jumble of clashing hues springs up

FORGET EVERYTHING I'VE EVER SAID ABOUT color. I am a failure. A hypocrite. A raiser of false hopes.

Color combos have always stymied me. I've had this dream that my spring garden would be all pastels; my summer garden would move into tawny sun-drenched colors, and autumn would be ablaze with brilliant reds and golds. Alas, it is still a dream.

I knew something was amiss when some perfectly gorgeous red lilies bloomed in July. Problem was, they were coming up through the foliage of a Spiraea that not only had dying pink blooms, but also had lost the freshness of spring. The satiny sheen of the brilliant lilies made the shrub look particularly dingy.

Now I look down my front path and see lots of color. Trouble is, it's a mishmash, thanks to my latest design technique—cram and jam. Really, when one has so many plants crowded cheek by jowl, there is little technique left to you, unless you want to thin out a lot of stuff. I simply can't bear to do that. Yet.

I've tried to keep color associations in mind even as I cram another plant in. What I didn't count on is that blooms of one season overlap those of the other. So here I am in August with exquisite hydrangeas blooming in violet, pink and blue.

And, within a slug's throw, I've got red lilies, orange daylilies, mustardy sunflowers, apricot coneflowers, and red, yellow and pink roses. And the most beautiful blackspot-free rose of all is a froth of orange sherbet. Instead of a symphony of color, my August garden is belting out hard rock.

To make matters worse, nurseries—sensing that plant lust is getting a second wind—have rolled out a fabulous array of color. So—and this is where the hypocrisy comes in—my neighbor Rosemary and I went foraging at nurseries one warm Sunday.

It's a brilliant combination, for which I can take no credit, as it happened quite by accident.

Did we come back with cool greens, silvers and wine foliage to calm our riotous gardens? Oh no. We fell in with a bad lot—brick-colored *Coreopsis* and unusual but florid annuals with fiery orange and in-your-face yellow flowers. I swooned over plants in the most inappropriate colors and now realize that my garden style is emerging into what one might call the M&M garden.

It's not entirely awful. There is something lighthearted about it, or maybe I'm just in denial. Sophisticated, it is not. But then neither am I. Sophisticated people do not have four cats and a dog or name their cars. (By the way, Gertie, my beloved plantmobile, was not totaled after all and is back.)

There is one praiseworthy color combo. In a corner in the front I have a 'Hot Cocoa' rose next to a wine-leaved *Loropetalum* shrub with red *Crocosmia* growing between them. It's a brilliant combination, for which I can take no credit, as it happened quite by accident.

This strident colorama calamity would worry me more if it wasn't late August. I'm in my laid-back mode of not caring overly much if my garden is pristine or color coordinated or overgrown (which it is).

As I get older, I'm more and more aware about not crossing that line when a garden becomes work rather than pleasure. As Scarlett might have said, if she hadn't been busy digging up those carrots, "Spring is another day."

AUGUST 19, 2010

NO MIDDLE GROUND

Gardening magazines cover highs and lows

IT'S HARD TO KEEP UP WITH THE PROLIFERAtion of garden magazines, but I am giving it a good try. They certainly are piling up, and with the colder weather approaching, I'm hoping I'll have a chance to catch up on my reading.

I've noticed that the magazines seem to fall into two categories—the country/cottage group and the upscale designer group. You can tell the difference. Country/cottage garden magazines have pictures of smiling couples in their gardens holding cats or dogs. The dogs look loopy with their tongues hanging out, and the cats look embarrassed, like they'd rather be somewhere else.

Designer magazines rarely show the owner, but instead picture the designer or landscape architect looking very urbane in Ralph Lauren-type tweeds and English wellies (boots). These upscale designers seldom hold an animal, but they do occasionally hold a rake or shovel, which, given what they're wearing, is obviously only for symbolic effect.

Another difference is that in country/cottage magazines, you'd think that everyone has an acre with views of meadows beyond. In the upscale versions, you'd think everyone either lived in New York with a rooftop garden or in Los Angeles with a big pool and lots of cactus.

Country/cottage magazines carry advertisements for bunnies, steppingstones and birdbaths. The designer magazines carry advertisements for elaborate conservatories and bronze statues of wild boars, an ornament that continues to confound me.

I personally am in the country/cottage category, which I hesitate to call low-brow, but as Popeye once said, "I yam what I yam." Nevertheless, I kind of like looking at the upscale magazines and fantasizing about what those gardens would be like. Call it a guilty pleasure.

I find it fascinating the way they've disciplined gardens into kind of a graphic design with lots of "hardscape" and architectural plants. The difference between an architectural plant and all the rest, if you didn't know, is sort of like the difference between a runway model and the girl next door. You fantasize about one, but you have a long-term relationship with the other.

Upscale gardens also tend to have lots of concrete walls, glass and turquoise, a color that, along with flamingo pink, did not exist before the 1950s. There's water, but seldom in ponds. It comes running smoothly down a wall or disciplined into a channel.

Unless you live in a semitropical area with no hurricanes, which leaves California, these gardens are not very practical. They show outdoor rooms with fancy furniture, Oriental carpets and even lamps. Turkish lanterns and silken cushions are scattered about. It obviously never rains in these paradisiacal settings.

OK, that's my Casablanca garden fantasy. The alternative scene, which you often see in upscale publications, is what I call the Napa

> *There I was, hose in hand, wearing a flannel nightgown that had, Lord help me, skiing cats on it.*

Valley fantasy. There's a long wooden table in a meadow with checkered tablecloths thrown on at a rakish angle. The table is laden with baskets of baguettes, wine bottles, designer salads and some kind of fish on a ceramic platter from Tuscany. I know these tables do not exist in real life. A table with fish and no cats on it is a fantasy.

The newest vogue in these fantasy gardens is the outdoor shower or old claw-foot tub. These people obviously do not have a mail carrier or garden help or neighbors who drop by. I draw the line at this fantasy. No way am I going to be out naked in my garden at any time of the day. It's bad enough that I have been caught out in my garden in my nightie. It happened one Sunday morning when I was rolling up hoses in preparation for an afternoon garden tour. Suddenly, a man appeared in my garden and blithely announced he had come early to "beat the crowd."

There I was, hose in hand, wearing a flan-nel nightgown that had, Lord help me, skiing cats on it. So, it's a sure bet this man picked up on the fact that he hadn't wandered into an upscale designer garden.

OCTOBER 28, 2004

KEEPING IT FLUID
A fish mishap prompts a pond rehab

I HAVE FOLLOWED THE NEW POND PROJECT AT my neighbors' this spring with nosy interest. Rosemary and Walt decided not to move their pond closer to the house after all, because they didn't want to destroy a flowerbed. But they are enlarging the current pond quite a bit with Doug the Wonder Boy's help.

Not only is the pond now deeper, but they put in a large rock ledge where fish can hide. The idea was to raccoon-proof the pond naturally rather than relying on the electric fence. All the experts they have contacted about Goldie, their injured koi, agree that the nature of the injury indicates that it was the electricity that did it. She must have jumped up and hit the fence.

This is not to scare people away from electric fences but to suggest that these fences be placed back far enough that a jumping fish can't hit them. The koi experts also warn not to put electric fences too near foliage around a pond. If the foliage touches the fence and a fish touches the foliage, it can get a shock that way, too.

After weeks of recovery in a tub in Walt and Rosemary's basement, Goldie was launched into the new pond and, to everyone's relief, started eating immediately. Sparkle Plenty, another koi, was overjoyed to see Goldie and insists on swimming side

Fantasy gardens call for fantasy figures.

by side with her. We are all now re-considering Sparkle's gender and considering that a more appropriate name is Sparking Plenty.

Before the pond was complete, all the koi were in a holding tank, and Goldie went off her feed again. It seems any change is traumatic for her. Linda Montgomery, the koi health adviser who helped nurse Goldie, told Rosemary that Goldie is the canary in the coalmine if anything is "off," and she may be short-lived because of her injury.

Koi and their undersized goldfish brothers happily share the pond.

My own fish, just plain goldfish, were quite active and visible this spring, rising to the surface in a greedy frenzy every time we fed them. Now they are staying deep, and I just see flashes of gold below. They are no longer coming to the surface for the floating food, but the food does eventually disappear.

The change occurred after a blue heron was spotted gazing meaningfully into the pond. Obviously, my little fish have been traumatized and perhaps are in mourning for some of their lost brethren.

It is interesting to see that they have learned not to come dancing immediately up to the surface, lest there be another predator. Perhaps they will replenish themselves this year. We had baby fish only one year, and that was the year that we had no frogs. I suspect the frogs eat the fish eggs and perhaps some of the baby fish.

The herons, on the other hand, go for the largest fish. Rosemary says one of the koi specialists told her that herons will actually go to the edge of the pond and regurgitate something into the pond, then spear the fish as they swim up to what they think is food.

This reminds me of friends who years

earlier got the idea to put cat food out for the raccoons, hoping this would satisfy them and they'd leave the fish alone. That fantasy ended when they spotted a mother raccoon dropping the cat crunch into the pond as bait to attract the fish.

But the most aggressive predator story I've heard is about the heron that strutted into an art exhibit at Hughes Water Gardens a couple of years ago. The staff told me about it when I was out there picking up my annual banana this spring. One of the artists had a painting, fortunately a print, of a koi on an easel, and a heron pranced up and poked his beak right through it. That wasn't the end of it. The staff had to keep chasing the art-loving heron away for the rest of the day.

JUNE 7, 2007

❧

PERILOUS PROJECT
A 'simple' pavilion drags in complex problems

A GARDEN, I HAVE DISCOVERED, IS A JUNGLE filled with danger at every turn. I am not talking about beasties, sprinkler leaks, toxic plants or hoses to trip over. No, the real dangers are plant lust, visions of unachievable perfection and the incompatibility of one's vision with one's backbone and bankbook.

Now I have discovered an even more insidious danger: the out-of-control project. This year we have what I envisioned was to be a very small and simple project. We are building a small pavilion in the vegetable garden to replace a broken arbor. Now half finished, it is a simple structure, just four posts and a roof plus a stone floor.

But since the carpenter was here building the pavilion, it seemed to be a good idea to have him fix a few planks that were loose on the house. When he got in there, he found everything from dry rot to carpenter ants the size of Godzilla. So he ended up having to redo an entire corner of the house.

That of course led to the need to call a bug man to send the Godzilla ants packing back to Tokyo to fight the Mothra ants. Do you hear cash registers clanging?

Next, it appears the dry rot was caused by aged and leaky downspouts, so it looks as if an army of gutter men will be the next invasion. All in all, the

The pavilion before . . .

"simple" pavilion is turning out to be very, very expensive.

Even without these side diversions, the pavilion itself is making those money-pit slurping sounds that one usually associates with a home remodel. I would like to have left the pavilion open on all four sides, but because it backs onto a shared property line, for privacy's sake (neighbors' as well as ours), we are putting a back on it.

But really, who wants just a plain old back? Doesn't it need something to jazz it up? Of course it does. I knew just the thing. Insetting a stained-glass window would give us light and privacy. So I got down an old window I had that was the perfect shape and size.

Naturally, things couldn't be that easy, and they weren't. When we got the window out, we discovered it had little cracks and would be too fragile to install. Now I am fixated on having a window, but three antiques shops and one junk dealer later I grow queasy over the prices. I am wondering where this "simple" pavilion will take us next.

Oh yes, I forgot to mention, since it is somewhat wider than the old arbor, we had to take out the grapevine and a clematis. That means buying

. . . and after.

new vines to run up the posts. Already, I have a clematis and a climbing rose standing by.

It doesn't end there. Plants on both sides of the pavilion got trampled when the carpenter and his assistant hauled in lumber and other equipment. All this building was taking place in the rain, so the area turned into a swamp.

We must now decide whether to dump in lavish amounts of compost and replant or to cover the area with gravel and make little open areas. I suspect we will go in the latter direction, but the vote is split between Doug the Wonder Guy and Jim the painter.

Oh, I guess I didn't mention that when you replace gutters, downspouts and boards, the reality that your house needs painting slaps you in the face.

APRIL 30, 2009

SWIMMERS ANONYMOUS

In spite of its checkered past, the pond is back in the fish business

WE WENT OFF TO GET SOME FISH FOR OUR pond the other day. It's something I swore I'd never do again. Not with our spotty history. It all started years ago in another house with four fish. My husband, the World War II buff, promptly named them Ajax, Achilles, Cumberland and Exeter. These were the four British ships that pursued the German pocket battleship, the *Graf Spee*.

I was just going to call it a battleship, but my husband says I have to say "pocket," because it is extremely important for reasons I cannot fathom. I suppose it's like saying a botanical name without naming the cultivar. Anyway, the naming was a mistake. Once you name something, it is guaranteed to break your heart. The fish disappeared one by one, and we never identified the culprit.

But that was barely a tub of water, not worthy of the name pond. It wasn't until we were in our current home that we dug a real honest-to-goodness pond, which we stocked with koi. My husband promptly named them after World War II aircraft carriers.

It was a disaster. Raccoons from as far away as Medford hopped on trains to come up to Portland so they could raid our pond. A blue heron the size of a B-29 zoomed in with fork and knife in each talon. The worst incident, I'm sorry to say, was the work of one of our own. The Perp, a very fat cat, waddled upstairs into our den one night, a fish wriggling in her mouth.

I jumped up with a shriek, ran into the bedroom and slammed the door, leaving my husband to deal with things. Women's lib was set back 10 years that night. So was feline lib. The Perp was declawed the very next day.

When we put in a new pond three years ago, I established a new rule. I was firm. There would be no fish. Nevertheless, Doug the Wonder Boy dug this pond with straight sides, deep pockets and rocky shelves where fish could hide. "Just in case," he said.

That first summer, the frogs moved in. Then last summer, a great mystery occurred, even more fantastic than the chocolate cake that vanished and the subsequently sick dog. Fish appeared in the pond. Six or seven of them. Little gold ones, although Doug says he has spotted a black one.

The thing is, we didn't put the fish in. We bought only two water plants last year, and I'm sure there were no fish eggs along for the ride. Thus far, no one has admitted to stocking the pond. It remains a mystery.

We didn't feed the mystery fish for fear we'd attract raccoons. They survived just fine. In fact, they made it through winter and presented us with babies. The tiny offspring, however, seem to be disappearing, we suspect at the hands of the frogs. Or perhaps it is Petey, the turtle who lurks in the depths.

A blue heron also has been seen perching on our chimney.

With all these signs, you'd think we'd know better. But no. We decided the larger fish might be lonely. So off we drove to Hughes Water Gardens out on Stafford Road, where we became the proud owners of 15 comets. They are pretty orange and white fish, very spunky, not at all like the sullen koi that lurked there waiting to be gobbled up. I mean, let's face it, if a slow-moving obese cat like The Perp could snag one, they really had to be dull.

I'm hoping these are smart fish. I'm hoping the new pond's straight sides and deep pockets will protect them. I am hoping they are too big for the frogs to eat. But this time, I'm playing it safe. There will be no names.

JUNE 13, 2002

> *Women's lib was set back 10 years that night.*

꧁꧂

EYE OF THE BEHOLDER
The plastic flamingo runs neck and neck with velvet Elvis —or does it?

I VISITED THE JAPANESE GARDEN ONE GLORIous sunny day this fall. It was crowded, and I was forced to follow another couple closely on a narrow plank among the irises. So I couldn't help but overhear parts of their conversation.

The man said something deprecatory about gnomes, and the woman said she had some garden angels. The man responded that that was "marginal." I assume he meant marginally acceptable. His companion then murmured apologetically that her angels were small and discreetly placed.

I wanted to bop the guy on the head with a pink flamingo. Who was he to judge her taste? Shouldn't garden ornaments be selected for their ability to delight the owner, not to impress the visitor?

It was interesting, because that very day I had been reading an article in the very highbrow British magazine *Gardens Illustrated*. It highlighted a quote by architect Adolf Loos, who pronounced: "The lower the standard of a people, the more lavish are its ornaments. To find beauty in form instead of making it depend on ornament is the goal to which humanity is aspiring."

Silly me, I thought

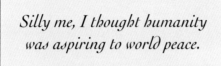

Silly me, I thought humanity was aspiring to world peace.

humanity was aspiring to world peace. Oh well, some will agree that this is an indictment of those of us who love our garden ornaments. Others will put this down as an example of pretentious blathering.

Lord knows, I've had ornament disasters that might have brought fines from the taste police. My list includes the blue gazing ball, the overabundance of bunnies, the rusty trellises, the fire-engine-red Adirondack chairs, the chipped-plate mosaic steppingstones and, gosh yes, even a gnome.

Velvet Elvis paintings have nothing on stylin' flamingos.

The gnome thing started when I spotted a special gnome that had been cast from an antique English mold. It had a very expressive face and none of the bland plastic sheen of a gnome you might find at your local market. Anyway, that's how I justified the love affair.

Then, one winter, my gnome lost his head, thanks to an errant branch or possibly too much gnomic partying. Who knows? By then, I realized gnomes were an infatuation and not a love affair, and I moved on.

Admittedly, I have been guilty of not showing the proper respect for pink flamingos. I would like to say I am sorry, but I just can't work up the appropriate repentance because pink flamingos make such a tempting target. And, truth is, I kind of admire people who have the good humor to include an object that is the garden equivalent of a velvet painting of Elvis.

Still, there is shocking news to report on the pink flamingo front, and we need to be sympathetic of our friends who are loyal devotees. The story was first broken by Dan Glaister, the Los Angeles correspondent of the British-based *Guardian* newspaper, which only goes to show that pink flamingos are capable of making international news.

He reports that pink flamingos may soon be an endangered species. Union Products of Leominster, Mass., the factory that has manufactured pink flamingos since 1957, is going out of business.

The story also quotes Robert Thompson, a Syracuse University professor of popular culture, as saying, "The pink flamingo has gone from a piece of the Florida boom and Florida exotica to being a symbol of trash culture to now becoming a combination of all we know kitsch, history, simplicity and elegance."

Wow, now that pink flamingos have been declared a symbol of "elegance," I know just what to get all my friends for the holidays.

DECEMBER 23, 2006

❧

ROSE RESISTANCE
A shocking desire for hybrid teas encounters an immovable object

I BLAME IT ON THOSE DARNED PLANT CATA- logs. Winter should be a time for sedate contemplation of practical matters in the garden. But then the catalogs arrive in the mail, and, before you know it, wild ideas are taking hold and plant lust is rising like sap.

This year, I have a bad case of it, and I blame it all on the Heirloom Roses catalog. After years of dismissing hybrid tea roses as impractical, I suddenly am developing a yen for them. I imagine their perfume. I have visions of cut flowers. I am blind to matters of black spot, as I look through the catalog and see those seductive acronyms, CB for continuous bloom and VDR for very disease resistant.

My history with roses is not stellar. When we moved into our house 22 years ago, it had a rose garden surrounded by boxwood hedges. But the house had been empty for a year, and all but a couple of roses had died. I planted new roses, which immediately began to fail, despite well-dug, compost-filled holes.

That's when I learned that you aren't supposed to plant new roses where previous roses had been. It seems roses, like agricultural crops, need crop rotation. The old roses leave microbes and other stuff in the soil that will attack the new roses.

So, over the years, after an unsuccessful

attempt at a white garden, the rose garden became a vegetable garden, which both Doug the Wonder Boy and I adore and whose bounty we share. Now so many years have passed, I'm sure the soil would once again be suitable for roses. Those little microbes surely will have died of old age.

Roses or veggies? The battle waged on.

I broached the idea of returning the area to roses to DTWB, pointing out that this is the season for bare-root roses. I made my approach very carefully as this could be a relationship-breaker. I mean, he has a record of knockout successes with vegetables, while I have a sheet of rose-killings that would make a felon blush.

I merely suggested that with all his other landscaping duties, the vegetable garden might be too high-maintenance. I was just thinking of him, I said, what with his having to plant and harvest vegetables each year. I shamefully omitted the maintenance roses would require.

He answered very carefully, in his usual polite way, so polite that only someone as practiced as I at watching him could have detected the slight rolling of his eyes. He didn't outright reject roses and agreed they were worthy of consideration and this would be a good place for them. But I could tell he was a vegetable man through and through.

The tip-off was his diversionary tactics. He started talking about tomatoes, saying maybe we shouldn't plant heirloom varieties this year as they don't ripen soon enough. Then we got into cucumbers (which both of us love when picked sun-warmed off the vine).

Zucchini came up, too, and he opined that maybe we could scale back there.

By this time I knew I'd lost the war, which was OK because I, too, love the vegetable garden, but for different reasons than he does. He wants healthy produce. I love the aesthetic of the late-summer vegetable garden, brimming over with fecundity and abundance when the rest of the garden is growing tired.

We ended the conversation with him agreeing to move the 'Westerland' rose, which is in too much shade. Still, I'm feeling restless. I think there will be some new roses, somewhere.

JANUARY 17, 2008

A LESSON FROM THE ENGLISH GARDEN
Perennials paint garden with changing panorama

DRIVE THROUGH A NEIGHBORHOOD IN THE Northwest and you'll gaze at some of the finest lawns in the world. You'll see an abundance of shrubs that would make gardeners in other parts of the country turn green with envy. You'll also see spots of color—annual flowers such as petunias and marigolds all lined up like good little children.

What you won't see as many of are perennials, those glorious arrays that make English gardens the thing that poets get silly about.

This is not to say that annuals are sec-

Visitors to the birdhouse make fascinating entertainment for garden kitties.

ond-class flowers; they have their uses. But, oh, to forgo perennials in a climate such as this is tantamount to a botanical felony.

Perennials are those flowers that bloom each year, unlike annuals which must be planted yearly. Some perennials, such as baby's breath, are short-lived, while others, such as daylilies, span generations.

The western areas of Oregon and Washington have, like England, some of the finest flower garden weather in the world—mild temperatures and abundant moisture.

But even gardeners east of the Cascades can grow perennials handily. The perennial gardens so much a part of those charming Colonial New England villages thrive despite colder winters and shorter growing seasons.

And don't worry if you've gotten a late start.

Thanks to seedlings, which are plentiful in local nurseries, you're in plenty of time for close-to-instant gratification this year. With wetter and grayer springs and temperate summers, a garden that peaks in summer is ideal. Plenty of perennials are at their best in summer, and many bloom well into fall.

Why perennials? They have four advantages over annuals:

• **You don't have to replant them year after year.** While they may be more expensive than annuals initially, they're a one-time expense. Many even multiply.

• **You can see the whole cycle of growth with perennials.** With annuals, you just plant them in the dirt where, after a while, they become a slightly bigger version of what you planted. You really need to go through a cycle of seasons to appreciate perennials. There's a thrill in seeing the first green shoots poking up after the gloom of winter. Then as winter yields to spring, tendrils unfurl and buds appear.

- **Perennials offer sheer variety.** They range from dainty nosegays to big, bold statements. A perennial garden can be in misty blues, pinks and lavenders or, if you're the torrid type, hot oranges, reds and yellows— and everything in between.

- **You get a changing panorama with perennials.** Some bloom two to three weeks; some span a season or more. A border of petunias will look the same all summer. But a perennial border constantly changes, as spring bloomers give way to early summer beauties, which in turn cede to late summer and fall glories.

So how do you go about planting a perennial garden? Other than preparation of soil, which is crucial, you can make lots of mistakes and still find success.

First, select a site.

Most perennials are sun lovers. Watch the pattern of sun throughout the day and select a spot that has at least six hours of sunlight (bright sun-dappled shade is OK). If possible, choose a spot that can be viewed from a window, deck or terrace. After all, perennials put on quite a show.

You needn't have a big area. Two of the best ways to incorporate perennials into your garden are in borders or islands. Borders are particularly effective along a fence or hedge. Or dig up the turf that edges a pathway. How about the narrow strip between the driveway and the house that you can't mow anyway?

Ideally, a border should be at least 6 feet wide if you want that lush English look. But break that rule if you don't have the space. A 3-foot-wide border along a front walk can be charming. On the other extreme, don't make the border so big that you can't reach in to plant and weed. If you plant a large border against a fence or hedge, leave a strip that will give you access to the back.

Another option is the island bed, which is simply a floating flower grouping in the midst of a lawn. If your yard is formal, a circular or rectangular bed will work nicely. If you prefer a more informal look, make the shape irregular. An easy way is simply to take a hose and drape it into patterns until you find one that pleases you.

Islands look particularly nice when they are anchored with a focal point, such as a birdbath or sundial, around which the flowers will cluster.

Work the dirt. If perennials are to thrive year after year, they need well-established roots. That means tilling the soil to a depth of two spade lengths (purists will insist 2 feet).

There are two ways to do this: The hard way is to turn over the soil one spade depth, then pile that somewhere. Till up the next level beneath that. When that's done, return the soil you set aside. The cheater's way is to rototill or hand spade to one depth, then buy some good topsoil to

Oh, to forgo perennials in a climate such as this is tantamount to a botanical felony.

raise the bed about 1 foot. Raised beds also have good drainage, which makes for healthier plants.

If your garden has hard clay soil, you will need to add soil amendments—compost and other organic matter, such as peat moss and steer manure, to keep the hard clay from compacting permanently. Otherwise, the soil will become impermeable to roots and water. Work enough amendment in to give your soil a soft, crumbly texture.

Now for the fun part—choosing and planting perennials. To achieve the lush look of English gardens, get several of one kind of plant so you can plant in drifts and clumps. Keep in mind how things appear in nature.

Set your seedlings on the prepared soil, and test your arrangements before settling them in. Keep seedlings together where you can keep them moist and wait for an overcast day to plant. New roots are so near the surface, they dry out quickly in the harsh sun. A run of drizzly days will give your seedlings a chance to dig their roots into the ground. If you must plant in the sunshine, watch that the young plants don't dry out.

Seedlings usually carry tags that tell you the height and spread of mature plants and how far apart they should be planted.

As you plant, loosely stagger plants with the tallest in the back (or center if it's an island bed) so that you descend to shorter varieties in the front. "Loosely" is the key word, because you don't want it to look like soldiers marching down steps. Bring some of the taller plants slightly forward, push some short soft clumps a little back. Have a tall spiky accent (iris or daylilies) interspersed throughout.

There are two basic plant forms; mounders and spires. Soft mounding plants such as coreopsis pull the border or island together and can be used profusely. Accent the mounders with spires such as delphiniums and lilies. It's also nice to vary textures, placing lacy or needle-leaved plants, such as artemisia and lavender, respectively, against strappy-leaved iris and daylilies.

Don't fertilize immediately. Soil amendments should contain some nutrients. You can wait until next spring when plants are better established. It's best to err on the side of underfeeding.

Remember, all of these do's and don'ts are simply guidelines, not rules. You'll want to experiment and see what you can get away with. Often horticultural accidents create the best effects and people will admire your artistic daredevilry. As flowers fade, pinch just the flower head off the stem. That is called deadheading, and it will guarantee longer bloom.

MAY 12, 1989

❧

JANUARY—TIME TO PLOT
No dirt under your fingernails, but planning is a thrill

GARDENING IS A LITTLE BIT LIKE BEING IN school. No matter what you're doing, you feel as if you should be studying for some test. With gardening, you always feel something should be done.

That's what makes January one of the greatest gardening months of the year. It's guilt-free. It's a time to plan and dream. Curl up with the new garden books, put an old movie on, and haul out some graph paper.

Chairs in a circle are too invitational to resist.

If you are planning a new garden or renovation of an existing one, here are some things to think about:

• **First consider your garden's overall structure,** not particular kinds of plants. Imagine where paths and flower beds will go. Think of them as shapes, bare of plants.

• **Look at the light patterns in your yard.** Where does the morning sun fall, midday sun, afternoon sun? What areas are mostly shady? This will help you site flower, vegetable and herb gardens.

The best gardens grow and change over the years.

• **What already seems natural, perhaps unconsciously so?** Are there worn areas in the grass where everyone walks? This means this is a natural area for a path. Is there a spot perhaps under a tree, where you often drag your chair to sit or dine al fresco? Here is a natural location for a terrace. There's no rule that says decks and terraces can be off only the back of a house.

• **Decide on an overall look.** Is your lifestyle informal? Are you more comfortable with straight lines and symmetry? Answers to these questions will determine whether you want to set out curving paths and irregularly shaped beds, or if you want straight lines and geometrical shapes.

• **Once you have settled on an overall design or look, start small.** You don't need to do the entire landscape in one year. Begin with a corner where you might site a garden seat at the end of a little cobbled path interplanted with moss, thyme and baby's tears. Or dig one new flower bed and make it spectacular.

Don't do anything else until you've got this area done. The best gardens grow and change over the years. They don't spring full grown like Minerva from Zeus' brow.

• **As you consider what plants you'll add, you don't need to plan** so that everything looks grand all at the same time. The border on the shady side of the yard may be spectacular in early spring with vivid bulbs. But when the trees leaf out and shade it, it will revert to a green woodland area with nothing more colorful than ground covers. But that's OK, because by then the perennial border on the sunny side of the yard will be the star attraction.

• **There's always a tendency to fall in love with a wide variety of plants** where they're spread before you like a feast at the nurseries. But a little discipline (a word that is anathema to most gardeners) can stand you in good stead. Decide early on if you want an overall delicate pastel look or the vibrancy of primary colors, then select accordingly.

• **Finally, don't think just in terms of what you will add.** Renovating a garden has just as much to do with what you take out or move.

It may seem heartless to take out a living thing such as a healthy tree, but if that tree casts so much dense shade that nothing else can have a healthy life over a large part of the yard, out it should come. Nothing can give such an immediate lift to a garden as removing a large, dark green tree or shrub that has grown out of proportion to its space.

JANUARY 11, 1991

※

ANTICIPATION IS PALPABLE
Before you jump in, know that planning saves labor

THIS IS THE TIME OF YEAR WHEN "GARDEN thrall" peaks. The signs are everywhere. Gardeners study weather forecasts, shovels poised and ready to spring into action at the first sign that there will be enough sun to dry out those clumps of clay.

On weekends, nurseries and plant sales look like a feeding frenzy as planting fever spreads like loosestrife. Visions of everything from rose-covered arbors to putting-green lawns dance in gardeners' heads.

But gardeners who are too ambitious now may find themselves enslaved to a high-maintenance garden. Believe it nor not, there may actually come a time when you want to do something besides work in the yard. Here are 20 tips for making life easier.

1. **Improve your soil with compost and amendments before you plant.** This is the one short-cut you can't skip. If you forget this step, nothing will be easy to grow.
2. **Reduce the size of your lawn.**
3. **Automate watering systems.** Water deeply and less frequently rather than lightly and frequently.
4. **Make perennials the backbone of your flower garden;** use annuals for spot color or pots.
5. **Plant flowers close** enough so that mature plants will crowd out weeds and support each other without staking.
6. **Choose disease-resistant plants.** There are, for example, hundreds of rose selections, so why choose the ones that are sure to get mildew in our climate?
7. **Don't fight problems; remove them.** If you have a messy tree or one that casts too much shade, take it out. The same goes for a bush that is overgrown. Rather than constant pruning, remove it and put in a daintier shrub.
8. **Opt for an informal look.** The more formal the garden, the more pruning and trimming is required to keep the look.
9. **Use ground covers** on slopes and under trees where mowing is difficult.
10. **When selecting plants, do a little research.** Find out what is invasive, what needs staking and what needs a lot of water so that you can avoid these plants.
11. **Limit plants to a few** that do really well with little care and grow them in large clumps.
12. **Make raised beds** where ground has poor drainage.
13. **Use slow-release fertilizers.** They're more expensive, but you don't have to fertilize as often.
14. **For potted plants, use a few very large pots and group them.** Small pots dry out quickly and need intensive watering.
15. **Make the best of a bad feature.** If you have a wet spot, put a pond in. If you have a shady area, make a green bower rather trying to grow flowers.
16. **Use a thick mulch** where ground is exposed to keep weeds out.

17. Don't plant messy trees by patios or drive-ways.
18. When you mow, leave the lawn clippings on the grass. They'll break down and add nutrients.
19. When you plant bulbs, dig a large hole and lay a group of bulbs in it rather than digging individual holes.
20. Take risks. For example, sow seeds directly outdoors instead of starting them indoors. Don't dig up dahlia tubers for the winter. There are plenty of years when the weather will be mild enough so that you won't lose them.

MAY 3, 1991

A SINGLE NOTE

Great monochromatic flower gardens observe texture, size and shape, as well as color

L AST SUNDAY WAS AN ABERRATION. IT WAS warm enough to sit with friends on the back porch and watch dusk settle over the garden. The women were talking about the garden bathed in moonlight; the men were at the other end of the porch talking about cars. Those of us at the romantic end of the porch were wax-ing lyrical about the white flower. As evening deepened, the palest flowers and silver foliage seemed to jump out with a luminescent glow, while everything else receded into mysterious shadow. It was so lovely that I began to have twinges for my late white garden.

It was an experiment, and not what most would term a raving success. The white garden was put in a patch where some roses had succumbed to a freeze. Since new roses do not thrive where old roses have grown, I decided to try crop rotation. Because the rose garden is defined with boxwood hedges, I thought it would make an excellent space for a white garden.

The design strategy was simple: I went to several nurseries and bought all the white flowers I could find and stuffed them in. Thanks to the good rose soil, the garden flourished. In fact, it flourished out of bounds, smothering the hedges and choking the paths.

The birds also gifted me with seeds. Two gaudy yellow sunflowers, one lovely pink mallow and three tomato plants sprouted in my white garden. Other than those deviations, the garden really was all white.

And therein lay its problem.

I suppose if seen by moonlight it would have looked romantic, but by day it was guilty of that most unforgivable of sins. It was truly boring. Awful would have been interesting. Bland was unforgivable.

Since then, I have seen some beautiful white gardens and have begun to analyze where I went wrong. The main problem is that I forgot that it takes more than white to make a white garden. It also takes the same kind of garden planning you put into any flower border or bed, regardless of color.

In my single-minded thrall with white, I had forgotten to take into account scale, foliage and overall plant shapes. So there were drifts of white cosmos leaning against equally floppy candelabra nicotiana, creating a vague,

> *Awful would have been interesting. Bland was unforgivable.*

shapeless mass. I learned the hard way that attention to combinations of texture, size and shape may even be more important when flowers are all the same color.

The lacy cosmos, for example, would have been better banked by a tighter, more disciplined neighbor, perhaps a stand of iris. The tall candelabra nicotiana could have been girded by a shorter, more compact plant.

By day, the best white gardens aren't

A beautiful stand of Astrantia major.

more to recommend them than color, such as interesting foliage or majestic size.

Acanthus, *Crambe cordifolia*, cardoon, *Cimicifuga*, *Astrantia*, Japanese anemones, lilies, *Eremurus* and iris are all fine examples.

Finally, the prettiest white gardens, with possibly the exception of England's Sissinghurst, aren't particularly big. An all-white garden is smashing if you have a small lot with masses of greenery.

all white. Nothing creates drama like a stand of glossy dark green leaves and white flowers. Ferns, hostas and other primarily foliage plants set off white beautifully. Tufts of blue flowers here and there also are pretty and give a bit of contrast. Buttery, but not orangey, yellows blend nicely with white flowers as well.

Great white flower gardens also don't rely solely on flowers. For one thing, white flowers don't last long, so long-term interest has to come from foliage. Silvery foliage is magical by moonlight. But by day it can wash out unless it, too, has a contrast. A glowing, burgundy-leafed bush can lift a banal silver border to the sublime. The contrasting color should, like spice, be used sparingly, but like spice, it is the sure antidote to blandness.

The best white flowers by day also have

But, in a big area, a monochromatic scheme can be too limiting. A white border along the narrow side of a house makes an enchanting, magical passage. If you have a corner for a secret garden, making it into a white garden can add to the mystery.

One of the most effective white gardens I have seen was a small circle set smack dab in the middle of a lawn. At the center was a magnificent pot with a small, silver-leafed tree. Bricks rimmed the pot as paving and white flowers and silver-foliage shrubs were planted around the perimeter. There was just barely enough room for a bench.

The circle, which was visible from bedroom windows, was called, of course, the "moon garden."

JULY 23, 1993

PLEASE, CALL THEM BACKYARDS

America, home of the hybrid garden

Rest your eyes on quirky garden art.

MUCH HAS BEEN WRITTEN ON HOW DIFFERent cultures approach gardening. No end of books extol the splendors of English gardening. You can find a variety of books on gardens of Italy, France, Spain, Germany, China and Japan. There are even writers who have discovered the New World. Local bookstores carry tomes on the gardens of Mexico and Canada.

But there seem to be precious few books that sing the praises of the uniquely American garden. There are probably three reasons for this state of affairs.

For one thing, the American garden is a slippery concept to define. Our gardens, like Americans themselves, are derivative of many cultures. Rather than being a drawback, that hybrid approach can be an asset. There is no denying that diversity adds to the richness of the American gardening scene. But it also makes the American garden difficult to pigeonhole.

The second factor that argues against a typical American garden is that there is no such thing as a typical U.S. climate. Few things define a garden as much as climate, and our country spans a wide variety of weather patterns. Imagine any other country that embraces looks that range from New England where the climate resembles northern Europe's to the desert Southwest where cactus flowers reign to parts of California and the South where conditions are downright tropical. The Pacific Northwest, at least west of the Cascades, comes closest to the temperate conditions that make England the world's premier gardening climate.

We can't control the first two factors, and we wouldn't want to. On the other hand, the third reason that American gardens aren't heralded is that they simply aren't appreciated for their own particular virtues. And we can do something about that. It's time to sing the praises of the American garden.

If you could think of one thing that makes American gardens a standout, what would it be? Liveability comes to mind. This is the common denominator that ties American gardens in all parts of the country together. In other cultures, children grow up with the warning, "Don't trample the flowers." Here

> *It's time to sing the praises of the American garden.*

in America, yards are where we send children to play so they don't trample the house.

American gardens are built around decks and patios. We need a place to put the barbecue and the table with the red-and-white-checkered tablecloth. In American gardens, such basics aren't something to be hidden away. Nor are the swing sets, sandboxes, badminton nets, hot tubs, and plastic wading pools. Americans don't look at their gardens as showpieces, but as living spaces.

If this makes for a quirky charm, it also makes for some bumpy aesthetics. When American gardens go bad, they get boring with their cement slabs and too perfect lawns and shrubs clipped to tight little balls.

Too often decks jut off the backs of houses like the bill on a baseball cap. Cement patios sit there like miniature helicopter pads. Swimming pools appear as unnatural forms that, for all their kidney shapes, don't fool anyone for a minute. Hot tubs seem to be a particular challenge. They either look like appliances exposed to the elements or are cutsied up with some prefabricated lath contraption that, contrary to disguising the hot tub, advertises its glaring presence.

The best of American gardens don't bypass the pleasures of the pool and hot tubs and kids' play areas. Nor do they try to disguise them. What they do is integrate them.

JANUARY 21, 1994

THE TIME IS RIPE
Open your senses to the garden in high summer

EARLY IN THE YEAR, I AM CONVINCED THAT spring is the best time in the garden.

Later, I will insist it's autumn. This, if I may state it baldly, is nonsense. After all, I know that the absolutely choice time in a garden is high summer.

Is this not, after all, the season we all wait for? Spring is the season when we pretty up gardens so visitors can enjoy them. In autumn, we clean up and plan for next year, the year we are convinced will bring our garden to perfection. But high summer is that halcyon hour we reserve for ourselves to enjoy our gardens just as they are.

Late lilies are blooming; sunflowers are shooting up; the dahlias are flaunting their brilliant petals like the floozies they are. A few leaves have browned, but who cares? Not us, when the air is abuzz with bees and the whir of hummingbirds, and dragonflies hover like iridescent helicopters above the pond.

Out in the vegetable garden, not so little green vines are devouring their trellises as tomatoes redden, pumpkins fatten and grapes threaten to ripen, which they never quite manage to do in my garden. No matter.

So what if the lawn has lost its freshness. Who cares if spiders have draped the foliage in gauzy nets and slugs have made lace of our hostas. Who has time to worry about perfection when one can pluck a ripe cucumber off a vine, get a whiff of the neighbor's barbecue or simply doze off on a balmy afternoon?

If young gardeners live for spring, we older gardeners embrace high summer as a garden's sublime moment. What a garden lacks in the freshness of spring, high summer more than makes up for with its fullness and fecundity. If spring is a pretty blossom, high summer is a ripe fruit, ready for the picking.

But, it's a fruit that must be picked lest it rot on the vine. And, by picking, I mean opening one's senses to the garden in its maturity and enjoying—not planning, not enhancing, not making to-do lists—but purely enjoying a garden.

We must ignore those magazines with their lists of chores for August. This is not the season for an angst-ridden pursuit of new plants. Nursery shopping should be a languorous stroll down seduction alley to discover a beauty here and there, not the frenetic cramming of wagons to fill in naked space.

Naked space! Was there ever such a thing? I can't imagine it, just as, come winter, I will look out at a mudscape and wonder if the flowers were a mere fantasy.

This is our seventh-inning stretch—that comfortable span of hammock suspended between a post that says "getting the garden ready" and a post called "putting the garden to bed." We must plunk ourselves into our hammocks—imaginary or real—and look, listen, smell and savor the garden with all the sleepy-eyed satisfaction of a plump frog perched on a lily pad.

August is a gardener's get-out-of-jail free card. We can be indolent. We need not feel guilty for chores undone. We are allowed to be self-satisfied. We might even linger, for once, at a bench without popping up to snatch a weed. Can we really do that?

And, oh yes, I realize I am awash in sentimentality, aslosh in clichés and, for all that, disgracefully unrepentant. After all, with all the poets stuck on spring, someone has to stick up for summer.

JULY 31, 2008

Wilbur, the garden cat.

Part 4

DISEASES AND SNAKES AND SLUGS. OH MY!

❧

When I return to a spot where there are dead slugs,

invariably there is a live one on top.

And it's not giving mouth-to-mouth resuscitation.

Weathervanes aren't just for farmers . . . here's a clever piece in the garden.

SLUGFEST

Mayhem in the garden

I THINK I OUGHT TO WARN YOU THAT THE CON-
tent of this column may be unsuitable for
some readers. Especially if you're squeamish.
It is a column about how formerly squeamish
and tenderhearted people can become ruthless killers.

Slugs will do that to people.

I was at a dinner party the other night
when the four women adjourned to the living room, while the men stayed at the dining
table. This was not gender-biased, mind you,
but rather due to the fact that we women were
gardeners who all work together, and, naturally, we do not talk about it enough at work.

I don't know what our husbands were talking about, but I do know that when one of the
women mentioned the word "bra," the men's
conversation stopped dead for a couple of seconds. So much for the "I didn't hear you, dear"
excuse.

Anyway, at
some point, the
subject of slugs
came up. One of
the women, Judy,
who is extremely

> *Every time your bare toe touches
> something cold and wet, well, your
> imagination just runs wild.*

ladylike, mentioned how she just had to get
out and slice and stomp those slugs. She used
the word "stomp" twice, and even I had to
wince. This is what some of us eventually
come to. Slug slayers. I know, because it has
finally happened to me.

For years I'd read that the only way to
get rid of slugs is to take a flashlight and go
out after dark and cut them in half. This
sounded distasteful in the extreme. So, like
everyone else, I started with saucers of beer.
But waking up to a heap of dead slugs in a
saucer is truly disgusting. Beer does not de-
hydrate the little beasts, so they still look
slimy.

Next, I tried slug bait, but that made me
feel guilty about what I was doing to the environment and also fearful lest one of my pets
get into it. Plus, my hostas and ligularia still
looked like lace curtains. I held out some hope
for the bullfrogs that moved into our pond
because I'd read they eat anything, including
slugs. But so far, they haven't made a dent.

Finally, this summer, I gave in. Armed
with a flashlight in one hand and scissors in
another, I went out into the wilds of my garden after dark. The first night, I snipped 100
of the beasts within a half hour. One night, I
reached the 200 mark, and lately the slug
population seems to be in decline.

This whole thing has been quite an education. No wonder saucers of beer and slug
bait don't work. They're set up to snare
maybe dozens of slugs, while the garden is
rife with hundreds.

As with any
art, technique is
all. It helps to
come at the slug
obliquely, so you
aren't really look-
ing at it. Just catching it out of the side of
your eye sufficiently to have a true aim. That
way, when you snip it in two, you don't actually see the gore.

Then, just as you snip, you scoop the slug
sideways with the scissors into the shrubbery.
That way the late slug is no longer lying all
bubbly in the middle of the path for you to
step on.

You will also discover that slugs are pack
animals. If you find one, you're likely to find
its buddies. And, if you thought that it was

not possible to find anything more disgusting about slugs, there's this: They seem to have cannibalistic tendencies. When I return to a spot where there are dead slugs, invariably there is a live one on top. And it's not giving mouth-to-mouth resuscitation.

Finally, here is something else important I learned. Open-toed shoes are not appropriate. Remember, you are going out in the dark with a flashlight, and you can't actually see much. So every time your bare toe touches something cold and wet, well, your imagination just runs wild.

AUGUST 29, 2002

A rabbit of the more tolerable variety.

MEAN THUMB

Pests can drive even the gentlest gardeners to the dark side

WHEN IT COMES TO RIDDING OURSELVES OF pesky critters, gardeners have been known to go to great lengths and even develop a brutal side. But, when it comes to furry critters, there's also an ambivalent side.

The other day I was walking with a friend in her country garden and she was complaining of the damage rabbits do. Then suddenly we came on a new bench—a bench carved with cute bunnies.

I myself have never had a bunny problem, but raccoons are another matter. They continue to come into our yard and visit our new pond, but I don't think they've had much success because it's deeper and has straight sides.

> *When it comes to critters without fur, there's really no ambivalence and little mercy.*

The other night, our dog Hector ran out into the yard barking his head off. When my husband went out to see what the noise was about, he found a mother raccoon and two babies looking longingly at the pond.

Suddenly, the mother raccoon turned on our dog and hissed, and poor Hector ran screeching back into the house, up the stairs and into my arms, where he had to be comforted for about 10 minutes. So much for hero dogs.

Actually, the raccoons may have done us a favor when it comes to other predators. This year for the first time, our fish have had babies, lots of babies. We think it's because the raccoons got the bullfrogs that had previously eaten up the fish eggs. Anyway, we found the remains of a frog or two last spring.

When it comes to critters without fur, there's really no ambivalence and little mercy. The other day I made a small donation to a worthy cause and was feeling a bit overly pleased with myself. I said something like,

"It feels good being nice." Without missing a beat, my husband said, "Does your being generous extend to my getting a bug zapper?"

I said no, but it didn't help when later that week we were watching television and a commercial came on. It advertised a gawky machine that looks like a cross between a robot and a vacuum. According to the voice-over, it emits an attractant that lures mosquitoes from miles around, probably as far away as North Dakota. Then, whoosh, it vacuums them all up.

I could feel my husband quiver in the chair beside me and thought, "Oh, lordy, he is going to want one of those." A few days later, Doug the Wonder Boy was over for dinner. Feeling sure I had an ally, I made the mistake of mentioning how disgusting bug zappers are with that whirring noise. Not to mention that they can also kill beneficial insects.

Well, silly me, I had forgotten that Doug, like my husband, had once been a little boy. He and my husband started talking about those "great" sizzling sounds bugs make when they hit the zapper. The two of them were going at it with great glee, and finally Doug said, "I may have to support Ted on the bug zapper." This, after I had slaved over opening boxes of a takeout dinner for them.

However, a gardener's brutality is most likely to emerge when it comes to slugs. There may be ambivalence about bunnies, but you just don't see cute slug benches. Even I have to admit I took on a challenge from a friend this summer to see who could scissor the most slugs. I think I may have won, too, but someone threw out the paper I was keeping score on. Some people have no respect for scientific data.

I like to think, however, that the differences are that I don't actually enjoy killing slugs, and killing them this way is more environmentally benign. But perhaps that's a rationalization. The best rationalization I've come across is in a book by Meg DesCamp called *Slug Tossing and Other Adventures of a Reluctant Gardener*.

DesCamp doesn't really want to kill slugs herself. So she tosses them into the street where cars can run over them and she, herself, can feel innocent of murder.

It's a whimsical book about DesCamp's first attempt at gardening, and slug tossing is just one chapter. It's a good read for those of you who are intimidated by gardening and think you must be born with a green thumb. It proves one does not spring full-blown into a gardener. No, some of us learn mistake by mistake, trial by trial, accidental success by accidental success.

DesCamp's book is based in Portland, so many of you will recognize familiar places and challenges. Maybe you've even run over one of her slugs.

OCTOBER 2, 2003

IN DEFENSE OF BATS
Forget the belfry, you want them in the garden

THE SIGNS OF HALLOWEEN ARE EVERY-where—witches, skeletons, ghosts, goblins and bats. Scary things. But wait, one of those creatures doesn't belong on our list of bad guys.

The little mouse-eared and brown bats that visit your yard are some of the best friends a garden ever had, as a lot of savvy homeowners are beginning to appreciate.

Suddenly, bat boxes are becoming a familiar item wherever birdhouses are sold.

If the idea of inviting bats to live with you seems blood-curdling, consider this. Bats eat insects—lots and lots of insects. According to the Audubon Society of Portland, one little brown bat can eat up to 600 insects in just one hour. Their favorite delicacy is mosquitoes.

They also pollinate plants.

And what of the myths about bats? They don't suck blood, at least not any of those in North America. (The infamous vampire bat lives only in Central and South America.) Bats won't fly at your hair either. "Well, they might fly at your hair if you had bugs in it," laughs Jennifer Devlin, education coordinator for the Audubon Society.

She surmises that bats got the reputation for flying at hair simply because they sometimes get trapped in a house. In their panic, they fly all over, including at you.

Devlin is on a campaign to separate fact from myth, and she has a program she takes on request to schools, garden clubs and community groups. "It's the most popular program we have," she reports.

One thing is true about bats: They can carry rabies. But the incidence in this part of the country is rare; in fact, rarer than among cats and dogs.

Even a rabid bat isn't likely to attack. Most people get bitten because they see a sick bat and pick it up. Devlin advises that sick or injured bats should never be touched. Instead, they can be scooped with a stick into a box. The Audubon Society does accept injured bats and has successfully treated and released some.

Right now bats need all the help they can get. Nearly half of the species in the United States may be endangered. Without these tiny flying mammals, farmers and gardeners alike might have to depend to a greater extent on pesticides. In England, all species of bats are now protected, and it's as illegal to kill a bat as it is to kill one of the Queen's swans.

All North American bats are insect-eaters. About 15 species inhabit Oregon, 11 of which live in the Portland area. The most common local bat is the mouse-eared bat (*Myotis* species). One endangered local species is the silver-haired bat that likes to roost in the bark of big trees such as ancient Douglas firs, according to Devlin. Townsend's big-eared bat also is a threatened variety.

Bats always have had a mystique. They are the only mammals that actually fly, rather than glide. They hunt at night, seeming to see in the dark. What they have is a sonarlike guidance system to detect insects and obstacles.

Bats are attracted to yards with water, such as a pond. Bat houses also are a good way to entice bats to take up residence. Houses for bats differ from those for birds in that they have inner partitions that create the crevices bats prefer.

The Audubon Society recommends hanging bat houses in a sheltered spot about 12 to 15 above ground. The bat house should be on the side of a building away from prevailing winds and unobstructed by tree branches or utility wires.

Although bat houses can be mounted on poles and trees, the society reports the best success with the houses that are attached to a building, which helps keep them warmer.

OCTOBER 25, 1991

NAIL THOSE SNAILS

Foreign gastropods are on the march

HAVE WE DONE SOMETHING TO IRRITATE France again? I thought we were friends after the ill-advised dust-up over "freedom fries." Did an Oregon tourist in Paris wrinkle his nose at escargot, causing France to unleash an army of snails on us?

All I know is that for the first time in 30 years of gardening I am facing an invasion of snails and seeing my hostas and dahlias reduced to tatters. I go out on nightly forays with my scissors, but somehow cutting a little shell in half is more disturbing than simply snipping a naked, slimy slug. That pretty shell blunts the killer instinct.

For one thing, you see snails in paintings and even children's books, but you never see slugs romanticized. I even found Web sites devoted to snails as pets and advice on how to attract snails to one's yard (I say yard, because surely anyone who exhorts inviting snails does not have a garden). Worse, I found a site for information on snail ranching.

Given all this snail-love, it somehow seems more heinous to dispatch a snail than a slug, although the two are virtually the same in the damage they wreak. It just goes to show that it's true what they say about clothes making the man.

Finally, after wading through all the snail lore, I found sanity on the Oregon State University Horticulture Department

> ### *Have we done something to irritate France again?*

site. Let me quote what OSU extension agent Robin Rosetta writes: "Exotic snails are getting a toe-hold into the Pacific Northwest and the only thing between them and global domination is a vigilant public." Cute, that "toehold" reference.

Oregon's Department of Agriculture confirms that snails pose a serious threat to agriculture and the nursery trade. In 1983, the department instituted a quarantine against brown garden snails (*Cantareus aspersus*), the most common of the snails found in the state. Host plants imported into Oregon must have a certificate of compliance showing they were examined and found free of snails in every phase of their life cycle.

Still, the slimy invaders, originally introduced into California in the 1850s for food, are finding ways in. In the past decade, according to OSU, there were 12,000 mollusk "interceptions" made during routine inspections at U.S. ports, airports, and border crossings. That includes 121 interceptions at the Port of Portland.

I am trying to envision an interception. "Hey, Mr. Snail, where's your passport? Do you speak English, or only French? You must leave immediately." Apparently, shiploads of tiles are a favorite transport for snails.

Some opine that our newly perceived Mediterranean climate is a factor in the proliferation of snails. *The Journal of Pesticide Reform*, published by the Northwest Coalition for Alternatives to

Pesticides, says the Northwest's wet, overcast and mild climate is perfect for these nocturnal creatures.

The coalition recommends a number of measures to control the snail population, principally by reducing habitat. That means clearing away debris such as bricks, boards, grass clippings and rock, where snails like to hide. They also note that mulch is a favorite habitat for snails, so they suggest not mulching around plants that snails particularly savor.

They also suggest we might not grow such tasty plants as hostas, delphiniums, dahlias, marigolds, strawberries, lettuce and other leafy vegetables. This seems pretty extreme, as does introducing snail predators such as snakes. Other predators include toads, frogs, birds, certain beetles, ducks and geese.

I notice that most of the advice about ridding one's garden of snails speaks in terms of "management" and "removal" and "hand-picking." No one quite has the temerity to use the word "kill," as in squash or snip. After seeing a few ravished dahlias, I learned to look past that pretty shell and see the slimy creature for what it is. Snip, snip.

AUGUST 16, 2007

❧

OLD WIVES, NEW WAYS
Before DDT, organic gardening was the norm and home remedies abounded

I WAS TALKING WITH FRIENDS ABOUT WHAT IT meant to be a green gardener, and one pointed out that going "green" is nothing new. It is really a throwback to the way people used to garden before chemicals such as DDT came into use.

My friend said that in those days there were a lot of home remedies, such as throw-

> *It's difficult to distinguish between the wise old-wives' tales and the silly old-wives' tales.*

ing boiling water on weeds. The problem with many of those old-fashioned methods for getting rid of weeds and bad insects is that it's difficult to distinguish between the wise old-wives' tales and the silly old-wives' tales.

Will grass clippings spread at the base of roses (but not touching the stems) deter pests? Actually, I tried this, and it did work. Apparently, they make a hot little mini-compost pile. Will a clove of garlic next to roses keep aphids away? The jury is still out. Will sprinkling water that you washed a cat in keep mice away? Why on earth would that scent deter mice if the actual cat (now very angry) that you washed isn't keeping them away?

Then there are the old-fashioned recipes that are just plain disgusting. The worst is the advice to collect dead slugs, worms, and insects in a bottle, fill it with water and let them decompose. Then spray the foul-smelling results as an insecticide. I personally would rather have the insects.

If you want a good source for organic gardening, get yourself a copy of Ann Lovejoy's *Organic Garden Design School*. This is a complete book offering everything from design advice to recipes for fungal sprays and composting. Lovejoy's theme is cooperation with nature, not control. Better yet, she makes a convincing argument that "green" gardening is actually easier and produces better results.

Tips for green gardening:

- **Plant trees.** If you don't have room, join a neighborhood tree-planting party.

- **Don't dig plants in the wild.**

- **Grow something from heirloom seeds** and share seeds from your crop.

- **Make your own compost** with grass clippings and other organic (nongreasy) debris.

- **Carpet your planting beds** with organic compost about 3 inches thick in late fall or early winter and again in spring.

- **Introduce beneficial insects** into your garden. They are beneficial if your nursery is selling them.

- **Have a small pond.** It will attract frogs, which devour slugs and insects.

- **Keep bird feeders clean.**

- **You don't need to limit yourself only to native plants,** but do use plants that are well adapted to our area because they originate from similar climates. They will require less coddling.

- **Site plants where conditions are appropriate.** For example, plants that swoon in afternoon sun should not be planted in a western exposure, where they will need excess water to stay healthy.

- **Avoid rototilling.** This chops up weed roots and creates more weeds.

Froggie love. Sculpture by Susan Nebeker.

- **To clear an area of weeds or grass** without chemicals, cover it with black plastic, cardboard or newspapers (weighted down with stones or bricks). Do this in the fall before spring planting.

- **Immediately remove diseased branches** or leaves from plants. If the whole plant is infected, remove it. Spraying may prolong its life a bit, but it will either die eventually or just go on looking sickly and possibly infecting other plants.

- **Use a reel mower.**

- **Get over your slug squeamishness** and go out with some scissors and slice those beasts in two. Really, is a bunch of dead slugs in a saucer of beer easier to stomach?

- **Develop a green attitude.** Some bite marks on leaves are natural. Pristine isn't natural.

MAY 17, 2007

✁

NO. 1 ON MY LIST
A dinner-party problem tests my virtue

I AM STRUGGLING TO STAY A VIRTUOUS AND organic gardener. But lately I have been sorely tried.

I had a dinner party for about 30 people in my garden. I wanted it to be perfect (which means I didn't do the cooking) because it was a fundraiser for a very worthy cause. Everything was ready when the guests arrived. Nothing could go wrong. Or so I thought.

Just before it was time to sit down, I noticed little green bugs in the glasses on the table under the tulip tree (*Liriodendron*). I frantically ran around cleaning them, trying to pretend nothing was wrong. Then, as I stood talking to a guest, I looked over toward the table. The sun was coming straight at me from the west in those low, late-afternoon shafts of light. And there, spotlighted in the sunbeams, I could see a steady rain.

> *I'm afraid it was what one guest inelegantly referred to as "aphid pee."*

But, alas, it wasn't a rain of water. I'm afraid it was what one guest inelegantly referred to as "aphid pee."

Aphids have now replaced slugs as my garden nemesis. They suck juice out of leaves and, while they won't kill healthy plants, they will distort and curl leaves and stunt growth. If you see street trees dropping leaves, it's not due to an early autumn. It's probably aphids. The worst thing is their sticky excretion, which is called honeydew. I am sure that anyone who has ever parked under an aphid-infested tree knows what this is like.

Since that evening, I have learned quite a lot about aphids. For example, if you see a lot of ants, it's an indication you have aphids. Ants love honeydew. They love it so much that they will ward off beneficial insects that eat aphids. I'm not sure how they do this. Maybe they wave little ant swords or shout obscenities such as "Your mother looks like a wasp." Anyway, one of the ways to control aphids is to control ants.

This is not the first time we've had aphids. Years ago, when we first moved in, we had a terrible aphid problem in the same tulip tree. The tree is too tall to hose off or spray, so we had the soil under the tree injected with an insecticide. The injections, which are said to be less harmful to good bugs than spraying, are effective only in spring when the sap is rising so that it draws the insecticide up into the foliage. These soil injections, by the way, should never be done near a fishpond.

The injections really worked, and we repeated the process for about five years. Then one spring we forgot to do it, and we still didn't have aphids. We thought they had gone away, and since I wanted to be as organic as possible, I didn't order any injections after that.

Then we started to get a little honeydew

drip. I bought ladybugs and let them loose in our garden, even though I read they would fly away. But they did hang around, and within a couple of weeks the drip would go away. That worked for a few years, and I was so pleased that I wasn't too bothered when a clot of ladybugs spent a winter in a corner of our den ceiling, although it was slightly creepy to see them there.

But now I'm wondering if our ladybugs have retired and moved to condos, because the aphids are back with a vengeance. I read that they can go from newborn to adult within a week, and they can produce 80 offspring in a week. Apparently, my tree is a regular aphid Club Med, because they definitely are having a good time and multiplying.

Since the ladybugs aren't doing the job, I started to look for other natural enemies. I learned that these include lacewings, which sound nice like ladybugs, and flower fly maggots and certain fly larvae, which sound pretty icky.

Another aphid fighter is a parasitic wasp that lays eggs inside the aphid, which causes (please don't be eating now) the aphid skin to get all crusty and mummified. You are supposed to look for these little aphid mum-

Dragonflies feast on mosquitos, aphids and other garden pests. This one is pure fancy.

mies to see if the wasps are doing their important work. However, since an aphid is only about one-tenth of an inch long, I am wondering how you can tell an aphid mummy from a speck of dirt. It's not something I want to investigate too closely.

All I can say is that the whole thing is disgusting. At least slugs are big enough that you can snip them in two, and they also don't you-know-what on your guests.

AUGUST 10, 2006

SNAKE EYES
Fear of wildlife slithers into view

JUST WHEN I THINK I'M A MATURE ADULT, along comes something like the Great Snake Incident. I blame my friend Carlene for what happened. She told me how one of her cats brought a snake in while she was home alone, and how she had to get it out of the house with a stick. The incident must have imprinted on me.

Because, only a week later, I went out at night to move a sprinkler, and there was a snake in the path. I wasn't sure at first if it was a twig or a snake. So I got as close as I dared. It was all curvy like a snake. I went around to another side, and sure enough I saw a stripe down its back.

I ran inside and screeched for my husband. He was upstairs and took his sweet time. I screeched again, and when he came down I was angry and said something about how traumatized I was and how he needed to respond more quickly.

We went outside with the flashlight, and I shone it right on the snake. He kept saying, where is it? And I kept saying, it's right there where the light is. I was getting really mad because he seemed downright pigheaded about not seeing the snake, and I definitely needed rescuing.

Then he leaned down to pick it up, and I screeched again. "Don't touch it," I yelled. "It might bite you." He ignored me, picked it up and snapped it in two.

It was a twig.

I was so unnerved by the whole incident that I made him go down the dark path and turn off the sprinkler because I was sure there was a snake lurking out there ready to jump at my ankles.

It seems to me that all those magazine articles about attracting wildlife to your garden are so much hoo-hah. What people really want is selective attraction. One man's sweet honeybee fertilizing the flowers is another man's vicious stinger.

If we are going to be candid, we have to admit that most of us actually don't want that much wildlife in our gardens. I have seen considerable handwringing over the damage done by those winsome deer and cute little bunnies. And anyone who owns a pond knows that raccoons are fond of re-enacting Sherman's march through Georgia.

Then, of course, there is the constant battle with slugs, snails, aphids and, for some, spiders. I happen not to mind spiders, which is good because right now they are so busy draping every inch of my garden with webs that you'd think Hollywood was about to start filming *Return of the Arachnids.*

When it comes to wildlife in the garden, most people have the welcome mat out for butterflies and diminutive birds, certainly something smaller than herons and hawks.

Bats, like snakes, are the subject of a great divide. Both can be great garden helpers. Bats are voracious mosquito eaters, and our locals are not at all like the bloodsuckers of vampire fame. Long ago, I put a bat box I got at the Audubon Society's store on the south side of the house in hopes of attracting more bats.

Since our garden snakes are not poisonous, they too should be welcome guests. However, I can't say I have a snake box. Intellectually, I accept that snakes are good for my garden. But when a snake, or maybe even a twig, rears its slithery head, intellect flies out the window.

Ever since the Great Snake Incident, my husband has taken to making remarks about rescuing me from the anaconda. Cute. I know I will not hear the end of this incident for some time.

JULY 27, 2006

GREEN BY DEFAULT
Good intentions are only part of the story

I'VE HAD A CHEMICAL-FREE GARDEN FOR YEARS. I feel a bit smug saying this, but the fact of the matter is that this isn't completely due to virtue. While I respect the environment, my "greenness" is partly due to a large dose of laziness.

Plants that require coddling are banned. I enjoy hybrid tea roses in other places, but not in my garden. I once pulled up a row of Exbury azaleas, to the horror of a neighbor who came over to lecture me about their value. Once they'd bloomed, their leaves turned a dirty white, thanks to a bad case of powdery mildew.

When my Japanese anemones developed a fungal disease, we replaced them with hydrangeas. When the Japanese maples died because of a soil-borne disease, we bought small Japanese maples with exceptionally pretty leaves and put them in large pots.

We lazy gardeners know that it's simply easier to avoid problems than to try to cure them. My attitude is that there are enough plants that thrive in the Northwest that I do not need to deal with high-maintenance prima donnas.

Having a mature garden helps. Over time, gardens tend to find a balance and grow more disease- and bug-resistant. OK, I admit this summer the balance got a little askew when the aphids made a mess. But the tardy ladybugs did show up, and we have no aphid problem at all now. We may have a ladybug problem, but at least they're cute.

Speaking of problems, I am reminded of something a colleague mentioned the other day. When her young daughter purchased her first condo, my colleague went over to help her plant a pretty courtyard. Things were going fine until recently, when the daughter called to say, "Mom, you've got to come over right away. It's an emergency."

> *We may have a ladybug problem, but at least they're cute.*

The emergency was slugs, the existence of which heretofore had not registered on the daughter. My friend headed over with a box of slug bait, but I think she should have headed over with scissors. I once considered the idea of scissoring a slug in half as gross to the extreme, but I am now completely converted. I am so good at slug snipping that I probably could qualify for the Olympic trials.

It's not that I get all the slugs. I still have holey hostas. But so what if I have a few holes? I just refer to them as my special lace-leaf plants. Sometimes, greenness is a matter of attitude, as well as laziness.

SEPTEMBER 14, 2006

SLUGGING IT OUT
A mulch of autumn leaves breeds an army of munchers

I WAS OUT CHECKING THE DREGS OF THE VEGE-table garden when Doug the Wonder Guy approached me looking stricken. "I did it," he said. "I'm the guilty party." I wondered what on earth he was talking about. Had he pruned my chocolate mimosa again? Had he eaten the last piece of pie sitting on the kitchen counter? Had he let Ernie the dog escape from the yard?

"I'm responsible for the slugs this year," he confessed. Since he looked so bereft and contrite, I resisted the urge to whap him on the side of the head with a cabbage and, instead, listened to his story. It seems DTWG had a bright idea last fall, which I have to admit sounded reasonable. Instead of putting all of the fallen leaves into the compost pile, why not rake a bunch over our flowerbeds to act as winter protection?

That part of the plan worked. Even a newly planted crape myrtle survived last winter. But the carpet of leaves also did something else. It provided a perfect habitat for slugs to crawl under and deposit their eggs. Leaves are airier and lighter than most mulch but still retain moisture and some measure of warmth. Hence, by spring, I had half the world's slug population bounding out from underneath their leafy nursery and heading straight for the shoots of my newly emerging plants.

Over the summer, as I've whined about slugs ad nauseam, kindly readers have sent me slug remedies that will not harm my pets. Reader Linda Taylor swears by the herb borage, which she says slugs loathe. She places a borage plant at each corner of her vegetable garden and among her tomatoes.

Roger Ferguson asked if I was aware of the corn gluten-based slug remover, and no I wasn't. He says it is quite effective in getting the "little dears" to go away permanently and is still kind to the environment. Darlene Sanman passed along advice that slugs prefer the thin-leaved hostas.

I have noticed that they don't touch some very thick-leaved greens, such as *Podophyllum*, that enjoy the same conditions as hostas—shady and moist. Truly, it helps to have a thick skin. Carole Trenko wonders if I've tried late-winter slug control with ammonia. She credits this advice to the late Elsie Skinner, longtime president of the Northwest Hosta and Shade Gardening Society.

In late February before shoots emerge, she advises sprinkling about half to one cup of a mixture of one part non-sudsy ammonia and four parts water onto the crown of hostas and other susceptible perennials. This does in the slug eggs. There seem to be dozens of environmentally friendly ways to control slugs. All work to a degree. They probably can do in a zillion slugs, but my problem is that I have about a centillion.

I think, given DTWG's epiphany, that the most viable solution is to smash or spray the ammonia mixture on the eggs during winter. They are, I'm told, underneath anything dark and moist, such as boards, pots and, alas, masses of leaves. They look like milky-white caviar (sorry if I've put you off that delicacy now). Otherwise, if they hatch, my slugs will mount armies and march forward with impunity in spring.

No matter that they lose companions to boiling water, diatomaceous earth, salt, copper barriers, beer, oat bran, ducks and chickens, salt and various spray mixtures. There are still enough survivors to munch everything in their slimy path.

And, of course, I will try readers' suggestions. This is war, after all, and I am glad to have allies. And I'm really glad that baby slugs are not cute.

OCTOBER 22, 2009

> *If they hatch, my slugs will mount armies and march forward with impunity in spring.*

Part 5

THE RESTLESS MONTHS

❧

Right now, I want it to be spring.

I can hear things throbbing and pulsating and poking up in my garden.

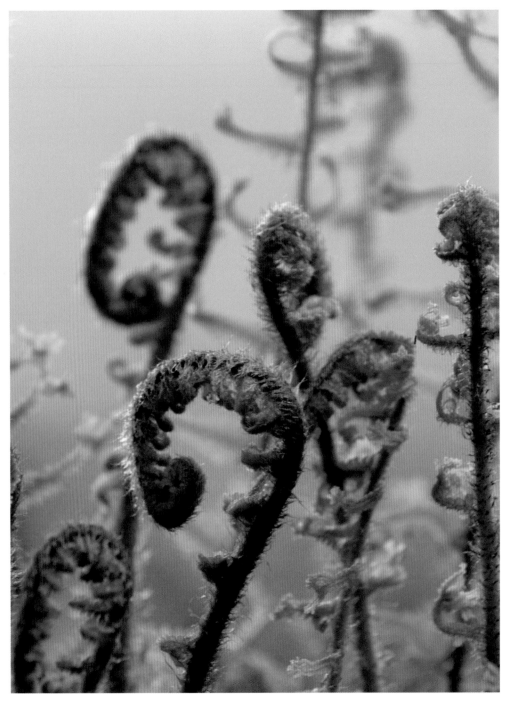

As the fronds unfurl, so does the hope of spring.

ALL WOUND UP

I'm ready to spring into action

I AM WALKING AROUND LOOKING LIKE A RELA-tively normal and calm woman. But inside, I am going, "Oh boy, oh boy, oh boy. Gardening season is starting!" If I were a dog, my tail would be wagging 50 miles an hour.

Oh yes, I know I'm rushing things. We could still have a late February freeze. We've even had snow in early March. It could—and likely will—rain until the Fourth of July. But, as Woody Allen once infamously said, the heart wants what the heart wants. And right now, I want it to be spring. I can hear things throbbing and pulsating and poking up in my garden.

It's the season of delicious anticipation. We gardeners want to dance a jig. We want to write poetry full of horrid clichés such as "season of renewal, reawakening, birdies singing." And most of all, we want to buy plants. No matter that the ground is soggy.

I used to wonder why the gardening shows took place in February, long before gardens were in bloom. Now I know. Those clever show people are catching us when we are most vulnerable, just as we are crawling out of hibernation. They recognize the primal beat thumping away in our hearts.

But enough of this silliness. It's also time to get practical. At last we can actually do things in the garden. It's time to prune roses and late-flowering vines. And while you're pruning, cut back hard those plants you've grown for winter bark color, such as shrub dogwoods and willows.

> *Keep an eye on weather reports. This is Mother Nature's most fickle time.*

They'll grow back by next fall, and the new growth will give you brilliant color. You can also cut back your beautyberry (*Callicarpa*), which otherwise will be a shapeless mass in spring and summer.

It's remodeling time. Unless the ground is terribly soaked, you can transplant shrubs and begin dividing perennials. You can start fertilizing, especially the vegetable gardens and lawns. Cut back those grasses you left for winter color so that new shoots have room to sprout. Start some seeds, but indoors.

Oh me, oh my, what a delirium of splendid activity lies ahead. But don't let it make you rash. Keep those tender plants under protection. Don't sow seeds directly in the ground. Remember, it's the soil temperature, not the air temperature, that matters, and the soil is still cold.

Except for deadwood, don't prune anything that blooms in spring. (If your garden is dull at this time of year, search out some early-blooming beauties. Even a small garden has room for a daphne, flowering quince (*Chaenomeles*), star magnolia (*Magnolia stellata*), and a hellebore or two.

If you have the room, a must-have (but woefully underused) early flowerer is our native flowering current (*Ribes sanguineum*). It's modest sized and early and long blooming. Oh, and one more practical word, before I lapse into a rhapsody of silliness over approaching spring. Keep an eye on weather reports. This is Mother Nature's most fickle time.

But most of all, celebrate the season. Make a wish on the first daffodil you see. Put sprigs of daphne in bud vases. Dance a jig around the unfurling ferns. Go out and get a flat of primroses. Go for the gaudiest neon colors with the little yellow eyes winking up at you. They are the happiest of all flowers.

While you're at it, buy some pansies too. You don't even have to plant them. Set them on your kitchen windowsill, and they will make your heart sing. "Oh boy, oh boy, oh boy."

My imaginary tail is wagging at the thought.

FEBRUARY 21, 2008

DEEP THOUGHTS
Pondering, planning for the future

THEY CALL LATE AUGUST THE DOG DAYS OF summer. Possibly, that's because most of us have little energy to do more than lie around with our tongues hanging out.

But in case anyone should wonder, it's not that we aren't doing something. Gardeners are tricky. We may give the appearance of just lying around, but we, like the dogs, are having deep thoughts.

In fact, this is a very dangerous period. This is the time when spouses should be nervous, because we are thinking up the projects that will make their backs give out later in the fall or spring. This is when we speculate where we'll put the new pond or where to dig up the next patch of turf.

As we cast our eyes over the yellowing lawn, we are seeing the new deck in our mind's eye or the place where the brick terrace will go. We are siting the greenhouse and redoing the flower borders. Some of us are even mentally blowing up the entire ter-

rain and wondering what it would be like to start all over again.

Meanwhile, our unsuspecting spouse is flipping the chicken on the barbecue, barely aware of what is going on as we think these deep thoughts under cover of lying on the chaise with the latest mystery.

While taking this mental inventory of the garden, we should entertain some medium-deep thoughts about pesky but necessary planning details. If we don't take note of them now, we will surely lose sight of them when the next season of activity starts.

And, unlikely at it seems at the moment, that could be pretty soon. Already a hint of gold, albeit dirty gold, dapples some trees. In a few weeks, the official close of summer rite will be upon us—the setting out of the ornamental cabbages.

So, here are some things to add to your planning repertoire:

• **Check out what's got to go, and be brave about it.** Gardening 101 is all about putting things in. Graduate school is about learning what's got to come out. The tree that casts too much shade, the shrub that's grown out of proportion, the rose that spends most of the summer dotted with black spot, the flowers that don't perform well—outta here. It's a tough discipline to learn, particularly when we have introduced and nurtured the offenders.

• **Note who's lying down on the job.** Such is our aversion to staking that, by now, half the flower border may be horizontal. Certainly the daisies, the crocosmia and the yarrow are having what the British call "a little lie down." So mark out a perimeter where the stakes are going to have to go. If you wait until spring, you won't believe that those perky little green things will ever get fat and floppy.

- **Those misty days of autumn—if they ever come—will be prime time for moving.** So think about what's got to pick up and where it's going to go. Take an inventory of what has grown too close, what has gotten hidden behind something else or what can be brought together for a smashing color or texture combination.

- **Make a list of what needs dividing,** but don't stop there. Where will the newly divided clumps go? Remember to figure in how much room they'll need where they're mature. If you don't have room, it may be time to farm some divisions out to friends.

- **Ponder the palette.** Now's the time to decide what parts of the garden need a wake-up call. Where can we introduce jolts of color? Maybe the pastel garden needs some deep purple or blue to bring it out. Maybe it's time to be madly adventuresome and try—gasp—primary colors. Perhaps the green garden can jump from pretty to spectacular with the addition of a scarlet or variegated leaf.

> *I'm beginning to understand how those bimbo-esque girls get away with things. Cuteness is a terrific distraction.*

- **Finally, cast an eye over the whole look.** If something about the garden design doesn't quite work, more likely than not it's because of proportion. Most of us, when we put something in, err on the side of timidity—

too skimpy borders, curves that are a bit too flat, walks that are too skinny. A bit of recontouring can do wonders for the overall look.

But think this all out now. September's coming soon and, with it, the box of 500 bulbs you ordered.

AUGUST 21, 1992

PANTING FOR A PROJECT
When it comes to gardening, logic grows weak

ON GROUNDHOG DAY, I CARRIED ANDOVER Ernie out into the backyard and held him up. The sun was shining, and he cast a shadow. Ernie is our dog, and we live on Andover Place. It was the best I could do under the circumstances in that no groundhogs were hanging about.

Ernie, who is a very silly dog, enjoyed the whole adventure. I don't know if that meant we would have six more weeks of winter, but I doubt it because Ernie is one of those "liar, liar, pants on fire" creatures. He certainly fibbed when he wrote that letter to me, with the help of a vet, saying he was looking for a home and was a very good doggie that did not dig.

Not only did he dig up the purple tulip bulbs we planted last fall, but he is the prime suspect in the disappearance of a rare and expensive plant I splurged on last summer.

Cobblestones, embedded pieces of glass and tile, stained cement—release the artist in you.

The angst is that, despite all attempts at positive thinking and logic, I do not have a project. How could I have forgotten that gardening, like any passion, is not about logic? I feel aimless and unfocused without a project. I told my friend Denise that I don't have one, and she just rolled her eyes.

I swear I have no project. Well, except for little things. For example, I have three large, round water bowls that disappear completely once surrounding foliage spreads out. I've thought about pulling the three out and grouping them in a sunny spot and filling them with water lilies. But how should I group them? Should they be in a triangle or all in a row? Where can I put them?

Then there's the 'Westerland' rose that we moved last fall after it was rudely crowded out by a ninebark shrub (*Physocarpus*). This rose grows tall and, although not a climber, could use something to lounge against. Surely I have room for another arbor. In fact there's a little opening in the boxwoods surrounding the vegetable garden that empties onto a path by a long border.

And, now that I think about it, there's a little secret spot under an arbor in front with nothing there but a couple of chairs. Possi-

Twice, I found it flopping on the ground, badly in need of resuscitation.

After replanting it a third time, I put a wire cage over it. Alas, someone moved the cage, and the plant was gone, leaving no telltale signs, not even a leaf. I'm beginning to understand how those bimbo-esque girls get away with things. Cuteness is a terrific distraction. But I digress, if only to disguise the fact that I have gone from euphoria over the nearness of spring to mid-February angst.

bly we could tuck in a round of cobblestones or, better yet, a concrete round embedded with colorful tiles and glass.

I must also decide what to plant in the wasteland where I dug up the huge Hosta Hotel for Insatiable Slugs. Any new plant must take shade and moist soil, and be about as tasty to slugs as cod liver oil.

Plus, I'm sure to have bare spots after last December's freeze.

Oh my, I am beginning to feel a pulse.

Possibly, Ernie isn't the only "liar, liar, pants on fire" gardener around here.

FEBRUARY 18, 2010

CRAZY FOR MARCH

Hello, garden fever; goodbye, common sense

IT'S HERE! MARCH, MARCH, MARCH! I AM doing my little Snoopy the dog dance of happiness. Poke, poke, poke! I can hear my plants coming up.

It is a dangerous time. All those best-laid plans and resolutions are about to fly out the window. I'm talking about those resolutions not to put in so many marginally hardy plants, the resolutions not to go for the latest exotic, but to stick to tried-and-true. Out goes the plan to limit one's palette, to focus on foliage, not ephemeral flowers, and to avoid being distracted by what's in bloom this moment. Forgotten is the sensible advice about making lists of plants we need and sticking to them and then buying only what we can plant within the week. Is such a thing even possible when we are in the thrall of March Madness? I think not.

Sports fans think March Madness is about men's college basketball. We gardeners know that long before the NCAA finals, we tended to go slightly nuts in March, and maybe "slightly" is too faint a word.

With plant lust upon us, I am going to share some advice about shopping for plants that does not call for restraint, since I know that this is not the time to mention that nasty word.

1. **Check out what's in other people's wagons.** They've already done the Big Search and may have found treasures you missed. And don't overlook the shade section. That's where some of the choicest plants live.

2. **If you have an established garden, forget the old advice** to buy plants in threes, fives and sevens. If you love something, buy it.

3. **Always buy a plant that you've never heard of.** It's fun to see what the mystery plant does.

4. **Check mature size.** That plant may look like a cute puppy now, but it could grow into an SUV. You don't want to spend your time whacking it back every year, only to have an unnaturally shaped plant.

5. **Be careful of euphemisms** for aggressive spreaders. More growers are now labeling plants as spreaders or invasive, but not all. The term "tends to spread" may turn out to mean this plant will be like Sherman marching through Georgia.

6. **If you see a gorgeous bloomer,** buy the one that is not quite in bloom but has lots of buds. But don't limit yourself to plants in bloom or bud. We have a long season, so leave room for plants that will take you into fall.

7. **When you select a plant,** walk around with it and check out potential compan-

ion plants that might go with it (an excuse to indulge even more). For example, if you select a hosta with gold margins, look for golden *Corydalis lutea* to cozy it up to, since they take the same conditions.

8. **Check out plants in the nursery's garden,** even if it's just a parking strip, to see what they'll look like with maturity or to get ideas for combinations. Investigate Seduction Alley, that display of plants the nursery sets out so you have to walk through them. It's a great way to find out what's the latest and greatest.

9. **Always go with a companion,** the kind that when you are tempted to buy too much will encourage you. That way, when you go home, you can blame your excess on her.

10. **Finally, when you see something special, buy one** for yourself and one for your neighbor/friend. It will make you happy.

MARCH 12, 2009

✧✧✧

PLEASE MR. POSTMAN
Tempting garden catalogs stir the imagination and put rare ornamental plants at out fingertips

MORE DROOL-INDUCING PHOTOS THAN Victoria's Secret.

More haunting descriptions than Brookstone.

More eye-numbing selection than Sears, Roebuck and Co.

If your thumbs are greenish and twitching, you know what we're talking about.

Garden catalogs. Thick and glossy, or slim and funky, they're here, and more are arriving daily. Soon you'll have a wheelbarrow full to tempt you to overwork your plastic.

Browsing through them is a great way to the dreary winter. And they're an efficient and entertaining tool in planning your garden. They put photos, colors, heights, textures, hardiness and growing conditions at

> *You never know when the sun will break through.*

your fingertips, making an easy task of deciding how to fill the front bed, the shady spot in back or the vegetable garden in your climate zone.

Catalogs are a good way to find rare and unusual plants and to keep up on new plants and trends. For example, Forestfarm in Williams offers 200 to 400 new plants in each catalog, owner Peg Prag says.

Oregon and Washington are hotbeds of garden mail-order sources, which means many of the plants and seeds we can order are grown in a climate zone similar to ours. In the United States, only California has more mail-order garden sources, followed by Oregon and then Washington.

There can be downsides to buying plants by mail. The products might be more expensive than in local nurseries, although bulbs often are considered to be a better buy by mail. The plants might be smaller than you'd buy locally, and you can't see the quality. Shipping has some risks, too, though most reputable mail-order firms guarantee their product.

And for many of us, gardening is not always a planned-in-advance activity, which catalog shopping requires. You never know when the sun will break through and bring the urge to plant something right now.

JANUARY 15, 1998

✧

DON'T BE FOOLED BY SPRING'S FALSE START

Seduced by the scent of spring? Better nip that impulse in the bud

FEBRUARY IS THE MOST DANGEROUS MONTH in the garden. There's usually a week or so of unseasonably mild, sunny weather that causes buds to swell, shoots to rise and our heads to fill with visions of spring in glorious Technicolor with tweety-bird sound effects.

But don't fall for it. It's false spring, an annual bit of trickery to seduce us.

You will hear it in small talk all over the city. "Guess spring is early this year," they'll say in the grocery line or on the elevator Monday morning. Depending on the year, they might

Untimely pruning may spoil your chances for gorgeous roses like this one.

add something about the cause being that weird El Niño thing.

Of course, they will forget that every February, practically since recorded history, local gardeners have been suckered into thinking spring has come early.

Dizzy with sunshine, many of us react to false spring by rushing out to prune roses. Some rummage through seed packets and start sowing sweet peas directly in the ground. Others start digging the vegetable garden, unmindful of the sucking sound effects from a shovel dipping into muck.

And if the bluebird is a harbinger of spring, then the harbinger of false spring is the guy—every neighborhood has one—who dons Bermuda shorts and hauls out a lawn mower.

Then, wham, in comes a cold front that nips those little buds, blackens those brave new shoots and sends us into an equally cold sweat.

Did I prune my roses too early? Yes. Do the burnt tips on the leaves mean my bulbs are all dead? No. Do the browned buds on trees and shrubs mean I've lost this year's blossoms? Maybe. Wait and see.

Snow and ice snap branches, but they seldom deflower or kill an entire plant. However, a warm spell that wakes plants up from their beauty sleep can be deadly.

It starts plants budding and sending out new shoots. If this thawing period is followed by more cold, a plant has lost the protection of dormancy. There might be no false spring this year, and there might be no late cold spell, but both have happened often enough to take precautions.

The first is patience, a virtue that does not

come easily to those of us who dabble in the green arts.

Except for cleaning up storm damage, don't prune roses until late February. Even a week can make a difference in whether roses thrive or take a dive. At higher elevations, it won't hurt to wait until March. The only downside to late rose pruning is that you push back spring bloom a bit. You also can add extra mulch around more delicate plants to keep them cold and dormant. Hybrid tea roses, daphne, ceanothus and gunnera all could use protection.

Tamp down the ground around any new trees and shrubs you planted in late fall that might not have established roots, and add mulch there as well. Soil that thaws and then freezes causes shallow-rooted plants to heave, leaving some roots exposed. Plants with high tops—roses, shrubs and new trees—are particularly susceptible because the wind catches them and adds to the rocking motion.

Seeds are another area that calls for patience. Even if your soil is well drained and crumbly (and if it is, I am insanely jealous of you), most seeds simply won't germinate until nighttime temperatures are at least in the 50s. So, for now, stick to sowing indoors, in cold frames or in greenhouses.

Above all, if your soil is anything but well drained and crumbly, don't try to dig early. You can destroy the structure of soil by digging before it has dried out.

Should false spring waltz in this year and send you into such a frenzy that you simply must do something in the garden, go after slugs. I've already discovered baby slug nests under rocks. And even in their cradles, they were swapping recipes for hosta shoots a la mode.

FEBRUARY 5, 1998

∽✗✍

THE SAP ALWAYS RISES
Fidgeting with hope and worry, gardeners look ahead to spring

I SELDOM REMEMBER DREAMS, BUT THE OTHER night I woke from a dream in which I was chipping the frozen bodies of my little goldfish out of our pond. That's when I realized that I was more worried about what damage the weather had wrought than I'd been willing to admit.

I won't know for some time whether our fish survived. In winter, pond fish stay burrowed in the mud and don't start swimming around until the water reaches about 55 degrees. They should survive if the pond didn't freeze all the way down, and, since we have a couple of deep spots, chances are they'll be all right.

The plants I am most anxious about are my new roses. I don't think we'll have much problem with established roses. But last year I was walloped by a renewed passion for roses and planted about 10, and some didn't get in until fall. Now I worry that the newbies might not have made it.

So far, the only major loss we are sure of is a massive laurel that had been limbed up as a tree, an impractical arrangement if ever there was one because it kept suckering up from the ground.

Doug the Wonder Guy (remember, no more "Boy," as he has turned 40) sawed it down after it divided into a perfect V under the weight of the snow. He didn't cut it all the way back, but it's been sufficiently trimmed so that the telephone pole that it masked in the back alley is now visible in all its inelegant glory.

Review photos from last summer to create a to-do list as gardening season approaches.

As I look out, the pole seems to mock me with a neon glow. If I were really evil, I would go out and plant a kudzu vine at its base. Everyone seems to be doing winter cleanup. If the sounds in my neighborhood are anything to go by, this has been the winter of the chain-saw massacre.

The symphony has all the marks of a prelude. Spring may still be far off, but by February we Northwest gardeners start getting fidgety. My neighbor Rosemary and I had lunch at our local bistro, and owner Li Doyle was talking about her seed starts. Other neighbors came in, and somehow the subject of gardens came up. I run into these conversations everywhere I go. Obviously, the sap is rising, and I don't mean in the trees.

People seem to be approaching this gardening season with greater impatience than in past years, along with a good dose of ambivalence. On the one hand, gardeners are fretting about losses, whether fish or plants. On the other, I detect a sense of gleefulness about new opportunities. There is, as they say, always a silver lining, and to gardeners nothing is so utterly thrilling as a bare patch of earth.

All of us have our hopes for this spring. I'm hoping my fish and roses made it. Doug the Wonder Guy is hoping that the ubiquitous wild morning glory may have been a casualty of the weather. But I do not share his optimism.

I believe that morning glory is like uranium with a half-life of a zillion years. Kitties Wilbur and Orville, when they can raise their lazy selves from the center of the bed, are hoping the pond fish will indeed be frozen and are envisioning tasty treats. Ernie the dog is hoping that better weather will bring out lots of new scents. He can spend an hour zigzagging around the garden, sniffing away, while we stand there freezing, waiting for him to attend to his business.

My non-gardening husband, Ted, is just hoping that we've finally gotten all the holes in the fence patched so Ernie can go out on his own.

FEBRUARY 5, 2009

TAKE IT OR LEAVE IT
Let the tips fall as they may

I STILL REMEMBER A TIME ONE OCTOBER WHEN I saw a young woman select a $40 bougainvillea and cart it off. And I still remember her look of "you crazy old lady" when I tried to warn her. Clearly, not everyone wants advice, but almost every gardener yearns to give it. It's in our blood. So here are my top 20 tips for fall.

1. **Don't play zonal denial now.** Wait until spring, when your semitropical plant will have a chance to gain a toehold long before freezing weather.
2. **Go overboard on bulbs.** By next spring, you'll still wish you had planted more.
3. **Select diminutive varieties of bulbs** for early bloom. Ground huggers hold up better to spring rains.
4. **Don't be besotted by tulips.** Expand your horizons.
5. **OK, go ahead and be besotted by tulips.** But stick to one color for a great dramatic effect. I'm partial to purple.
6. **Don't mark places** where you planted bulbs with bone meal if you have a dog.
7. **Don't pick the "last rose of summer."** Picking is a form of pruning, and you

don't want to trigger new growth with cold weather about to set in.

8. In general, avoid fall pruning. Wait until plants are truly dormant.

9. If you can add only one plant now, make it a witch hazel. Not only will you get glorious fall color, but it will give you scented winter bloom.

10. If you have room for a second plant, make it *Rosa moyesii* 'Geranium.' This *Rosa* has gorgeous hips.

11. Hold off on adding mulch until the weekend after Thanksgiving. Mulch now will keep soil from cooling off. You want to let the soil cool because this will signal your plants to go dormant, which will protect them from cold.

12. You can never have too many hellebores.

13. Dig out any rogue plants that have taken over and use the newly bare space to plant bulbs. Then in spring you can decide what you really want to go there.

14. Don't cut back the foliage on marginally hardy perennials. The foliage will protect tender plants' crowns and increase chances of winter survival.

15. Do cut back the foliage on any plants affected with powdery mildew or other diseases. Leaving foliage on helps the disease winter over. Dispose of the diseased foliage; don't put it in your compost pile.

16. Rake up large leaves (such as maple leaves). Left on the ground, they will form a mat that can harbor diseases and insects.

17. Save conifer branches blown down by the wind to throw over your flower and vegetable beds when it's time to mulch.

Make the effort to put in more bulbs this fall.

They add a measure of protection but still allow air circulation.

18. Autumn is an excellent time to rearrange the furniture; that is, to move plants around. In the Northwest almost any plant is movable. A misty day is the best time to do this.

19. This is the best time of year to shop nurseries for plants with good fall foliage color.

20. Drain your in-ground sprinkler system before there's a freeze. We forgot to, and now we have more leaks than the White House.

OCTOBER 12, 2006

❧

WAITING FOR A SCHEME TO SPROUT

What would spring be without the annual project?

HERE IT IS MARCH, AND I HAVE NOT GOT A project. You would think I'd be happy

A sign over the door labels the little outbuilding, not the "Potting Shed," but the "Pouting Shed."

that, after 20 years, the garden is more or less finished. But no, I'm not. Of course, there is absolutely no space to do something new, but that has never stopped me before.

It's not that there aren't things to do. Certainly I must wage war on weeds. Last year they got out of hand, especially in the gravel paths. The front border against the holly hedge definitely needs reworking. It looks nice in early spring when the hardy geraniums and lady's mantle fluff out like peacock feathers in a romantic haze of color.

But then the geraniums collapse into an unpretty mass exposing flat leafless centers, and the filmy lady's mantle flowers turn an unsightly brown. Both have to be cut back, and I am left with scandal of scandals, exposed earth, which I try to fill up with annuals. The effect is, predictably, a hodgepodge.

So certainly there are things to do. But these aren't exciting. They are like replacing the water heater or washing the windows. In fact, weeding is very much like washing windows in both its utter necessity and its utter banality.

> *A couple of skylights would brighten the place up. I can feel my heart flutter.*

Always there have been annual projects to look forward to: a pond, a knot garden, a new vegetable plot, a sitting area with a fire pit, a little "bus stop" sheltered bench, reshaping the back lawn or taking out the front lawn entirely. These were exhilarating, and the anticipation of "The Project" was something to be savored over the dreary winter months.

It would start with an idea, expressed timidly to Doug the Wonder Boy. "Perhaps, we could put a path around the pond where the lawn gets so soggy," I would say. He would get that saintly expression of forbearance, as in "Uh-oh, here it comes." But before long, I had a partner in crime. Under Doug's direction, the new path would not just go around the pond, but extend all around the lawn. The lawn would become a floating island of emerald green.

We would delight in the new project. We would talk it out, get out measuring tapes, arrange hoses, fantasize what it would look like and shamelessly revel in our cleverness. Each year it was a delicious experience, a rite of spring, a quickening of pulses in tune with nature reinventing the garden around us.

But now I am getting desperate. No project has emerged, and here we are with spring galloping up.

I have paged through garden magazines for ideas. I always thought a pergola would be nice, but, no, really that is too much. Restraint is such an irritating virtue. I'd adore a tiered fountain dripping water music, but such a conceit, while exquisite in a courtyard, would not work in our informal garden. I've always fancied those little espaliered fruit trees, but we've run out of walls.

The fantasy of fantasies is an attached conservatory, where one could sit on chilly but sunny days reading the latest mystery with a lap cat. The room would be filled with the earthy scent of potted plants, and there would be a little round table, like those in French gardens, where one would take tea and eat chocolate-covered cherries. But that would

necessitate winning the lottery, and one would have to first buy tickets.

But perhaps the little back shed could be fixed up. We could sweep out the cobwebs, scrub the walls, wash the windows. A decorative painted floor might work. A couple of skylights would brighten the place up. I can feel my heart flutter.

I told my husband I must give Doug a call. I believe I detected a note of resignation in his voice as he said, "This sounds like chapter one."

MARCH 1, 2007

GOOD NIGHT, DEAR GARDEN

It's time to tuck in those tender plants for their wintertime beauty rest

I AM HAVING A HARD TIME GOING DORMANT. What with summer not getting a start until August and the lovely, lingering fall, it's hard to shut down systems. Yet, in my heart of hearts, I know it's time to start putting the garden to bed. After all, I will need to hibernate the next few months, living off of tea, leftover Halloween candy and garden books, so that I can re-emerge in spring ready to terrify my husband with yet another "little project."

So, like the Olympian athlete who knows she must go to bed on time, I am turning to the chores that will put the garden to its winter rest. First, I will lay in some newspapers, sacks, old blankets, sacks of compost, or anything that can be thrown on for quick protection. Then I will begin a weather watch.

At first sign that nighttime temperatures will dip into the 30s, I will hasten to throw protection around the delicate plants. These divide into two groups. The first includes newly planted and divided specimens that do not yet have established root systems. The second group is the marginals, plants that aren't quite at home in our climate zone and make it through some, but not all, of our winters.

These include hebe, daphne, ceanothus, lavatera, jasmine, senecio, and several of our favorite hybrid tea roses.

So, why the Band-Aid treatment with newspapers and old blankets; why not just compost the whole garden? The key to composting is timing. Shoveling compost on is like putting a great downy comforter on your garden. If you do it too early, when the soil is still warm, it will keep plants from going dormant. You want your plants to take a few mild frosts to put them to sleep.

Then, when they are dormant and the ground has cooled, you lay compost down to keep the earth cold, not warm. This insulation will keep plants from coming out of dormancy during that false spring we frequently have in late January, early February. That's when we lose our roses. And that's why roses survive winter in colder places such as New England. The snow there acts like an insulating blanket that keeps plants from waking up too early.

Order your compost now, but don't put it on until after Thanksgiving. Compost should be at least 3 inches thick to do some good. If you use leaves, shred them to keep them from forming an impenetrable crust. Hay, barkdust, mushroom mulch, newspapers—almost anything that acts as a blanket

will work. But not straight manure. At this time of year, you don't want to fertilize and stimulate tender new growth.

Next come the roses. Hold off picking those last blooms. Let roses form hips, a process that sends a message to shut down. Next, resist the urge to give them a good pruning. It's true that a number of garden books recommend fall pruning, but most of those books are written for the rest of the country where the last frost can come as late as June. Under such circumstances, if you didn't prune in fall, you wouldn't have roses until August.

But here, we can prune as early as mid-February with relatively little risk that a late frost will kill new growth. So, give roses an extra bit of toughness by leaving them unpruned through the winter. Just trim, not prune, enough to keep roses from whipping around in the wind. With climbers, tie down long stems. If you have standard roses, wrap the stems about the same time as you compost. Plants with tall, skinny stems tend to get X's in their eyes at the first sign of cold winds.

Don't overlook evergreens either. Skinny, tall fir trees that get too dense turn into sails in the wind. If you've got such a tree near the house, open it up by thinning out a few branches to allow the wind to pass through.

Finally, take fuchsias, geraniums and houseplants into shelter. Bring in thin pots, too, and turn over water containers so they don't break when water freezes and expands. Then, say good night.

I can re-emerge in spring ready to terrify my husband with yet another "little project."

NOVEMBER 5, 1993

LIVING IN THE ZONE

Will that lovely plant survive in your microclimate?

JANUARY AND FEBRUARY ARE THE DEADEST months for outdoor gardening. On the other hand, they are great months for reading garden books and planning where and what to plant come spring.

If you're a new gardener, you'll come across such terms as "climate zones" and "microclimates." You'll also note that most plants described in books or on seed packets have a number after them. These indicate the coldest climate zone that a particular plant can survive in.

Climate zones are based on national weather data compiled by the U.S. Department of Agriculture. These zones are based on normal winter temperature ranges and do not take into account a record-breaking freeze, so they cannot guarantee a plant will survive.

The United States is divided into 10 climate zones, with 1 the coldest. If a book has a 4 after a plant, it means that plant will survive winter temperatures in zones 10 through 4, but not the colder zones 1 through 3.

Daphne odora, *beautiful but delicate.*

In addition to having a cold limit, some plants cannot take extreme heat either. Others can take the summer heat, but they can't take a warm winter because they need a cold-invoked dormant period in order to bloom. For these plants, you will see a number range, such as 4-8. This means that, in addition to not surviving in the colder zones 1-3, the plant cannot survive in the warmer temperatures of zones 9 and 10.

The maps are very general and don't factor in minor elevation changes or other local features. For example, they show the Portland–Vancouver metropolitan area and the Willamette Valley as zone 8. But if you live in the Portland hills or on the east side exposed to Gorge winds, you probably have a zone 7 climate.

The extreme coastal section of Oregon is in zone 9, although some tropical plants from zone 10 can survive in the vicinity of Gold Beach and Brookings. The maps place narrow strips east of the Willamette Valley running down to the Rogue Valley and along the Columbia Gorge in zone 7. Northern Central Oregon is in zone 6, and the eastern side and southeastern corner of the state generally fall in zone 5. The central highlands of the state are the coldest and fall in zone 4.

Local features in these areas that may modify climate zones are principally elevation and river valleys. For example, areas along the Snake River Valley, including Boise, are at least one zone warmer than most of Eastern Oregon.

But climate zones should be used as a

guide, not a rigid restriction. There are other factors that explain why gardeners in Bend can grow some of the flowers listed as hardy only to Portland's zone 8 temperatures. In addition to local geographic features, there are a number of site-specific conditions that can affect what grows in a specific place. Within each climate zone, there are microclimates.

For example, an area in full sun against a south facing wall will be warmer than any other area of your garden. It may have a microclimate that makes it as warm as zone 9, even though you are located in 7 or 8. This means that you may be able to grow some varieties of flowers and fruits or vegetables here that you could not grow even a few feet away.

One might think that a sunken area of the yard would be sheltered and would thus have a warmer microclimate. But in fact, colder air tends to collect in lower areas, and such a pocket may have a microclimate a whole zone cooler.

Factors that normally produce a warmer microclimate are south facing slopes, areas next to heat-radiating buildings or walls, and areas that are sheltered from wind. In Oregon, these garden areas are fondly known as red tomato territory.

JANUARY 12, 1990

PUTTING STRUCTURE TO THE TEST
Points to consider in the months ahead

IT's HARD TO LOOK AT A LANDSCAPE WHEN it's in full leaf. Your eye notes the perfect rose, wanders down the billowing border and stops at the spreading shade tree. You see elements, but not the whole. And if the whole doesn't quite come together, it's difficult to see why.

But as leaves fall and flowers fade, the bones of the garden emerge. As the landscape becomes spare and while the weather remains mild, it's time to look at overall structure and make adjustments.

Structure is what pulls the garden together, however subtly. It's what gives the winter garden substance. With it, the garden has a Spartan beauty even in the dead season.

Structure comes from the shapes and patterns of the garden and the relationship of its features. These elements provide a framework that, when done right, pulls all the parts together harmoniously. The true test of a harmonious garden is that it works even when there aren't flowers in bloom.

This is the time to take a hard look and ask some questions. Here's a checklist to get you started:

• Do the lawn areas and flower and vegetable beds have pleasing lines and proportions even when bare?

• Are there adequate paths and do they make sense; in other words, do they lead either eye or person to a natural point? Do the paths follow natural travel routes, or is there a worn spot across the lawn?

• Is the terrace or sitting area where it should be, or did you tend to drag chairs away from the terrace over toward the big shade tree? There's no rule that says a deck or terrace has to be attached to a house. A sitting area should be where, in fact, it's most comfortable to sit.

• What's the view from the windows you most frequently look out? Are plants located sensibly for the best progression of bloom? For example, are the early spring flowers that bloom when it's too cold to go out near the house and visible from windows?

• Are trees, large shrubs or decorative objects sited to best advantage? Do things look a bit bland? Maybe you need a tree or large object to add a little drama. Conversely, if things look a bit thick out there, maybe it's time to thin out. One of the quickest ways to convert a dank, dark yard is to take out an outsized tree or bush.

• Is there a theme throughout, either informal flowing curves or formal angles, or is it a mishmash of both? It's hard to be disciplined when there are so many styles to choose from, but it may be time to decide if it's going to be rectangular beds or loose flowing curves.

The coming bare season is the chance to catch those small details that might have escaped notice before. The garden just may need fine tuning, but what a difference fine tuning can make. Here are some things to look for:

• If the curve of a lawn or bed doesn't seem quite right, the most common problem is a shape that is too flattened to be a pleasing curve but not a straight line either. Have the courage to make a good healthy arc.

An early attempt at shaping the edge of a flower bed may have produced lots of small in-and-out scallops for a too-busy look.

Early spring (before the blowsiness of summer) highlights the structure of the garden.

Sculpting the edge into a simpler, long sweep of curve may be just what's needed.

It's not unusual to be a bit reserved in the first attempt at a perennial border. But the result may be a skimpy, shallow border where plants have no choice but to line up. Digging out three or four more feet will give room for the sweeps of flowers that give borders that lush look.

It's also a good time to look around and decide if and where new features should be added. With major additions, such as arbors, gazebos, greenhouses, pools and ponds, you'll want to live with the shape and site for a while to make sure it's the best spot. Map out where you want the feature, either by digging up turf, roping off the area or some other marking device. Then live with it through the winter. If it still feels right in the spring, go ahead with the project.

Looks aren't the only thing on the autumnal check list. It's also a good time to check out if the yard works well on a practical level:

- Are there sharp corners where it's hard to mow? Gently rounded corners are not only easier to mow, but they almost always look better.

- Are there places where you have to lift or drag the lawnmower because they're hard to get to? Consider ground covers as an alternative to lawn in such areas.

> *Structure is what pulls the garden together, however subtly.*

- Is it easy to water the yard, or are there odd corners that the sprinklers don't catch and you have to haul a hose to? If so, replan these areas and think about attractive pavings or plants that take drought.

- Are things easy to get to? An outdoor eating or cooking area should be handy to the kitchen. The route to a compost pile should be a fairly straight line, no matter how lovely a winding path may be. If you've got several loads of grass clippings to carry every time you mow, the winding path will lose its charm quickly.

- Are the paths usable? They should be wide enough to allow a wheelbarrow through.

- Is the garden maintainable? This is difficult to face up to, because there's always the temptation to expand. Were there areas you meant to get to all summer to weed, but never found the time? Perhaps some of those flower beds should be converted to pretty, textured ground covers. Perhaps small, no-care shrubs should replace flowers that need a lot of staking or trimming.

It's not just a season to think of additions, but also of paring back. When a garden becomes more work than fun, it's time to cut back.

OCTOBER 20, 1991

Part 6

MISTAKES, MISHAPS, AND DO-OVERS

❧

Very few of us have horticultural backgrounds,
and some of us even fell sound asleep
when our post-lunch biology class covered botany.
Yet we manage to have gardens.

A lush, mature garden can only mean there were lots of errors on the way.

GETTING THERE, ONE MISSTEP AT A TIME

Mistakes are part of the fun

SOMEONE RECENTLY ASKED ME IF I HAD EVER made any gardening mistakes. Well, let me see.

There is of course the first pond that leaked like a sieve, the fine crop of algae we raised in it and the mosquito colony it supported. Then there were the raccoon wars, the invasion of the blue heron and the honeymooning ducks that laid eggs all over the yard.

On the plant side, you'd have to count the innocent but unwise introduction of the invasive bishop's weed, the black plague sweeping through our roses, and the debacle of planting 300 Red Emperor tulips that subsequently bloomed right in front of the orange-pink camellias.

And let's not forget the runaway ribbon grass, three trees crashing down in various stages of their careers, the summer of dripping aphid juice, the tragedy of the frozen hebe hedge, and the ancient sprinkler system that breaks every year, leading to embarrassing letters from the water bureau.

I also seem to remember laboriously double digging my first flowerbed, not knowing you had to add organic matter, and seeing it return to the consistency of a Los Angeles freeway the following year. Then there was the time a teen-age helper thought that doubling the amount of recommended fertilizer would be even better for the lawn than the normal dose. The lawn was a perfect lemon yellow for my first-ever open garden.

> *The lawn was a perfect lemon yellow for my first-ever open garden.*

But other than that, it's been smooth sailing. As for writing about gardening, I have had relatively few unpleasant experiences. One that comes to mind is the time years ago that I wrote about hellebores and recommended a place to go if you wanted to see fine examples of this plant. An angry head gardener called me to say that if he wanted publicity, he would do his own, thank you very much.

I said I thought his was a public garden. Well, it is, he conceded, but went on to say memorably, "We don't want just anyone there." So I told him, darn, I'd have to cancel the visit I had planned for the Hells Angels Hellebore Club.

Most reader letters are delightful, but there are the occasional ones that take me to task. One anonymous reader regularly writes whenever I mention weather and invites me to go back to California or sometimes to go straight to a place even hotter than California. I also once got a letter from a prisoner who said he thought he and I could make beautiful flowers together, although he did not quite word it so delicately.

Still, as time goes on, the missteps seem to be a bit smaller, although just recently I raved on about planting an espaliered apple tree with branches bearing six kinds of apples grafted to the main stem. One week later, I read the advice of fellow writer Vern Nelson, who warned never to buy that kind of apple tree because the different types of apples will all grow at different rates. Sound advice, but, alas, too late.

So, it's obvious that the journey down the garden path has a few bumps. On the other hand, the one thing I have to say about gardening is that the stumbles have been almost as much fun as the strides ahead, and there aren't many endeavors that you can say that about.

AUGUST 1, 2002

⌒⤬⌒

THE BAD AND THE UGLY
Some ideas should go straight to the compost heap

DESPITE A GROWING GARDEN ENTHUSIASM and sophistication, there are still some bad ideas out there. I mean really bad ideas.

No, I'm not talking about gnomes and flamingos, for which I nurture a secret affection. Also, bad ideas are not the same as mistakes, which we all make and can put down to learning experiences. A mistake is something like deciding to douse the pots on your terrace with fish fertilizer just days before you have an outdoor dinner party. The cats enjoyed this; my dinner guests did not.

Bad ideas, on the other hand, are more in the nature of things the perpetrator does not regard as a mistake, at least not immediately. Bad ideas are things like using an old toilet as a planter (petunias do not make it look cute), laying down fake turf (unless it's in a stadium) and attempting do-it-yourself projects that should be left to a professional. Even so, these are minor-league bad ideas. The following are major-league bad ideas.

The other day I saw a picture of an outdoor room in an upscale garden magazine. It was one of those little trellised areas with fabulously expensive outdoor furniture around an outdoor fireplace with a flat-screen plasma television over the hearth.

People, people, we are talking about gardens. Gardens are places to sit in and smell the flowers, enjoy the fresh air and listen to the birdies sing. If there is one place a television doesn't belong, it's in a garden. And, if I'm your neighbor, I don't want to hear "American Idol" contestants warbling over the back fence.

Another bad idea is a growing trend to put huge homes on tiny lots. Despite a sagging housing market, it seems more and more high-end homeowners are buying up little cottages and bungalows on premium land, then tearing the existing houses down. What goes up in their place are the mansions, and sometimes the McMansions.

Instead of a cottage nestled in a garden, there is now a behemoth that spreads its expensive stone-clad wings out to the lot line, chomping up garden space as it goes. This has the look of a large, evil-looking cat confined in a canary cage. It's not large homes that I find objectionable, but rather the loss of proportion with the land they sit on.

Not all bad ideas are new trends. Disneyland pruning has been going on for a long time. By that I mean hacking rhodies and other large-leaved shrubs to resemble lollypops and beach balls. Large-leaved plants should be left to grow into their natural graceful shapes or at least pruned to look natural. Gardeners who want topiary should confine their creative urges to small-leaved plants. Af-

> *There are several reasons why nude gardening is a really bad idea.*

ter all, didn't God invent boxwood just so we could play with clippers?

And here's one bad idea that trumps them all. I saw a magazine announcement that May 3 is the fourth annual Nude Gardening Day. It turns out there are even several Web sites devoted to nude gardening. Setting aside one's moral stance or natural prudishness, there are several reasons why nude gardening is a really bad idea.

Let me count the ways: sunburn, nettles, thorns, chilly weather, rain, mosquitoes and, ouch, errant pruning shears. Plus you have to consider that today the neighbors likely have cell phones with cameras, and they may also have kids who like nothing better than posting photos on the Web.

But the really overwhelming reason it's a bad idea is something else. We must remember that, in gardening, one has to spend a lot of time bending over. A backside, even one modestly cloaked in stretch pants, is not a pretty sight. I rest my case.

APRIL 10, 2008

❧

TIME TO PUT DOWN NEW ROOTS
Mild and misty days make autumn the perfect season to relocate unhappy plants

IT'S MOVING SEASON IN THE NORTHWEST. THE conditions that make for ideal planting also make for ideal transplanting. The ground is warmer and drier than in spring, and the days are misty and mild, so plants can be moved without going into a Camille act.

This makes it the perfect time of year to correct mistakes. Mistakes, you say? Look around and listen to your garden. It will tell

you quite bluntly where you have gone wrong. My own garden is a regular cacophony of nagging.

For example, the monkshood and plume poppies that have become leaning towers of Pisa are screaming to be moved to a sunnier location where they won't have to crane their necks to get a few rays. The hostas that spent most of the summer with toasty edges are insisting that they be shifted to shadier locales. The temperamental hydrangea that sagged if I wasn't at its beck and call with the hose also cries to move toward the shadows.

Of the two dogwoods that came down with the dreaded anthracnose, only one has responded to three years of spraying. The other is begging for a mercy killing. The buddleia that was supposed to be a dwarf variety grew up to be a basketball player and wants to move out of the flower border and over toward the fence where it can get as tall as it wants to be.

Some plants have been indiscreet and must suffer the consequences. The sweet autumn clematis that was supposed to cover the arbor over the gate now has taken over the gate, the fence and the nearby rhododendrons, and is eyeing the roof with malicious intent. It will be replaced with a daintier variety.

Out will come the coreopsis to be banished forever since it refuses to stand up straight and spends most of the summer in a messy sprawl. The crambe will move into the spot vacated by the coreopsis. The crambe turned out to be bigger than expected and its leaves, although lovely, rudely covered a small but charming water trough.

Other plants haven't misbehaved at all; rather, they have performed admirably in relative obscurity and are asking to come closer to center stage. The witch hazel blooms sweetly in winter but is so far out back that no one ever notices it. It will move to the front yard where its delicious scent can tantalize in the quick dash between garage and house on stormy days.

The beautiful Japanese blood grass turns out to be incredibly well behaved in that it hasn't spread at all. So the clumps, now polka-dotted around, will be clustered together for a more natural look.

Roses love circulating air around them.

Whew, what a nag this garden is. But thank goodness. There are some things you just won't get out of books. You have to open your eyes and look. The books say, for example, that monkshood prefers shade. But tell that to mine that are leaning at 45-degree angles toward the sun.

This is the season to pay attention to the excellent advice your garden is giving you. In spring, everything will be fresh and new and you won't remember how things actually performed when the heat was on, so to speak.

The best tip your garden will give you is not to fight Mother Nature. If you've got shade, don't yearn for pretty sun plants, but opt for a gorgeous, lush shade garden. If there's a soggy place in the lawn that never quite dries out, turn it into a bog garden verdant with iris and ligularia.

If there's a spot where there's more moss than lawn under your trees, you need to think about opening it up so light can get through. Or maybe your garden is telling you this is no place for a respectable lawn. Attractive stonework or ground cover may be better choices.

Continued problems with black spot or powdery mildew are signs that your roses are telling you they need to be moved where they will get better circulation or that you shouldn't be watering them overhead.

Did some of your old perennials let you down, performing as wimpy specters of their former selves? Some may be signaling that their useful life is over. Perennial doesn't mean forever. It only means that the plant comes back more than two years. Some perennials are short-lived.

If newly planted perennials didn't plump out, they are complaining that they have soggy feet thanks to our insidious clay soil. Lift them out, set them aside in shade with moist newspapers over the roots. Then work in a lot of compost. If you've got a whole flowerbed or border that has been desultory from the start, take out everything and put in a raised bed. The next message you will hear will be a chorus of thank yous.

Perennials that have good, healthy foliage but have fewer flowers than in previous years are begging to be divided. Flowers with brown centers are sending the same message.

The messages are all there, easy to decipher if you're observant. A plant that looks unhappy is unhappy—where it is.

OCTOBER 15, 1993

❧

LEARNING TO REST
Sit back and appreciate the big picture

A GARDEN HAS MANY MOODS, SO I'M FINDING out. Sometimes it is an Eden, and other times it is a vicious jungle. This spring, I certainly have seen both sides of this two-faced domain.

One morning I opened my front door to find the encroaching jungle up close. I literally could not get off the porch.

Sometime during the night, the wisteria over the porch, laden with prodigious blooms, had collapsed, bringing down a rotting wood trellis that had held it in place. It lay in a tangle, its purple petals carpeting the front terrace.

Doug the Wonder Boy and a helper managed to rope it back up, but only after severely pruning the monster. Even worse, the wisteria's swan dive exposed the upper facade of the porch, which needed painting badly after having been covered with wisteria.

Normally, I would have called our favorite handyman, but he was out of town. I knew this because he hadn't come to fix our stove, which has been out of commission for six weeks. Being without a stove hasn't been a big problem in our house; I would have panicked if it had been the microwave.

By this time I was in a state, feeling overwhelmed and wondering if it was worth it to keep up such a large garden. It just seemed to be taking forever to get the garden in shape.

Then, later that same week, I came home from work and did some watering by hand. After I finished, I strolled out to the front, which I call the sun-catcher terrace because, when the rest of the garden is in shade, it gets the very last of the western sun.

Then I did something I almost never do. I went in the house and got a Coke and a book and came back out and just sat there. Hector the dog was at my feet, and our two youngest cats, Orville and Wilbur, took turns jumping on my lap and purring maniacally.

It was the most pleasant experience. From my vantage point I looked out over the flowerbeds and saw a paradise. The colors were all blurred together as in an impressionist painting.

It was quite a different perspective for me. Usually, I am looking at the ground up close, seeing just the weeds, the nasty seedlings of some spreader or the bare spots between plants.

I could not see all these problems from my chair. It was a lovely moment, and I remember thinking that, really, this is what a garden is all about. I must remember to sit in it for a while or merely walk in it without thinking of things I need to do.

I won't, of course. I will fall back into my habit of walking around thinking about what needs to move and wondering why I bought that terrible Lavatera and worrying that we should have cut back the now-monstrous beautyberry.

But I wonder whether that is such a bad thing. Is it having a garden or the act of gardening that brings more pleasure? I'm not sure. Does a painter get more joy from creating a work of art or from the end product? The question is relevant because, while I don't think of my garden as a work of art, I do think of it as a creation.

And, is it even more relevant that these thoughts are tumbling about because I am getting old and silly and not thinking about

> *Is it having a garden or the act of gardening that brings more pleasure?*

important things, such as why hasn't the handyman come to fix my stove? And, given I have a garden to tame, do I really care if my stove gets fixed?

JUNE 1, 2006

❧

RELAX THE RULES
Remember, gardens are for experimenting

WHEN I BEGAN TO DEVELOP A GARDEN IN earnest, I obsessed over what style I wanted. I was convinced I had to choose a distinct look—cottage, woodsy, Asian, and on and on with much wringing of hands.

Fortunately, at some point, a great bolt must have come out of the sky and knocked me and my gnomes over, because at last I realized I didn't have to pick and stick to a certain look. For me, that was terribly freeing. For the gnomes, it was a mortal blow.

> *These days, to the extent that I have a design plan, it's cram and jam.*

There are a lot of design rules. Most make sense and are a good way to start. They are well documented, so I am not going to repeat them. I have evolved my own set of design principles, which I will share with the caveat that they are not sanctioned under any respectable garden style.

The eraser approach. There's hardly anything you can do in a garden that can't be undone nicely if it doesn't work out. I once made a white garden that turned out looking like a washing line rather than a sub-lime echo of Sissinghurst's famous white garden.

Today, it is the vegetable garden, and the only trace of my pale pretension is one white rose. Some changes have worked. Others, such as an ill-fated herb garden, haven't, and that's when I apply the eraser theory.

Urban relocation. It would be nice to know where everything should go right from the start. Professional designers often lay out a landscape design that shows everything in its place. I don't have that skill. So, every spring we dig up plants and relocate them, sometimes because they've become too big where they are, sometimes because they're in the wrong lighting conditions. More often, it's just because I think something will look better in another place. So long as you do this on those drizzly spring days, even large plants can survive the upheaval.

Heartless editing. For most of us, it's hard to do away with a plant, and it takes awhile to get up the nerve to remove something such as an overgrown tree or shrub or simply something that never seems robust but doesn't have the decency to die on its own. But few things can reinvigorate a garden more than removing a plant that's not working out. And, yes, I do try to find a home for the healthy evictees.

Saying no to (most) pruning. It took a while to realize that not everything needs pruning. If a plant is healthy, letting it grow to its natural graceful shape can be very advantageous. Fluffy shrubs are lush, and lushness covers a multitude of design faults. Doug the Wonder Guy and I still have skirmishes over this issue. I think something happens to people's brains when they get hold of cutting instruments.

Going with one's gut. I've learned that my gut, rather than my heart, is a better guide

The dogwood tree, or Cornus controversa, *appears in variegated form here.*

when it comes to design. My heart has led me into disastrous affairs with inappropriate plants, faddish follies and over-the-top looks, such as last year's excessive use of pots. When something doesn't feel right, it probably isn't. That's where one's gut feelings come into play.

The old lemonade theory. Some of the best things in our garden grew out of disasters—or lemons. When a falling limb smashed our gazebo, we thought about rebuilding, for about five minutes. Then we decided we liked the open space and made a cobbled circle with a fire pit.

Once after an open garden on a very rainy day, visitors made a muddy wreck of the lawn around the pond. We graveled the area and reshaped the lawn, to much better effect. This year, after an arbor collapsed, we built a little pavilion in its place.

Moderation in everything, including rules. These days, to the extent that I have a design plan, it's cram and jam.

JULY 9, 2009

❧

A NEW LEASE ON LIFE
Nature's ecosystem kicks in to save the terrible pea-green pond

REMEMBER THE SAGA OF OUR POND? IT HAS been The Project for the summer in our garden.

When last you heard, we were in deep despondency. The pond had turned an opaque and truly disgusting pea green. Mosquitoes had arrived from all over the country, and soon larvae carpeted the surface. The pond even had a tree fall across it during a storm. It was not a pretty sight.

Since then, surprising developments have taken place. Seems there is something to this ecology stuff after all. First, the water plants went right to work competing with the algae for nutrients. Within about three weeks, the water had cleared. A larger recirculating pump also certainly played a part.

But the real clearing began with the plants—water hyacinths, water lettuce, four water lilies, a stand of flag iris and one umbrella plant. About half the surface is covered with plants.

The plants weren't the only thing that worked. The gambusia, the little topminnows that vector control supplies, made mincemeat out of the mosquitoes. In no time at all, the black, squirmy larvae were gone. The gambusia were so delighted with their new habitat that they went and had babies. The only trouble is that, being black, the babies are hard to see unless the sun is shining on the water. This summer, we have been able to see them for a total of about five days.

But it gets better. One morning when I went out to feed the fish, something squawked and jumped into the pond. It happened so fast that I only caught the motion out of the corner of my eye. It happened twice more, but again so fast that I caught only the motion. One morning, before approaching the pond, I scanned it afar through binoculars. And there he was, a perfect little, bulgy-eyed frog sunning himself on the rocks at the edge of the pond. He's about 3 inches long. We have named him Prince Igor.

That's not the end of the pond population explosion. Once more, when I was feeding the fish, I was stunned to find another new resident. A turtle stuck his head up. And he's not one of those dinky little play turtles. Shelly (we name everything) is about 5 inches long.

A pond has its own ecosystem and invites some predators.

Claire Puchy, who heads the nongame wildlife program at the Oregon Department of Fish and Wildlife, cautions us not to be too overjoyed with at least one of the new residents. In her words, if the frog is a bullfrog, "It will eat just about anything, including your fish and your turtle."

We could, however, be lucky and have a Pacific tree frog, which is native to the area. Unfortunately, our research tells us that tree frogs tend to be under 2 inches. So either we have a tree frog on steroids, or a teen-age bullfrog that can grow up to 8 inches. Personally, I think frogs stop being cute once they exceed 3 inches.

Puchy believes it likely that Shelly is a painted turtle, which she says is primarily vegetarian. That would be nice, because the turtle book we got at the pet store used some hostile words to describe many turtles, words such as "cannibalistic" and "omnivorous."

We've also got snails, but they're no mystery because they probably came in on the water plants. The only thing we didn't seem to have is the goldfish. We had put a number of inch-long feeder fish in several weeks ago, and saw only one or two rare glimpses. Suspicion immediately fell on Igor and Shelly.

So off we went to the fish store to get some fish that weren't bite-sized. Because of the price, we ended up with only two koi, at least 6 inches long. No sooner had they darted into the pond, then all the goldfish, which apparently had spent the summer hiding under the flag iris, darted out to greet them. They looked a lot like tugboats surrounding two large ships. And the goldfish have at least quadrupled in size. In fact, they look like they might be able to take Igor two falls out of three.

The next step is naming the pond. Given the way things have been going, we're thinking about Jurassic Pond.

AUGUST 20, 1993

MISTAKES AND MISHAPS
Learn from other gardeners' trials

THE SEASON IS YET YOUNG, AND ALREADY disasters have struck. Gardening can be a risky business, and I won't even dwell on the bit about Doug the Wonder Boy falling out of our neighbor's giant rhododendron.

Of late, I have heard of several garden misadventures. I am passing them on, not to be negative, but in hopes of preventing similar tribulations.

I have a friend who redid a front yard and set out new plants, then mulched them heavily. Despite a spate of rainy days, the new plants acquired a scorched look, and some

Make sure containers can drain properly, or learn the hard way.

just up and died. My friend's theory is that the new organic mulch was too "hot," and burned the tender new plants.

I've heard of fertilizer burning plants, but homicidal compost was a first for me. The solution, I would imagine, is to mulch in fall or winter, not just before planting. Ironically, you can also have problems with mulch that isn't "cooked" enough. It will have viable weed seeds.

My own little disaster was easy to remedy. I noticed that after heavy rains some of the containers that held trees were filling with water despite the drainage holes. The problem was that the larger containers were sufficiently heavy that they sank into the mud, which plugged up the drainage holes. We set them up on bricks, and they seem to drain just fine now.

More than one friend has reported a problem with a leaky pond. While raccoons won't swim, they will wade in a shallow pond, and their claws can shred a liner. My own pond was leaking a bit, and it turned out that the liner had sagged on one side. All we had to do was pull it up and anchor it with more rocks.

There are several approaches to pond building these days, ranging from stiff and flexible pond liners to spray-on materials. Given the many misadventures I have heard of with ponds, I'd recommend getting professional help if you are doing anything much bigger than 3 or 4 feet in diameter.

One of the biggest mistakes I made with our first pond was to build a little bank on its far side. Somehow I had forgotten about soil erosion, and of course every time we watered, more and more of the bank slipped down into the pond.

Speaking of disasters, we are having an "I told you so" moment at our house. Last year we removed some grass around our pond and laid a gravel path on sand where the grass used to be. We cut corners and didn't put landscape cloth down before the gravel. Now there are several little green tufts coming up through the gravel. Our path resembles an army of caterpillars with Mohawk haircuts on the march.

As far as plant disasters from the winter cold, the only victim was our red-leaved banana. We had even wrapped the stem the way they do in the Portland Classical Chinese Garden. I know, I know, many of you have bananas that survived. I'm happy for you.

Just about every clay pot that we didn't take into the greenhouse for the winter is cracked or broken, so there's another lesson on the need to be diligent about putting things away. Or, better yet, we should invest in good thick pots that can withstand the cold. One thing I will caution about is that if you are using a pot for a water garden, be sure it is glazed inside as well as on the outside. My experience is that all unglazed pots eventually leak.

The biggest disasters I see around town are pruning horrors. People are still whacking back shrubs and giving trees flattops instead of selecting branches to prune out and open up the plant to highlight its natural shape. I read this radical idea somewhere that if you want a 4-foot shrub, you should plant a shrub that matures at 4 feet. And, I might add, if you want a lollipop, you should buy one at a candy store.

MAY 24, 2007

TALLYING YOUR LOSSES

It isn't always obvious which plants have survived a sopping, shivering winter

I COULDN'T HELP BUT THINK OF THAT SCENE at the railroad station in *Gone with the Wind* where all the injured soldiers were laid out. That's what my garden looked like after the big freeze in February. Plants were sprawled everywhere. Even the winter-loving hellebores were drooping.

By now, you've probably inventoried your own garden to determine the survivors and the plants voted "off the island," so to speak. But don't do anything rash. Sometimes it takes weeks to tell if something is really lost.

Several years ago, the foliage on my *Acanthus mollis*, which is normally evergreen, disappeared entirely during a cold spell. I was

> *Those snobby hybrid teas are always thumbing their noses at me.*

sure it was a goner. But in mid-June I saw little green shoots coming up, and, sure enough, it came back. It took about a year to become really lush again.

There are several plants, such as hardy fuchsias, that are usually evergreen in our winters but deciduous in colder areas, where they are still hardy. When we have a cold spell, they think they are in Minnesota and die back to the ground, then make a comeback.

On the other hand, some plants that appear to have survived may be dying slowly. Not everything turns brown right away; it can take weeks for freeze damage to do its dirty work. I've had plants, especially roses, that sprouted leaves after a freeze, then turned toes up. Of course, those snobby hybrid teas are always thumbing their noses at me, and this is just one more "gotcha."

To check woody plants, scratch a bit of bark off a twig. If the inside looks white or greenish, it's probably a survivor, but if it looks mushy or black, it's likely in its death throes. You may

Abutilon, *a notoriously delicate plant.*

not know what made it and didn't make it until early summer.

So, while you'll want to be patient with some plants, there are others that should just get the yank. These are the ones that survived but were so ravaged by the cold that they have lost their looks. Silver-leaved plants, such as lavender and *Santolina*, will likely be leggy, if they made it at all. If a plant doesn't flourish, you've got to be tough and dispatch it.

In a way, you could look at this winter as a two-tier plant test. Because before the freeze, there was the deluge. Our saturated clay soil may have done in as many plants as the cold. At least you know that any plants that survived in reasonably good shape both are cold-hardy and can take soggy soil.

It will be interesting to see what all this does to the growing fascination with tropical-style plants. Last year there were certainly a lot of bananas and palms at nurseries, something you wouldn't have seen a decade before. And *Canna* and *Phormium* (New

Zealand flax) are almost staples now. I suspect that, despite this winter, most of us will continue to push the zonal envelope. It seems to be part of a gardener's nature to gamble with Mother Nature.

There are "plants" that took this past winter in stride. I noticed that Doug the Wonder Boy, in a fit of whimsy, divided the fake purple-flowered plant somebody mysteriously planted in my garden last year. I am happy to report that it survived the deluge and freeze in fine shape and continues to bloom.

MARCH 16, 2006

༄

CONSERVE YOUR FLOWER POWER
When blooming beauties woo you, try to save space for later

ALL LAST SUMMER I'D NOTICED A LITTLE shrub with apple-green leaves. For the life of me, I couldn't remember what it was. Then, one morning when I opened my front door to get the paper, I got a glorious surprise. My mystery shrub was covered with enormous blooms in the loveliest cherry-red.

Somehow, I had completely spaced out on the fact that, the previous fall, I had planted a hardy hibiscus called *Hibiscus moscheutos* 'Lord Baltimore.'

The moral of this little story is that, in

the thrall of gorgeous spring flowers, one should not fill up only on what's about to bloom. A wise gardener will save some room for plants that will bloom further down the line.

I need to remind myself of this because I flunked the "planning-for-later" test the first time I bought plants this year. I went in late March to the Amity Daffodil Festival, where several nurseries had booths.

I managed to load down my new plantmobile with an assortment of plants. Incidentally, we named the plantmobile Gertrude in honor of Gertrude Jekyll, thanks to a reader suggestion. The runner-up reader suggestion was Lloyd, after the late Christopher Lloyd. So thank you, dear readers.

But I digress, as usual. Anyway, it wasn't until I got home that I noticed that all my plants had one thing in common. They were all in bloom.

This was not smart. But how could I resist them? There were some tiny *Iris attica* plants, which can only be described as saucy. There was a new *Geum* introduction appropriately called 'Marmalade.' And, of course, there were hellebores galore. They are this year's hot plant, and I am either becoming a collector or running amok. It's hard to tell the difference.

I also picked up some woodland plants with lacy white flowers and attractive leaves.

They are called *Mukdenia rossii*. I'd never heard of this plant before, and I suspect that was part of the temptation to get it.

Daylilies, darlings of midsummer.

Next came the charming *Omphalodes cappadocica* 'Starry Eyes' that was winking at me and just too adorable to pass up. By this time, I was dizzy with plant lust, and

You must try to remember that the garden year does not end with the crescendo of June.

when someone stuck something called *Lathyrus vernus* 'Alboroseus' into my hands, I didn't even pause before plunking it into my box. I came home to discover that, underneath that fancy appellation, I had purchased a mere sweet pea.

Once again, I had been seduced by the charm of bloom. So now I must mentally write on the blackboard 100 times, "I will remember plants that will bloom later."

Dear readers, I can only warn you. This month you will be assaulted by everything from jewel-like primroses to stately delphiniums. You must try to remember that the garden year does not end with the crescendo of June.

If you want flower power in midsummer, look out for the likes of bee balm (*Monarda*), lily of the Nile (*Agapanthus*), sea holly (*Eryngium*), red-hot poker (*Kniphofia*), beard tongue (*Penstemon*), meadowsweet (*Astilbe*), hardy geranium, masterwort (*Astrantia*), phlox, daylilies (*Hemerocallis*) and the late-blooming Oriental lilies.

For late summer and into fall, look for sneezeweed (*Helenium*), crocosmia, sunflowers (*Helianthus*), flowering sage (*Salvia*), hardy fuchsia, bluebeard (*Caryopteris*), Russian sage (*Perovskia*), black-eyed Susan (*Rudbeckia*), toad lily (*Tricyrtis*), monkshood (*Aconitum*), *Anemone japonica*, aster, bugbane (*Cimicifuga*), stonecrop (*Sedum*) and those newly "cool" dahlia cultivars.

And, by all means, save room for yet another hydrangea. Like hellebores and dahlias, hydrangeas are enjoying renewed popularity. Personally, I like to see an old girl treated as the hot new thing.

APRIL 13, 2006

DOUBLE THE TROUBLE
Digging twice wasn't the answer to happy plants

PROBABLY THE STUPIDEST THING I'VE EVER done in my garden involved my first attempt at making a flower border. I say "probably" because so many things have fallen in the "stupid" category. I don't mind because few venues are as forgiving as gardening. It's not as if you're Michelangelo and you accidentally chip off David's nose and can't glue it back.

I'd read that the proper way to prepare a border is to double dig. The protocol calls for digging down a spade length, breaking up the soil and setting it aside. Then you dig down another spade length and break up the clods at this lower level. In those days, I had a working back, and I even cajoled my non-gardening husband into helping. We both felt virtuous about what we'd accomplished.

But somehow, I'd missed the part about adding compost, so I merely shoveled the top layer back on. It was nicely broken up, but it was still heavy clay soil that eventually reverted to the consistency of a Los Angeles freeway.

I planted my border, and while the plants survived, they did not thrive. Eventually, I saw the light, and on a gentle misty day we dug up all the plants in the border, wrapped their roots in wet newspapers and set them in shade.

By then we had ordered a mountain of compost and another mountain of good topsoil that had been well mixed with compost and manure. We didn't double dig this time, having realized it was a procedure designed for masochists, fanatics, or world-class gardeners, none of which fits us. We simply dug some of the compost into the top layer of the soil. Then we piled the good topsoil over the bed to a depth of about a foot.

Once everything was replanted, the results were almost immediate. Within weeks, the plants grew robust. It was like seeing a skinny found puppy fill out once it got good nutrition.

Now, 20 years later, that back border still has the best soil in the garden. You can stick a shovel into it and it is soft and crumbly. It also drains well and apparently is home to a nation of earthworms. We add an inch or two of compost twice a year to all our beds and don't make much attempt to scratch it in, since by now the plantings are too close. But it gradually works into the soil so that we rarely need fertilizer.

This is a graphic example of why gardeners harp on the need for amending soil, espe-

> *It was still heavy clay soil that eventually reverted to the consistency of a Los Angeles freeway.*

cially if you have heavy clay soil, as most of us do in the Willamette Valley. When people tell me they don't have a green thumb, I tend to think the color of their thumbs isn't the problem. The problem is likely the blue-black color of their sticky soil, a sure sign of compacted clay with zilch drainage.

I learned several things from my ghastly mistake.

First, I learned that friable soil is the foundation of a great garden. No amount of clever design will help if plants don't look healthy.

Second, I learned the importance of adding organic compost to ensure better drainage. It's also important to add if you have sandy soil, which drains too freely and loses nutrients. Compost is the miracle worker for both extremes.

Third, I learned the unimportance of double digging. If you need good soil at a greater depth, just make raised beds by adding well-mixed soil on top. Raised beds don't even have to look raised, and you don't need smelly railroad ties around them. Once the beds are planted, you won't be able to tell there's a little mound in there.

I launch into this annual nag about soil because, with the advent of February, we

Japanese anemones, surprisingly, rarely need staking.

are going to start to have fun. The garden will be waking up, the plant sales and garden shows will be hopping, and nurseries will be hauling out their stocks.

So, before the fun starts and the array of new plants robs us of lucid thought, here's a reminder of first things first. Remember to lay the foundation—good soil—before putting in those plants.

And if you're looking for a great Valentine's Day gift for a gardener, you can't go wrong with a sack or load of chocolaty topsoil. Just don't push things too far and forget the real chocolates. (Cherries in mine, please.)

FEBRUARY 7, 2008

❧

DIG 'EM, DIVIDE 'EM, DUMP 'EM

Editing your garden is as simple as pulling off a Band-Aid

THE DESTRUCTION DERBY IS ON. THE YARrow that lies supine despite the best efforts at staking is gone. The climbing rose that is a virtual test ground for the dreaded black spot is being yanked out. The dogwood that never recovered from anthracnose despite a strict spraying regime has been chopped down.

November: the cleanup month. And cleanup means more than raking leaves. It takes a while, unfortunately several years for some of us, to gather the courage to remove plants. The truth is that some plants, such as the sickly dogwood, deserve a mercy-killing. Others, such as the black-spotted rose, need to be dispatched with little mercy.

This is a hard truth to face. That must be why so many of us still have houseplants long after they've gotten leggy and that white salty stuff has formed around the rim of the pot. The sight of a sickly plant seems to bring out the missionary zeal—the by-gosh-I-could-save-this-soul syndrome.

At some point comes the breakthrough revelation that you actually can discard a plant and not be struck dead by a bolt of lightning. The discovery applies to the outdoors as well. So screw up your nerve, arm yourself with the proper tools and yell, "Off with their heads!"

Here's what to look for:

Shrinking violets: Start first with the obvious, the spindly, the less-than-healthy ne'er-do-wells. Put them out of their misery. Sometimes, it makes more sense to be the Terminator than Florence Nightingale.

Mega-monsters: Next, take a look at those shrubs that looked so dainty 10 years ago when they went in. Now they look like The Blob. Instant surgery can do wonders.

Takeover artists: Yes, there can be too much of a good thing. Lady's mantle, red valerian, purple fennel, plume poppies and their ilk are all lovely, but they multiply like rabbits. Time to thin the herd.

The fungus magnets: You'll find plenty of these in the rose garden. Hundreds of rose varieties are available; so why nurse along those that spend the summer looking like overly powdered ladies, thanks to an advanced case of powdery mildew?

Urban sprawlers: A few plants are worth staking—delphiniums, for example. But is it really worth putting up with the long-

Every path, every pond you imagine—make it twice the size.

stemmed marguerites, the ill-smelling yarrow and others that tend to lie down on the job?

(Note that some plants that only appear to sprawl actually are reaching for the sun. Move them to a full-sun location. The ones that can't stand up on their own, even in direct sun, are the problem; be brave and cast them into the outer darkness.)

Dubious achievers: Think back on the past year. Remember the five-minute wonders? They're the ones that you watch and wait for all summer. When they finally bloom, it all seems to be over before you can dig out the camera. Unless you've got a large spread, you've got to rethink whether you really have room for such poor performers.

Prima donnas: The breadth of plants that do well in this mild climate is astounding. So why put up with labor-intensive problems? If you've got something that constantly demands to be watered, fertilized, sprayed or cut back to stay at its prime, consign it to compost.

Ugly ducklings: This is an entirely subjective category, as beauty is truly in the eye of the beholder. We've all tried something that sounded interesting but turned out less than elegant. For me, it's *Phlomis*, that odd little plant whose whorls of yellow flowers grow around square stems. It is indeed interesting—but not really pretty. Just one plant is enough.

There's nothing like a good thinning to rejuvenate a tired garden. Won't it be fun when you have all that space to try something new next spring?

Anybody want some *Phlomis*?

NOVEMBER 6, 1992

CAN I GET A WITNESS?
There's no court of appeals when the garden lays down the law

I KNEW IT WOULD HAPPEN AS SOON AS I WROTE about the loss of my beloved *Cercis canadensis* 'Forest Pansy' and consoled myself with reports that this particular redbud "doesn't do well" here. Within days, kindly people began calling and writing in about their thriving, years-old 'Forest Pansy' trees, and inviting me to come see them.

This also happens when I have had plants die in winter only to see the same plants deliriously happy and alive in a neighbor's yard. It seems to be one of those perverse laws of gardening. I believe it is the law of paradoxical hardiness.

Then there's the law of inopportune obsession. It hits when you have been standing in a long line for the cashier at a nursery. Just as you finally get near the front, you will see a plant you just have to have in someone else's wagon. This is the plant that is always at the farthest outback of the nursery, thus invoking the law of pernicious positioning. You will return to be at the end of the line again.

The most famous gardening law is the law of malicious timing. That's how gardens manage to hit their peaks of perfection either the week before or the week after a big event. If your daughter is getting married in your garden, you can be assured that the roses will have gone over and the lilies will not have opened. And, in my case, the aphids will have staged a mass invasion with the ladybugs hot on their tails, but not hot enough.

A corollary for those planning a garden event is the law of opportunistic pandemonium. We can expect a number of disasters before an open garden. Mine have included the burned lawn incident (too much fertilizer), the swooning trees (twice), the world's largest wasp nest, the broken sprinkler system and, most unfortunately, the great aphid peeing festival.

Another operative law holds that as soon as you finally get the gumption to pull up a tiresome, boring plant, you will see it in another garden looking absolutely stunning. The phrase "What was I thinking?" will fill the thought balloon over your head. This is the law of ineffectual regret.

Still another law is that when you plant a rose that everyone insists doesn't get black spot, yours will get the beastly disease. You will have been a victim of the law of perverse exceptions.

Then there is the fact that, with years of experience and supposed knowledge, you simply cannot grow a certain plant. Thus you smugly determine it is finicky or too tender for our climate. Shortly thereafter you see it thriving in the garden of a friend who is an absolute beginner. This is the law of advantageous ignorance.

Oh, there are a lot of garden-related laws.

> *It seems to be one of those perverse laws of gardening.*

No matter how carefully you calculated the compost you ordered, it will always be one wheelbarrow short (law of perpetual miscalculation). High winds will blow in from the coast just after you've spent all Sunday raking leaves (law of the irresistible provocation).

The gorgeous peach-colored flower ordered from a catalog turns out to be flaming pink (law of capricious inconstancy). The exotic and expensive seedling purchased in a spring sale disappears by midsummer (law of inconspicuous consumption). The terrific free plant turns out to be invasive (law of roguish germination).

You decide not to spend the money to have a professional install some garden feature and opt for DIY (law of wildly misplaced confidence). Just as you've torn apart the garden for a new project, your in-laws from out of state call to say they're coming for a visit (law of coincidental aggravation).

Finally, you would think that after 20 years in my garden, I would remember what I planted where. Yet every spring, "mystery" plants poke up, and some remain unrecognizable until they have weeks of growth on them. This is the law of perpetual perplexity.

NOVEMBER 9, 2006

❧

ONLY HUMAN
Gardening luminaries kill plants, too

IN JUNE, I WENT TO ONE OF THOSE GARDEN seminars that are sponsored by *Horticulture* magazine and feature Very Important People.

About 250 people gathered on Washington's Bainbridge Island to hear about plants from the likes of Helen Dillon, a garden writer whose Dublin, Ireland, garden is world famous; Thomas Fischer, editor of *Horticulture*; Dan Hinkley, plant explorer and a director of the fabled Heronswood Nursery on Bainbridge Island; and Thomas Hobbs, British Columbia floral designer and author of the knock-your-socks-off school of vivid planting as embodied in his book *Shocking Beauty*.

I tell you all this so that you know that the words I am about to relate fall from the lips of the gods and goddesses of gardening at the Olympian level, and I am not just talking geography here.

During the first day, when we could stop from quivering with excitement, we heard about the speakers' latest plant loves. Far from being stuffy and superior, they talked just as much about plants they'd lost as they did about their successes.

Helen Dillon took her theme from Alfred Lord Tennyson's line "'Tis better to have loved and lost than never to have loved at all." Why, she asked, do we always say a plant has died? Why can't we just say, "I killed it?" She can handle plants dying, but she despises plants that die "badly," that is, plants that take their time shuffling off this mortal coil.

Dillon holds that you should regularly walk around your garden and demand of each plant that it justify its existence. If it looks nice for just one week, out it should go. With only a couple of exceptions, she is pulling out all her hostas, which someone described as slug caviar. Her view is: "If you catch 500 slugs in your garden, you should know that the remainder are saying, 'Good, there's more for us to eat.'"

Horticulture's Fischer opined that gardening should be classified as a subcategory of

We gardeners are (more than) prone to excess.

compulsive behavior. His theory is that plants have evolutionarily developed a manipulative behavior. They have learned to make themselves so attractive that they get us to buy them. Hobbs referred to this phenomenon as "the green needle."

Fischer noted that some plants such as gentians seem to be very "killable," and I have to admit mine, too, are in the deceased category. At one time or another, at least three of the speakers had lost a *Cercis canadensis* 'Forest

> "Some plants are so beautiful that you just need to kill them again and again."

Pansy,' an exceptionally pretty small tree with dark red heart-shaped leaves. I was feeling very "neener, neener" at this point, since mine continues to thrive.

Fischer also said, "Some plants are so beautiful that you just need to kill them again and again." This perfectly describes my relationship with the lovely shrub *Melianthus*. I am on my third one now.

Hobbs may have gotten off the best line of the day when he talked about falling in love with a plant

(*Podophyllum* 'Kaleidoscope') that cost $60 for a 4-inch pot. "But how much do shoes cost?" he asked.

He told Helen Dillon that she didn't have to forgo all hostas. He described *Hosta* 'Sagae' as so tall (4 feet) that the slugs can't see it. He also revealed that the picture of the amazing red ornamental rhubarb (*Rheum palmatum* 'Atrosanguineum') on the cover of *Shocking Beauty* was taken in the late Rosemary Verey's garden. It took the plant 40 years to get that color, and even then it's green again by June.

I am happy to pass this along because there are a number of us who have lusted for this plant, bought it and wondered what we did wrong when it didn't turn red. Mine, however, did turn dead.

All the speakers, somewhat hypocritically I think, cautioned discipline. "Select, don't collect," advised Dillon. That advice, of course, all went out the window the next day when they turned us loose in some gardens followed by a shopping spree at Heronswood.

I am only slightly sorry to report that my friends and I lusted and lost some money and, possibly, our good sense.

JULY 8, 2004

❧

LETTERMAN LOOSE IN THE GARDEN
The talk-show host inspires top 10 list of garden mistakes

T HE PROSPECT OF TELEVISION TALK-SHOW host David Letterman doing one of his irreverent "top 10" lists on gardening is enough to make you shudder.

His top 10 "mistakes gardeners make" probably would have some things like making pegs out of slugs, letting the kids do the pruning and spreading fish fertilizer just before the garden wedding.

Well, of course, that's humor, not real life. Or is it?

I seem to have an uncomfortable memory about dousing the deck plants with fish fertilizer shortly before company. In my zeal to have healthy plants, I seem to have forgotten what the aroma would do. The cats, however, had a great time at the party. In the context of having humbly learned by trial and lots of error, here is a highly subject list of top 10 mistakes gardeners make.

No. 10—Getting overexuberant with color: Salmon-pink geraniums and mustard-yellow marigolds need some buffers, like blue or silver or just plain green foliage. And red salvia practically should be banned. (As mentioned, this is a highly subjective list.)

No. 9—Using big chunky barkdust as groundcover: Leave that to McDonald's. In the home garden, use a finer grade for mulch, or better yet, plant so closely together that you can't see any ground. Under shrubs, use real live ground covers.

No. 8—Growing sun-lovers in too much shade: This will guarantee you spindly, bloomless plants. So what if you can't grow roses? A whole world of lush, gorgeous, shade-loving plants are waiting for you to get to know them.

No. 7—Being afraid to remove any living plant: Homeowners are loathe to take out a tree or shrub or plant, as if anything living is sacrosanct. But we're not talking about clear-cutting here. Sometimes the best thing you can do is remove a plant that has become overgrown and shapeless or casts too much shade.

No. 6—Making flower borders too narrow: And compounding the error, some gardeners line them all up against the perimeter of the property. This will guarantee a stringy look. What's the point of having flowers if the beds aren't wide enough for a luxuriant look?

No. 5—Thinking that if some fertilizer works well, a little more will make things really grow: What it will grow is giant yellow spots in your lawn. Believe me, I know. And it takes about three years for the lawn to grow back.

No. 4—Putting in flowers before shrubs. It's easy to fall in love with flowers when you're starting a garden. But sooner or later, especially come winter, you'll wish you'd added some shrubs for backbone. It's harder to find space for them later.

No. 3—Buying plants because of their beautiful blooms: It's hard to think about

You might want to take a second look at color combinations.

asters now, when all those blooming bleeding hearts are beckoning. But judging a plant by its flower will get you a garden that looks gorgeous in early spring, then does nothing the rest of the summer.

No. 2—Skimping on plants: An iris by itself can look a bit strange: a whole clump is stunning. Think in terms of planting in drifts, like nature does.

No. 1 mistake gardeners make— Ah, pruning. What is it about pruning? Hand mere mortals a pair of shears or clippers and some primeval urge takes over. If you are going to cut a tree or shrub down to stumps, why not take it all out and put the poor thing out of its misery? Taking shears to shrubs and rounding them to perfect little balls only works if the intent is bona fide topiary. Otherwise, open up the shrub, but leave it generally to its natural shape.

MARCH 20, 1992

Part 7

SHRUBS AND TREES

Frankly, whacking is my favorite pruning style.

And pretty much the only one.

A young birch dances in the breeze.

THINK AHEAD

Small trees can give huge satisfaction

I'M A FIRM BELIEVER THAT NOTHING STAMPS A garden as one's own as much as planting a tree. Not only does it demonstrate faith in the future, but it also shows a generosity of spirit. It says you are willing to invest in something that another generation (or maybe a subsequent owner of your home) may enjoy even more than you.

If all that do-good symbolism doesn't get you, there's the fortunate fact that many trees will grow sufficiently fast to give you, if not immediate satisfaction, at least reasonably swift satisfaction.

Since most gardeners these days live on ever-shrinking lots, smaller ornamental trees that peak around 25 feet are enjoying great popularity. A point in favor of small trees is that they tend to give dappled shade rather than heavy shade. Dappled shade will allow you to plant under your tree, especially lovely little spring bulbs.

The first thing to do is consider what you want most from a tree: shade, spring flowers, autumn color, fruit, great bark or just an overall graceful shape. Then, if you're like me, after you have considered all this, you will go off to a nursery and buy the first tree that shakes its pretty foliage at you. That's how I came to be the proud owner of two new variegated dogwoods.

In the 20 years that I have been in my garden, I have planted a number of trees. Besides the dogwoods, they've included two stewartias, two Japanese snowbells, one magnolia, two Japanese maples, two crabapples, one apple, one cherry, one silverbell, one katsura, one mimosa, one dove tree and the late, lamented redbud known as 'Forest Pansy.'

Most are doing fine, but some are not.

I have had mixed results with *Stewartia pseudocamellia*. I had two of these trees planted mere feet apart. The leaves on one browned, but the other remained entirely healthy. We took the bad one out and eventually moved the healthy one to where we had lost a Japanese maple to verticillium wilt (a fungus affecting many maples in Portland).

It was a dumb move. Now the formerly healthy stewartia is showing signs of wilt. The lesson here is that if you see signs of disease in your neighborhood, such as branch dieback or leaves that turn brown around the edges, make sure you choose cultivars that are resistant to common diseases. Maples are affected by verticillium wilt, while certain dogwoods are particularly vulnerable to anthracnose.

You can do an Internet search for these diseases and get quite a lot of information, including lists of trees that are susceptible or resistant to the disease. You can also check with master gardeners or nursery experts. In particular, if you are buying flowering cherries, crabapples or dogwoods, search out varieties that resist disease.

Diseases don't necessarily rule out acquiring some lovely trees; just don't plant them in the ground if the problem is a soil-borne fungus. I have several Japanese maples that are doing quite well in containers. I chose varieties with particularly attractive leaves or sculptural shapes.

> *If you're like me, you will go off to a nursery and buy the first tree that shakes its pretty foliage at you.*

October is a great month for planting trees (as well as shrubs), because the soil is still warm and relatively dry. We probably won't see such good planting conditions again until very late spring, which in these parts can be the Fourth of July. Also, of course, autumn is an excellent time to select plants for leaf color, which I think gives more punch to a garden than flowering trees.

But don't do what I did. One day at a nursery I spotted a gorgeous tree glowing orangy-red in the sun. It was an Asian pear (*Pyrus pyrifolia*). I stood staring at it, trying to decide whether I should buy it. While I was dithering, one of the nursery staff rolled up a dolly and carted the tree off. Someone else had beaten me to it. I still think about that tree.

These are by no means the only terrific small trees (30 feet or less), but they are ones I have experience with, either in my garden or in a friend's.

• *Acer griseum* (paperbark maple): Autumn color, beautiful bark; considered by many to be the most beautiful maple.

• *Acer shirasawanum* 'Aureum' (golden full moon maple): Golden leaves.

• *Cercidiphyllum magnificum* (katsura): Autumn color; considered by some nurserymen to be the most beautiful tree.

• *Clerodendrum trichotomum* (harlequin glory bower): Leaves smell like peanut butter; not my favorite, but I have friends who love it.

• *Cornus alternifolia* 'Argentea' (pagoda dogwood): Shrubby, heavily variegated foliage.

• *Cornus controversa* 'Variegata' (wedding cake tree): Gorgeous layered structure and variegated foliage; considered by me to be the most beautiful tree.

• *Fagus sylvatica* 'Tricolor' (tricolor beech): Pink, white and purple leaves; eventually tall, but slow-growing.

• *Halesia carolina* (silverbell, snowdrop tree): White bell-like blossoms in late spring; resembles a styrax.

• *Magnolia stellata* (star magnolia): One of the first trees to bloom in spring.

• *Magnolia wilsonii*: Huge fragrant white flowers on small tree; considered very special among magnolia lovers.

• *Malus* 'Molten Lava' (crabapple): Disease-resistant variety.

• *Styrax japonicus* (Japanese snowbell): Graceful tree with white flowers.

SEPTEMBER 28, 2006

BY THEIR LEAVES
Foliage is the key to practical plant purchases

IN THE FRENZY OF SELECTING NEW PLANTS, IT pays to pause and think about what they will look like when they're not in flower. More than once, this thought has stopped me in my tracks from buying a tree or shrub that looks fabulous in bloom but may just be a dark mass the rest of the year.

It is one thing if you have a grand estate

or country manor. You have room for plants with ephemeral effects. But most of us, with our urban lots, must be much more practical, which means selecting plants that look reasonably good in or out of bloom.

Of course, we buy a number of flowering perennials principally for their leaves. These include the likes of *Rodgersia*, *Canna*, *Acanthus*, *Anthriscus*

Japanese maples offer a wonderful variety of leaf color, shape and texture.

sylvestris, *Ligularia* and the ubiquitous *Heuchera* varieties. While the flowers may be charming, the leaves are spectacular.

Many perennials also happen to flower, but their flowers are insignificant or secondary. You wouldn't plant a *Persicaria virginiana* (used to be called *Tovara*) for those teensy flower spikes that one book describes as "dun" colored. And most people don't plant *Hosta* for its bloom, although some cultivars do produce lovely, if fleeting, flowers.

This brings us to those valuable double-duty plants that let you have your cake and eat it too, so to speak. They have both spectacular flowers and great foliage. Think about peonies (*Paeonia*). Most of us select them for the flowers. But, when the scarlet shoots poke up in early spring, is there a prettier foliage plant? I don't think so.

The beauty of lady's mantle leaves (*Alchemilla*) is well touted, but other fabulous double-duty plants, such as colewort, are underused. Colewort (*Crambe cordifolia*) sends up in June a huge spray of white flowers that

resemble baby's breath. They hover above heroic-size, rhubarblike leaves.

The bright feathery flowers of *Astilbe* light up shade, while the foliage is as lacy as any fern. After the purple flowers of *Iris pallida* 'Variegata' die down, you'll still have a handsome clump of green-and-yellow striped swordlike leaves. *Agapanthus* 'Tinkerbell' has lovely arching green-and-cream strappy leaves.

One of my favorite perennials is yellow wax-bells (*Kirengeshoma palmata*). Even if it didn't produce buttery-yellow flowers in late summer, I would still grow it for its elegant maple-like leaves and glossy black stems.

Perennials aren't the only flowering plants with stellar foliage. The introduction of dark-leaved varieties of dahlias, such as 'Bishop of Llandaff,' has made them popular foliage plants.

There's also common old nasturtium (*Tropaeolum*), whose leaves, when you think about it, are very pretty. And they grow in soft mounds that make a lovely fast-growing ground cover for bare spots. They're annuals, but they often self-sow and come back.

These are just examples. If we just look with fresh eyes, we'll spot many more plants whose leaves alone make them garden worthy. And, while we're being practical (and this may be my last practical thought before I am completely sucked in by plant lust), there's another thing to think about when it comes to foliage on flowering plants.

The leaves of some flowering plants disappear or, worse, just get ratty after they bloom. Take lilies. Few things look as glorious as a stand of lilies in bloom, but also few things look as unsightly as the browning stalks after they bloom. Oriental poppies (*Papaver orientale*), bleeding hearts (*Dicentra spectabilis*) and the blue-flowered varieties of *Corydalis* are other examples of perennials whose leaves shrivel up after they've bloomed.

Such plants should be tucked in where their dying foliage will be quickly covered by other plants. They are not edging plants. Fortunately, lilies have the good manners to grow straight up through other plants. They can also be grown in pots and removed after they have bloomed.

APRIL 6, 2006

❧

SUBSHRUBS: PLOP THEM IN, BE HAPPY

Perennials are so last month. Now I'm thinking bigger. Lavender, Russian sage, rock roses . . .

I HOPE YOU DIDN'T PULL UP THAT SORRY-looking hardy fuchsia. I almost did, because the poor thing looked like tumbleweed. But then I noticed a little greenery peeking up from the bottom. Hardy fuchsias are among those plants that often stay evergreen but will lose all their leaves in a freeze, which does not mean they're goners.

Some plants are good at

Cistus *'Snowfire.'*

playing possum, like certain clematis. They'll look dead and stringy, with stems that resemble raffia. Then they'll amaze you by leafing out.

Hardy fuchsias are to be distinguished from those tender plants you put in hanging baskets. Often sold as *F. magellanica*, hardy fuchsias may die all the way back in winter but will come up from the roots. I mention this because I have now moved on from my annual thrall with perennials and am turning my attention to shrubs, particularly a class of shrubs known as subshrubs.

I don't think this is a scientific definition, but rather descriptive of small woody plants that seem to be a cross between shrubs and perennials. These include lavender (*Lavandula*), santolina, bluebeard (*Caryopteris*), rosemary (*Rosemarinus officinalis*), artemisia, Russian sage (*Perovskia*) and germander (*Teucrium*), among others. Rock roses (*Cistus*), cape fuchsia (*Phygelius*), and Jerusalem sage (*Phlomis fruticosa*) may not officially be subshrubs, but they resemble them. With the exception of fuchsias, which can take shade and need moisture, the rest are sun lovers.

I suppose heathers (*Calluna*) and heaths (*Erica*) could be called subshrubs, but I won't bother with them. I refuse to consider a heather or heath because you can't just buy one. Before you know it, you simply must have great mounds of these soft, cushy plants. Knowing my lack of restraint, I'm not about to get started.

What I like about subshrubs is that they can be plopped into a hole and will fluff up and fill it in no time, unlike some perennials that may take a couple of years to get real heft. Many also make good pot plants, especially the fuchsias.

Bluebeard and Russian sage have the advantage of blooming in late summer when we're hard put to find anything else with blue flowers. I do have reservations about Russian sage, however, because I saw it in glorious abundance in a garden in Provence. It was about 5 feet high, billowing out in a great smoky cloud. After that, I could not look at mine without thinking, "You wimp."

> *Anyone who has grown lavender knows what I mean.*

Many so-called subshrubs are Mediterranean plants, so that makes their hardiness iffy. They survive all right, but tend to come back with bare woody stems. Anyone who has grown lavender knows what I mean. These are not plants that should be pruned down to old wood, because they won't come back. If pruned at all, it's best done gently in late spring, or right after they've bloomed.

I think of it as shearing, like we do to our Himalayan cat Yeti, whose long hair is full of knots by spring. You can prune down lower (on the shrub, not the cat) if you see new growth lower down, but don't cut off the new growth.

And a final word of warning: It's popular to make hedges or knot gardens out of santolina and germander because their leaves lend themselves to clipping like boxwood.

I lined an herb garden with germander once. That led to the coldest winter in eons. When it comes to many Mediterranean plants, the adage is true—plant only what you can afford to lose.

MAY 6, 2010

❧

TARGET AUDIENCE
Perhaps a few military flourishes would lure my husband into the garden

MY FRIEND CARLENE TALKED ME INTO TAKing a bonsai class with her. It's not something I am particularly interested in, but I was afraid she'd never cook her great "heart attack potatoes" again if I didn't go.

I brought my humble little bonsai back to my office, and Scott, one of the bright young men who work in our department, dropped in. I was surprised at how interested he was in my bonsai. Then he explained.

He said his wife hates bonsai, but he thinks they are kind of neat. He also said men tend to like them. I had, in fact, noticed there were several men in the class. Scott said bonsai appealed to men because—and I'm not making this up—they could imagine little soldiers stuck in the little trees all shooting each other.

This was a revelation. Suddenly, I realized that I had been using the wrong approach all these years in trying to interest my husband in gardening. I should have made the fire pit look like a bunker. The gazebo would have made a fine fort. The pond would have been ideal for little submarines, destroyers and cruisers. The vegetable patch could have been called the "green zone."

I can see it now. On the first nice day I'll say to my husband, "Honey, do you want to go out for some field reconnaissance?" instead of saying, "Let's take a walk around the garden." Maybe he would weed if I called it a search-and-destroy mission.

I have often wondered if gender plays a role in garden approaches. Certainly men seem to be more attached to lawns, vegetables, and roses. And pruning. It's been my experience that men like to handle loud, gas-powered implements in the garden.

"Honey, do you want to go out for some field reconnaissance?"

But maybe they just do that because we women feign weakness when it comes to lugging this equipment around.

I did some research on the Internet to see if there was any information about gender differences in gardening. I found a scholarly paper published in 2000 called *I Never Promised You a Rose Garden: Gender, Leisure and Home-making in Late Modernity*, published by Mark Bhatti and Andrew Church, both faculty members at the University of Brighton.

The paper cites data that more women fall into the "horticultural hobbyist" category; that is, serious gardeners who work hard in the garden. Men dominated the "leisure gardener" category, defined as someone who enjoys the garden but lacks the time and skills to garden. Men also dominated the "investor gardener" category, people who primarily see gardening as a way to add value to the house.

The researchers do not, however, make note of the fact that until recently, there were fewer women in the work force, which might account for the fact that they had the time to be horticultural hobbyists.

The researchers also described the garden as a negotiated environment, where men did more of the mowing, digging, planting, pruning and weeding and women did more of the "artful," creative work. Women were more of the "idea gardeners." Men, on the other hand, according to the paper, tend to want gardens to be tidy.

I also found a provocative article by writer Michael Pollan from the July 21, 1991, *New York Times*, under the headline "A Gardener's Guide to Sex, Politics and Class War." This certainly sounded promising. Alas, it did not live up to its racy title, but was nevertheless enlightening. Pollan observed that women dominate garden writing, while men dominate nature writing.

He notes that nature writers are observers, admiring nature from a distance. The gardener, on the other hand, "understands that nature and culture need not be antagonists." I don't know what this says about gender, but it's a fascinating article and worth Googling even if there's nothing sexy there.

Finally, I found a Web site offering photos of men gardening. The men are doing prosaic things such as hoeing and are fully clothed. There is no such site with photos of women gardeners, which may say quite a lot about gender fantasies.

FEBRUARY 15, 2007

LAST DAYS OF THE LOCUST

Removing an ailing tree can be a costly, complicated process

ON THE HOTTEST DAY OF THE DECADE, THAT 103-degree scorcher in July, my door bell rang. It was our neighbor to the west, informing me that one of our trees had dropped a huge branch onto their driveway.

I shuffled through the heat into the alley between our houses. Sure enough, there was an enormous branch from a tall locust hanging off of the cable and phone wires.

I called a tree service, and they came right over. With some huffing and puffing, they got a rope around the branch and pulled it down without breaking the wires. The following Sunday, my doorbell rang again. This time it was my neighbor Rosemary to tell me I had another branch down. She had actually heard it fall from four houses down. It was in the same place, only bigger, and this time it was hanging off of a Portland General Electric wire.

Since it was on a hot wire, I called PGE, and a crew came right out and removed it. Their forester, a very nice woman named Pam, came over a few days later and told me what I already knew. The tree was a goner and needed to be removed. I had nurtured a hope that the utility would remove the tree, since it was hanging over their line.

Alas, it was only over a distribution line to our house, not over a high voltage line, so it was my responsibility. Pam let me down easily. I could see the sympathy in her eyes as she broke the bad news. I tried not to cringe as I saw $3,000 fly out the window. Actually, because of the size and the need to rent a 62-foot bucket truck, it turned out to be $4,000.

On the day of the big removal, I got home from work at 6 p.m. to find that the crew from the tree service was still at it. So I got a soda pop and sat on my back terrace and watched the big operation. There was a lot of yelling and grunting and, of course, the loud noise of chain saws and the thud of big pieces of wood hitting the ground. Occasionally I heard a sharp retort like, "Oh, poop," only the word they used wasn't exactly "poop."

This was kind of worrisome because I imagined someone sawing his foot off or dropping a huge branch on one of his fellow workers. But it turns out these people really knew what they were doing, and the sudden outbursts applied to the bees' nests they found (more than one) and the opossum they surprised, which was probably also thinking, "Oh, poop."

The tree, which had towered over our three-story house, is now down, and all is safe, even if I am substantially poorer and the opossum has to find a new home.

AUGUST 26, 2004

LETTING GO OF SUMMER

The grand show is over, but autumn has its own beauties

AH, FALL. IT WOULD BE THE PERFECT season if only. If only winter didn't follow. If only it came without cleanup chores. If only I hadn't acquired too many pots and tender plants that need moving. If only I could still bend over sufficiently to get those bulbs planted.

There are certain phrases we gardeners tend to repeat. One is, "You should have been here last week." Another is, "I'm sorry, it's

Groupings of pots make a magical effect; just remember, they'll need watering more often.

such a mess." This hypocritical pronouncement usually comes after you've spent the entire week feverishly cleaning up for your garden guests.

And another oft-repeated phrase is, "I'm not ready for summer to be over." We start uttering this sometime in August, and by actual fall, it has reached mantra status.

I always get a bittersweet feeling at this time of year. The first trigger is when the *Rudbeckia* lose their petals. The dark cones are indeed attractive, but the fleeing petals remind me that the grand summer show is over. Another sign things are changing is when you wake up one morning and find the basil has turned to black slush.

It's not that autumn isn't beautiful—as gorgeous as spring, actually. Each year about this time I pull out one of my favorite books, *The Garden in Autumn* by Allen Lacy. It's the best reminder that this is not only a grand season, but also a lot more than foliage color. The book is relatively old, published in 1990, and may be out of print. If it's not available in bookstores, you can get it online. Plus, there's the good old library.

Lacy's book is not one of your glam coffee-table books, but it is filled with pictures of lush late-season combinations. Lacy describes flowers that linger from summer, flowers specific to autumn, grasses and berries, plus shrub and tree foliage.

Each year this book helps me break through the melancholy over summer's end and reminds me of what pinnacles an autumn garden can reach.

> *I come upstairs to find that tendrils of wisteria have grown a foot into the room. This is some nervy plant.*

This season also is, as we've been told repeatedly by garden experts, a fine time to plant, especially woody plants, which seems to be gardenspeak for trees and shrubs. My focus this year, however, will be on thinning out rather than planting.

Our wet cold spring had an effect that few of us predicted. It was as if our leafy plants, especially shrubs and vines, suddenly went on steroids. Shrubs sprouted to enormous proportions, and the vines—what can I say? They seem to be trying to swallow the house and doing a pretty good job of it.

In fact, I am thinking of radically pruning the wisteria covering the back porch. We hacked it back several times this past summer, but that just seemed to provoke it. Some days, when it has been warm enough to leave the door to the porch open, I come upstairs to find that tendrils of wisteria have grown a foot into the room. This is some nervy plant.

I got out Cass Turnbull's excellent *Guide to Pruning*, and she confirms, "Wisteria is Latin for work." She does not recommend taking the vine down to the ground, but she does recommend taking out 90 percent of the new growth and doing it before winter, when the vines become stiff and woody.

I also like the fact that she says she "whacks" her wisteria back, since, frankly, whacking is my favorite pruning style. And pretty much the only one.

SEPTEMBER 25, 2008

CATCH THE SCENT

Even a single shrub can cheer you amid the chill

Winter has a gift for you, even if you don't cultivate a four-season garden. Can you guess what it is? It's scent. And, if you have a small space, one select shrub is all you need.

There is nothing quite like getting out of the car on a cold winter day and trudging through the rain with a bag of groceries, then suddenly catching a note of witch hazel on the breeze. It can't help but lift your spirits.

Winter flowers, most of which bloom on shrubs, have an almost heartbreaking sweetness about them. They are light without the cloying heaviness of, say, lilies or hyacinths. Perhaps it is the sharpness of the air. I have a theory that winter flowers have an emotional pull because they are such a delicious surprise, coming as they do out of the seasonal wasteland. With the garden largely bare, the flowers of a single shrub can send a clear, clean note.

And, oh gee, I sound like one of those starlets pushing her new perfume. Hands down, my favorite plant for early winter scent is witch hazel (*Hamamelis*), and a close second is viburnum.

You have to get up close to sniff the flowers of viburnum because it doesn't project like witch hazel, but the flowers—at least on my shrub—last from early November to February. I have been warned, however, not to take viburnum into the house, where the scent is said to turn "catty."

To get the most out of winter scent, consider placement, which I seldom do in spring or summer (when my style tends to cram and jam). Years ago, I moved my witch hazel from the far back of our garden to out front beside the driveway. Now I can catch the scent every time I get in and out of the car.

Since many winter-blooming shrubs are large and ungainly when they are not in bloom, it's a good idea to push them toward the back of beds where you can grow clematis vines over them the rest of the year.

If you want the best winter scent of all, visit a nursery in winter and walk through the greenhouses. The spongy soil and humusy aroma are sure to make you nostalgic for spring. I always think of it as the scent of hope.

Aromatic Winter Shrubs

Witch hazel: Mine is *Hamamelis* x *intermedia* 'Pallida,' but 'Primavera' and 'Jelena' are said to be superior in the perfume department. Still, there are many delightful cultivars, so talk to your nursery people. Medium shrubs.

Fragrant winter-flowering witch hazel.

Viburnum: *Viburnum farreri* and *V.* x *burkwoodii* come highly recommended, but I love my old and common *V.* x *bodnantense*, which blooms from November to February. Mostly large shrubs, but *V. farreri* 'Nanum' grows to only 3 feet.

Daphne: My common *Daphne odora* blooms early and profusely and smells divine, but *D. laureola* (which has an evening scent) and *D. mezereum* also are praised for winter scent. Small shrubs.

Wintersweet: *Chimonanthus praecox* may take seven years to bloom, so look for a larger, older specimen. Large shrub.

Mexican orange: *Choisya ternata* blooms lavishly in late winter, with flowers lasting two months. Medium shrub.

Winter hazel: *Corylopsis pauciflora* is not really a witch hazel but does resemble one. I include it here because many people rave about it, but, alas, I have never had any success. It, along with keeping pets off furniture, is one of my great failures. Medium shrub.

Sweet box: *Sarcococca hookeriana* var. *humilis*, syn. *S. humilis*, is said to be "powerfully fragrant" in late winter. Some *Sarcococca* are large shrubs, but this is only 18 inches high and works as a ground cover.

Winter honeysuckle: The name *Lonicera fragrantissima* says it all. It's not a vine but a large, arching shrub.

Boxleaf azara: I hear that *Azara microphylla* flowers smell like chocolate. I may order one on the spot. Large shrub, but slow growing.

DECEMBER 25, 2008

❧

SNAP, CRACKLE — THERE GOES THE NEIGHBORHOOD

A raging spring storm on the eve of a garden tour tests the nerves of even the most placid gardener

WEDNESDAY, MAY 19, DAWNED FAIR AND bright. But shortly after noon, a nasty tree-hunting storm began to gather force. By 2 p.m., it was proceeding with the intensity of a heat-seeking missile—toward our house. Weather forecasters tracked its progress as it skirted around trees that heroically flung themselves in its path.

Meanwhile, back at our place—Ground Zero—the Pond Committee was busily surveying its work and pondering the fact that gravity-defying sediment had entered our water system. When the deluge hit, the committee members took cover with our three cowering dogs under the porch. That's when it happened.

A great gust blew, and—snap, crackle and pop—down came an elderly honey locust, collapsing out of the west border. It smashed a little copper arbor, pancaked the water iris, sliced off half of the beloved purple plum tree, and came to rest at the tip of the herb garden.

When the dust had settled, about 50 feet of tree stretched diagonally across the back lawn. Branches from every tree in the neighborhood, and probably some from Beaverton and Gresham as well, dotted our yard.

It could have been worse. The tree fell

Make room for dense plantings as well as open areas.

Everyone came to gawk and offer advice. "You could just leave it and pretend it's the new forest look. After all, everyone knows you've gotten pretty sappy about foliage these days," said one friend. "You could put a picture of a triumphant spotted owl on top and say it's part of an ecology message," said another. "Carve it up and pretend it's art," said yet another.

The tour organizers came to look and lied politely, saying it wasn't so bad and everyone would understand. The friend, whose garden I considered sending the tour to instead of my own, astutely read my mind and hastily offered her gardener to help with cleanup.

The next day, friends and helpers showed up with chain saws and a chipper. By the end of the day, the felon tree had metamorphosed into firewood and was stacked in the back shed. The branches had been chipped and now carpeted the paths.

almost exactly between the house and the gazebo. On the other hand, it could have been better. We were four days away from a garden tour, and ours was one of the open gardens.

When something like this hits, you have two choices: 1) hysteria; 2) look at things philosophically and remember you'll laugh about this in six months.

Naturally, I chose number one.

First, I called the tour organizers and said we'd have to cancel. Then I made a list of all the friends that I could hit up for last-minute open garden substitutes. Then I had a bag of M&Ms. Well, OK, two bags of M&Ms.

We reaped the benefits of buying locally when Garden Ventures, which made our arbor, brought over a new copper leg and a blow-torch to remove the broken one. The little arbor is back up, though leaning slightly to the right.

That compensates for the red plum, which, sheared completely off on one side, now yaws to the left. It was pruned and painted to hide the gaping scars. Frankly, it looks pretty weird, but it will probably live. The squirrels have returned to the tree, although they seem pretty irritated that we haven't gotten the squirrel-accessible bird feeders back up.

With all this help, we elected—in the

spirit of "the show most go on"—to open our garden for last Sunday's tour. With that decision, the garden organizers holstered their weapons, and the friends who suspected we'd try to hit them up as replacements returned to answering their phones.

After The Great Tree Disaster, everything else fell into perspective. We hardly noticed that an army of slugs, mistaking our garden for Georgia, had marched through it, pillaging as they went. It didn't phase us that black spot descended like the blight. We pluckily plucked off the spotted leaves so everyone would think our roses were the exception.

We handled the weeds with equal aplomb, carefully digging the first hundred out by their roots, then, when no one was watching, snapping off the remaining thousand by their tough little heads. Never mind that they'd sprout back up the moment our backs were turned.

We were even philosophical about the rhododendron blossoms, which, glorious just a few days ago, now hung like sodden brown rags. We didn't even particularly mind that the garden tour would fall exactly one day after the peonies, camellias, lilacs and bulbs had dropped their last petals and just one day before the roses, iris, delphiniums and foxgloves popped open.

As for the holes, we just went out and bought very big, very expensive plants and wedged them in, hoping no one would notice those black plastic pots.

I'd like to say the tour went swimmingly. Well, it almost did, if you overlook the fact that Ralph the dachshund mistook the leg of the first visitor for a lamb chop.

MAY 28, 1993

INTO THE WOODS
My 10 favorite trees and shrubs — for now

L AST WEEK I BARED MY SOUL AND ADMITTED to some of my favorite perennials. I am thus exposed for the plebeian that I am (lady's mantle indeed) and as a hopeless romantic (how else to explain bleeding heart).

So here are my top 10 favorite woody plants. As with last week, it was a herculean task to keep this list to just 10. I kept thinking about all the other favorites and realized that the term "favorite" is not only relative, but also may be fleeting. Next week or next month, I could be in the thrall of some other plant. Still, these below have stood the test of time.

• *Acer palmatum* 'Butterfly': A Northwest garden without a Japanese maple is, well, almost like a Japanese garden without a Japanese maple. Because we have a soil-borne fungus in our neighborhood that attacks maples, I am limited to growing my maples in containers. The lightness and delicacy of this cultivar are ideal for a pot. It has deeply dissected leaves edged with pink and cream, and truly they do flutter like a cloud of butterflies. (small tree)

• *Callicarpa bodinieri* var. *giraldii* 'Profusion': I still remember the first time I saw the stunning purple berries in a holiday wreath. I had to rush out and get a beautyberry immediately. The berries live up to the plant's common name, not just for their color but also for their shimmering opalescent quality. (shrub)

• *Clematis texensis* 'Etoile Rose': With so many gorgeous kinds of clematis to choose from, I found it almost impossible to name a favorite. I love them all but slightly favor the varieties with nodding, lilylike flowers. Some say the flowers on 'Etoile Rose' resemble tulips. (vine)

- *Cornus controversa* 'Variegata': This gorgeous dogwood has variegated leaves and tiered branches that grow in horizontal layers; thus it is called the "wedding cake" tree. The pagoda dogwood, *Cornus alternifolia* 'Argentea,' is a smaller look-alike and nearly as beautiful. (tree)

- *Cotinus* 'Grace': All smoke bushes have spectacular foliage, especially the purple-leaved varieties. However, to my eye, 'Grace' outshines them all because of the translucence of its leaves, which are heavenly when backlit by the sun. It's hard to describe the foliage color, sort of blue-green with a wash of wine. (shrub)

- *Daphne odora*: The sweet scent of early-blooming daphne is the perfume of promise. It's the promise that gardening season really has arrived, and winter is on the wane. Just one sprig in a small vase can lift one's spirits immeasurably. (shrub)

- *Hamamelis* x *intermedia* 'Pallida': I can't imagine a garden without a witch hazel, because I can't imagine getting through winter without its cheerful yellow flowers and sweet scent. And, oh my, the golden leaves in autumn are almost as spectacular as the winter flowers. (shrub)

- *Hydrangea aspera* (aka *H. villosa*): This is the queen of hydrangeas, tall and vase-shaped so it politely doesn't crowd its neigh-

A purple Cotinus—*not 'Grace' but still gorgeous. In the foreground is* Spiraea thunbergii *'Ogon.'*

bors too much. The leaves are velvety, and the flat purple flowers have a smoky quality that gives the shrub an aura of mystery. It's also wonderfully long-blooming. (shrub)

- *Rosa* 'Sally Holmes': Here's a rose that blooms repeatedly and profusely and is highly resistant to black spot. Need I say more? (shrub)

- *Spiraea japonica* 'Goldmound': This spirea is a common old girl, but there's nothing better for a reliable glow of golden color that won't outgrow its space. I just wish the flowers were white, not pink.

MARCH 30, 2006

Part 8

THE DULCY TOUCH

❧

I get all squishy from reader letters,
especially the ones that start out, "I feel I know you."
They make my heart sing.

Hide flashbacks to the innocence of childhood among the flowers. They'll delight you still.

WORKING FROM MEMORY

Experiences shape the gardens we plant

SOMETHING ABOUT WINTER MAKES ME INTRO-spective about gardening. Maybe it's the fact that I can't actually garden, so that forces me to think about it more. Lately, it seems that memories have been piling up, and it occurs to me that a garden is very much about memories.

Some will have shaped you positively, and others not so positively. For example, to this day, I detest ice plant because we had it in our parking strip, and every time you stepped out of a car, you felt it squish under your feet.

The ice plant should tell you I grew up in California. I recall my mother tending her roses and camellias, which she took great pride in. Given that we had hard adobe soil and intense heat, the camellias were in pots under a lath-covered patio. The idea of a camellia growing in the ground was unheard of, just as the idea that geraniums had to be in pots seemed strange when I moved to the Northwest. We'd had a year-round hedge of geraniums around the house.

My mother didn't focus on the "garden," but rather on those specific plants. In those days, the 1950s, none of our neighbors really had gardens. They had backyards, which were dominated by grass, barbecues (the real brick deals) and swimming pools. The lawn mower was king.

I don't remember too many specific flowers from my childhood, but some memories are associated with distaste. I had an aunt who cultivated dahlias and didn't like chil-dren. Visits to her home were unpleasant because she was always warning me not to touch things. It took me years to appreciate dahlias. Conversely, I adore calla lilies because a huge clump grew next to my grand-father's back door, and I adored him.

I detested, and still do, those horizontal junipers that were ubiquitous in the neigh-borhood. They were terribly scratchy when you were trying to retrieve your softball. On the other hand, I loved the hollyhocks that grew along my best friend's back fence. They seemed so romantic. For many years, I tried to grow them here, but our soil tends to be too rich for them to be successful. Now I con-tent myself with a lovely watercolor of holly-hocks hanging in my bedroom.

My first foray as a kid into gardening was in a little plot behind the garage. I didn't know anything about compost, so noth-ing much grew in the hard adobe ex-cept radishes and tomatoes, which collected disgusting, fat worms. I really don't like to eat tomatoes all that much, but I faith-fully plant them each year because the scent of their leaves fills me with such sweet nos-talgia.

Another scent that fills me with memo-ries is the aroma of burning leaves. Each fall, my father and all the neighbors would rake up the leaves and burn them in little piles. It was a rite of autumn.

While we didn't have slugs, we did have lizards. One day our cleaning lady was dust-ing my puppet theater, and a lizard sprang out and ran down her blouse. She ran into the street screaming and waving her arms, and all the neighbors thought she was quite

> *In those days, the 1950s, none of our neighbors really had gardens.*

mad. We laughed about this for years. Guilt-
ily, of course.

Somehow, all of these snippets from the
past must shape one's garden as an adult, so
I've often wondered how my dry, barbecue-
dominated backyard fits in. I think it helped
that I loved books, and children's books in
those days were always filled with illustrations of English-style gardens, such as *The
Tale of Peter Rabbit* when I was younger and
The Secret Garden when I was older.

The first time I became aware of a garden as such, rather than as a backyard, is
when we began visiting my mother's friend
Holly, who lived in the moist Bay Area. She
had no lawn, but rather gravel paths that
meandered through shrubs. There were a lot
of fuchsias, and I used to love to pop the centers open. I always did it sneakily because I
suspected I wasn't supposed to.

Somewhere around the fuchsia-popping
time, the idea of a garden began to germinate. By the time I was grown up and we
bought our first house, it was because of the
two gorgeous white birches out front.

DECEMBER 8, 2005

✤

HERE SHE IS, GNOMES AND ALL
I'll tell you no lies

RECENTLY, AT ONE OF MY FAVORITE NURSER-
ies, the proprietor remarked that he
had heard that I didn't like any plant unless it was "bone hardy." I didn't know quite
how to take the fact that I have been the subject of some gossip.

But I've learned that when you have a
choice between being irritated, confused or
amused, it usually works out best if you check
the amused box. I decided I had arrived in
some small way if I was the subject of gossip
in the nursery trade.

Like most good gossip, this little tidbit
about me was a tiny bit screwed up. I suspect
that it arose from a crabby column I did last
August. I wrote about watching young, pre-
sumably new gardeners walk out of nurseries with pricey shrubs such as bougainvillea
and tibouchina.

I don't mind tender plants, and I applaud

> *A garden should be fun, and for
> some of us, fun is a chance to be
> unrestrained and silly.*

experimentation. What concerned me is that
no one warned these green gardeners that
their plants were tender and would need protection. Nurseries, after all, don't have an
"annuals" section for shrubs.

Of course, if you are opinionated, and I
can't imagine anyone who gardens not being
opinionated, you are going to be the subject
of gossip. I don't mind being gossiped about,
but I would like everyone to get it straight.
Therefore, I am going to give you some guide-
posts to my idiosyncrasies.

• I believe chocolate is one of the great gardening tools.

• It's true that I have expressed fantasies
  about Harrison Ford, but I've lost interest
  ever since he left his wife and has been running around with skinny starlets. However,
  if he agreed to put in an hour or so of weeding each week, I might reconsider.

Whimsy in the garden. You know you love it.

• I am no fan of pink flamingoes and have been known to be quite rude on the subject. On the other hand, I have a soft spot in my heart for garden gnomes. I realize there is no logic to this, so don't try to figure it out.

• I do my best garden planning in the bathtub.

• I have no horticultural credentials, and you shouldn't listen to me if you want to know what to do. However, I believe I perform a service by making plenty of mistakes and then telling you what not to do.

• No one should ever write to me asking what I would recommend for keeping cats out of their garden. I have been spectacularly unsuccessful at this and am now the mother of an embarrassing number of cats and one dog.

• I agree that one should learn botanical Latin, but I don't have much patience with Latin snobs who look down on people who don't know Latin names. I think most gardeners will learn the Latin they need to know at exactly their own pace, which is the right pace for them.

• I agree with the experts who say gardens should have discipline and consistency. For example, one should use either all terracotta pots or all glazed. One should select ornaments with restraint. One should give the garden a focus and a color theme. I believe all these things, and yet I practice almost none of them. It's because I believe one thing even more: A garden should be fun, and for some of us, fun is a chance to be unrestrained and silly.

• Oh, and one more thing. There is no truth to the rumor that I am a chubby redhead. I don't know where those *Oregonian* people got that picture. I really am tall, blond and willowy. So get the story straight.

MAY 2, 2002

RAIN ON MY PARADE
You might think a columnist's work is easy, but . . .

HOMES & GARDENS' 10TH ANNIVERSARY reminds me of just how long I've been writing a garden column. Some people might think that writing such a column is all sunshine and roses. They would be very wrong. For one thing, the intrepid columnist faces no end of challenges.

No. 1 challenge: Demands are placed on you. When I first started writing about gardening, my editor looked at me earnestly and said, "Try to say at least one educational thing in each column."

Oh, I do try to hit the occasional educational note, but there are times when all you want to do is babble about how the sun is shining and what utter joy you feel because little plants are poking up, as if it's never happened before. Other times, it's gray and raining, and one needs to bare one's angst-ridden soul. It is difficult, at such times, to remember to say, "Be sure your compost is cooked before you put it on."

No. 2 challenge: Husband looks over shoulder. At times my husband has peered over my shoulder and noted that he doesn't see anything "educational." "What," I say, rather defensively, "you don't think that writing about The Perp is educational?" After all, she is an extraordinary cat.

No. 3 challenge: You are expected to know stuff. Not infrequently I have people wave a plastic bag at me. It usually has something dead and moldy in it that rather resembles ancient plant life that was buried with the mummies.

I am asked to either identify the mystery plant or identify the mystery disease that caused the plant to die. It is very sad to see the look in their eyes when I tell them I can't help. It is the same look of disgust and disappointment that kids get when they realize Santa is a sham.

No. 4 challenge: It is assumed you have a world-class garden. Someone once described Ringo Starr as being one of the top 1,000 drummers in England. I have always loved that description. So, I like to think that I have a garden that may be in the top 1,000 in Portland.

I am not being unduly modest. I am not a neatnik, so my garden is not pristine. I love to experiment, so my garden always has spots that are "works in progress." Restraint is not one of my virtues, so I have too many ornaments. I have no discipline, so my garden style is borderline hodgepodge.

Ah, but here's my defense. How could I report on all those mistakes if I didn't do the actual research?

No. 5 challenge: trying not to get all soppy over reader mail. I get all squishy from reader letters, especially the ones that start out, "I feel I know you." They make my heart sing.

I love the fact that they come in cards with flowers, pictures of gardens and pets and sweet sentiments. Oh, dear readers, I feel I know you too. Sniffle.

No. 6 challenge: facing tough questions. The most frequent are a) where's Doug the Wonder Boy; b) how much time do you spend in the garden; and c) how many cats do you have?

The answers are a) I would love to have people meet DTWB, but I don't invite him to

Cats are an essential to rank in the top 1,000 gardens in Portland.

garden events because he does, after all, have a life with his ladylove, Erica, and his new dog, Flora; b) I don't know because the time I spend is so erratic. There are times (spring planting season) when I'll stay out so long that I need a flashlight. Then days can go by with no garden activity; and c) too many.

No. 7 challenge: keeping the cats off the keyboard. I would write more about this, but someone has mentioned, rather snarkily, that this is not "educational."

MARCH 15, 2007

~⨯~

BARE FACTS

When 'pretty in pink' takes on a whole new meaning

LET ME SAY RIGHT OFF THAT BEING A CALEN-dar girl has never been among my secret fantasies.

But I had not counted on the drive of TV garden specialist Anne Jaeger, who talked me and others into posing for a calendar to raise money for a special cause, which you may have read about in "Homes & Gardens of the Northwest." Our Garden, a nonprofit, enables the inner city's neediest children to grow food and flowers and learn about nature, while earning the self-esteem that comes with accomplishment.

How can you say "no" to all that? I didn't. But then I started to worry. Anne had indicated that it would be one of those "bare it" calendars, but, she assured me, it would all be done in "perfect taste." In my mind, after a certain age the

> *In my mind, after a certain age the words "naked" and "perfect taste" don't belong in the same sentence.*

words "naked" and "perfect taste" don't belong in the same sentence.

She told me to think about how I'd like to pose, so I spent the summer thinking about it. I imagined twirling a parasol (beach umbrella-size, mind you) with only my head and legs showing. I saw myself standing in the middle of some shrubbery, never mind what I was mashing, with only my head showing.

You see, I am one of those people who declare they would never appear in a bathing suit, let alone in anything less. I would set off alarms if I were to go into Victoria's Secret. I'm not complaining, just stating the facts.

Anne told me I'd be Miss March and that I should think about what I do in the garden that time of year. Well, I'm trying to get everything planted in March, so I end up working late, sometimes by flashlight. When they came to shoot me, I was ready for them. I appeared in my flannel nightshirt, hat and boots. Talk about a thing of beauty!

About the only skin showing is a bit of leg below the knees and above the boots. The only bare babe on the March page is The Perp, who crawled into my lap just before the photo was taken and who looks quite lush and Rubenesque.

During the photo shoot, Doug the Wonder Boy appeared, and I tried to persuade them to use him, as he is by far the more decorative one in my garden. I was surprised they didn't, because some of the ladies attending the shoot were definitely eyeing him. (He has a girlfriend, now, so no inquiries.)

Oh yes, that's another thing about a photo shoot. It comes with an entourage. They are there to help "art direct" and tell you how lovely you look, even when you have toppled off your stool and have weeds in your hair and mud on your cheeks.

At one point, they tried to coax me into a shot that would make me appear naked. (Oh, I can hardly say that horrid word.) We pulled down my nightgown so it was under my arms. I stood against a high hedge and raised some pruning shears over it so that from the other side you could just see my head and bare arms.

I felt the nightie starting to slip and, in a panic, pressed myself into the hedge so there'd be no chance of spotting an errant piece of pink flesh. Later, I noticed blood running down my legs from all the scratches. I hadn't even felt them at the time.

So that is why, when you see the calendar, now available in local stores, full of lovely people standing in waterfalls, emerging from ponds, entwined with vines, covered with posies and all sorts of other poses suggesting various stages of "perfect taste" nakedness, there will be one aberration: Miss March is definitely the shy one.

OCTOBER 27, 2005

MEASURING TIME PETAL BY PETAL
Blooms and books that delight

GARDENING COMES TO THE FORE IN SOME OF the strangest ways and in some of the strangest places. Earlier this month, I spent a week in the hospital, and one would have thought that gardening would have been on the back burner. But no, it was amazing how it kept popping up.

I first noticed it because I was irritated about missing the lilacs. That's when I realized how much I'd come to reference time in terms of what blooms when. Late April, early May belongs to lilacs. I felt downright cheated to miss out on this year's show.

Next came bouquets from friends and colleagues at work. I was delighted because, believe it or not, in all my life, I've hardly ever

gotten flowers. I think people are a bit afraid to give flowers to someone who writes about them. I mentioned this to my friend Lynn, who brought me a May basket, and she said it was like the fact that no one invites her husband to dinner. Her husband, Dennis Baker, is the chef and owner of one of Portland's finest restaurants, Cafe des Amis.

Most of the bouquets were from florists, and they were splendid. But the favorites (the nurses certainly thought so) were bouquets picked by friends out of their own gardens. It was interesting to see how these personal bouquets reflected the people who brought them. Dear Lynn's May basket was full of bluebells, lilacs, a rhodie, and other assorted old-fashioned flowers in blues and violets. Lynn is a romantic who read me poetry but scoffed at the *People* magazine by my bedside.

Denise, on the other hand, is an exotic beauty whose self-picked bouquet reflected her love of vivid colors and dramatic shapes. It included some Rembrandt tulips in purple and peach, accented with pieris foliage glowing a rosy flamingo in the top leaves, backed by leaves in pure chartreuse. I never thought I could love a pieris, but now maybe I have to have one.

One thing I did learn about hospital bouquets is that arrangements with lots of lilies are not popular with the staff. In the garden, their scent is sublime, but in a small hospital room, the scent can be cloying. As I walked along the halls to build up strength, I noticed that the bouquets with lilies all seemed to be sitting on carts outside the rooms.

Doctors, nurses and aides came in to chat about gardening. They were particularly taken

> *The cats, of course, acted like, "Dulcy who?"*

with my flannel nightie decorated in a pattern of seed packets and gardening implements, a gift from two friends. You can imagine how sophisticated I looked, but at least it did close in the back, which is more than you can say for hospital gowns. The little hospital booties were an especially winsome touch. I am sure that I looked like a giant Mrs. Gnome as I trundled up and down the hall for my exercise.

On my way to the hospital, I grabbed a stack of books, and one was an old favorite, *Green Thoughts: A Writer in the Garden* by Eleanor Perenyi. Although it is more than 20 years old, it wears well, and I highly recommend it for someone looking for good bedtime reading. (It's now available in paperback.)

Each chapter is an essay unto itself, so it's perfect to be read in bits and pieces. Perenyi is unabashedly opinionated, which I find rather charming. If you want proof of the pudding, just grab the book in a store or library and scan the chapter called "Help." It will give you a great feel for the rest of the book.

When I returned home, I couldn't believe my garden after just a week. Who put the steroids in the soil? The daylilies and hostas, which had just begun to poke up, were huge. The rhodies were in full, exuberant bloom. I've never really been a fan of rhodies, but I may be about to change my mind.

How can one not like a plant that just explodes in a glory of welcome-home celebration? I mean, they were almost as happy to see me as my dog was. The cats, of course, acted like, "Dulcy who?"

MAY 29, 2003

SPOT REMOVAL
Relieve your lawn of dogs' bad habits

THE PERP HAS BEEN QUITE FULL OF HERself after having had her picture in the paper recently. Hector, our dog, is jealous and has gone into a sulk. As he points out so aptly, cat is not God spelled backwards.

He does not understand that staying under the radar is a good thing. Cats are excoriated for leaving little deposits in people's yards, stalking birds and chewing grass so they can run into the house and purge themselves on your best Oriental rug.

Dogs have gotten off relatively lightly in the PR department. But they do pose problems in the garden that must be dealt with. The worst is digging, and since I've never had a serious digger, I can offer no firsthand advice in that department.

But I do have plenty of experience with brown spots in the lawn and the occasional dead spot in the hedge or at the bottom of a shrub.

The best fix for that, I'm told, is training your dog to relieve itself at a proper spot away from the lawn. However, to some dogs, including ours, "training" is a four-letter word. They appear perfectly intelligent, but comprehend only the word "spoiling." So I decided to do a little research on the subject.

I read that you can prevent a brown spot from forming if you pour a bucket of cold water over the spot immediately after the dog has relieved itself. This probably will work if your dog has a routine and goes out about the same time each day. But it seems to me if you are going to be hanging around with a bucket of water at a certain time, you might as well be hanging around with a leash, which you can use to guide the dog from the lawn.

Hector and his ladylove, Flora.

Unfortunately, once you have spots on your lawn from dog urine, there is nothing you can do to get rid of them short of reseeding. You'll need to dig out the dead grass roots and fill the spot with new soil, rake it, then seed.

Then keep it well watered until the turf is established. Given that dogs express themselves daily, this seems a lot of work, and I'd recommend living with the spots unless you are having a wedding or an open garden—not that an open garden has ever led me to do that much work. Also, now that I think about it, training does not seem like such a bad idea.

I worry more about shrubs and hedges because they can't be easily reseeded. If the lower branches of a shrub have turned brown, you should immediately suspect Rover.

There are several dog-away products on the market, and opinions vary from "guaranteed to work" to "may give a measure of protection." If you go in that direction, be sure to read the labels carefully to make sure they do not contain stuff that you do not want to spray in your yard. If they say, "Keep out of the reach of tiny children, old grannies, and heirs who are eyeing you strangely," you probably don't want them.

Other recommendations I came across seem

> *Hector, our dog, is jealous and has gone into a sulk.*

to make sense. For example, several books advised putting a collar of something prickly, such as barberry branches, rose branches or holly leaves around trees and against shrubs that a dog frequents. This sounds a lot less silly than standing around with a bucket of water.

I also put a pot of flowers up against the spot in the hedge that Hector liked to mark, and so far that has worked. The bald spot hasn't recovered, but the pot hides it, and it also seems to deter our dog from using this spot.

Some people swear by putting out mothballs, garlic and freshly ground pepper to keep dogs away from favorite plants. I even found one book that recommended planting rue around tomatoes to keep dogs from eating your harvest. This is the first time I have ever heard of a dog eating tomatoes.

Oh well, when I was a kid we had a very fat dachshund that would lie under the canary's cage to catch the lettuce when it fell, so I guess tomatoes aren't that far-fetched.

MARCH 25, 2004

❦

MULTIPLE LISTING
Notes on scraps of paper mingle with weeds in my pockets

I'M A LIST MAKER. I WALK AROUND MY garden making lists of things that need to be done. Then I either lose the lists or leave them somewhere where they get so rain-soaked that I can't read them.

Occasionally I come across a scrap of paper with one of my lists. It will have anything from heavy-duty assignments, such as taking out the dead section of hedge, to lightweight items like removing the price stickers on a new pot.

I can't believe I've put that off. My mother used to drive me crazy because her pots still had price tags on them. I think every woman realizes at some moment with utter shock that she has become her mother. This price-tag thing is just further evidence for me.

My lists never seem to be complete, and the "must do's" on them never seem to all get done. A typical list will include such items as planting the mystery plant (another lost tag), moving the big urn to the front garden,

> *There is always a hose that leaks and a nozzle that doesn't fit tightly enough.*

thinning the camellia, straightening all the Pisa pots (as in leaning) and fixing the sprinkler head.

The last one has become a staple of my lists because there's always a sprinkler or sprinkler component that is broken, just as there is always a hose that leaks and a nozzle that doesn't fit tightly enough so that when you water, it runs down and soaks your front or squirts you in the face.

I once visited a 16th-century garden in Italy that had a grotto with tiny water outlets in the floor. The caddish prince who owned the place would invite his lady guests to walk into the grotto, whereupon he'd trip a device that would spray jets of water up their skirts. My watering apparatus comes with the same low comedy but without the prince. But I digress.

Sometimes I start lists of what's in bloom,

with the idea that I'll do this weekly. Alas, I never follow through, and by the time the next year rolls around, I can't remember what blooms when.

A much better idea would be to go around and take photos of the garden so that later you'd actually see what blooms when. My husband has a new iPhone with a camera, and I'd hoped he might do this. But he is too busy photographing our pets, the Ellises' new dog, and even the dog of the neighbor who is moving. My garden and I will have to get in line for pictures.

I also make lists of plants to buy but invariably forget to take them with me to nurseries. Once there, I fall victim to cunning displays of plants that were never on my list. It is not unusual to come home with a carful of plants, none of which was planned.

Still, I am compelled to make lists. If I didn't, I'd forget everything. That's not just because I'm growing old; I've always been that way. I make notes of things to remember, then stick them in my pocket. At the end of the day, I empty my pockets and find my little notes, another pen that has migrated home from the office and some scrunched-up weeds I've pulled as I walked around the garden.

This can be embarrassing. I'm constantly pulling out a tissue or a pen at the office only to have disgusting limp weeds flutter out.

What's even more embarrassing is that, on the day of our first open garden, I glanced over the shoulder of the person I was talking to and spotted, glaring almost like a neon sign, a price tag on a pot. Somewhere up there my mother is chortling.

JUNE 19, 2008

NETTLED
Gardening's perennial peeves

JUST WHEN SUMMER WAS AT ITS PEAK AND I was a veritable force of nature, spade in one hand and slug scissors in the other, the blow struck. I woke up one morning with a compressed nerve. An MRI and neck surgery followed quickly, and suddenly there I was, at the height of gardening season, laid up.

The cats were delighted, since they like nothing better than to cuddle up to a warm body on the hottest days of the year. But I was not delighted, and while I did not sink into depression, I did slither into a foul mood.

It seemed, therefore, an appropriate time to take off the green-tinted glasses and admit there are some gripes I have about gardening.

First off, we're not even going to talk about slugs because slugs, along with black-spotted roses, belong in the Garden Gripes Hall of Fame.

If you really want to know the critters that annoy me most, they are not slugs or raccoons or even fish-spearing cranes. My vote for the most annoying creature goes to aphids. Slugs may devour selected plants and leave slimy trails, but they are limited in their spread and don't climb trees. I don't have to drive to work with a windshield coated with slug slime.

You might expect weeds to come next on my pet peeve list, but I take weeds in stride as part of gardening. What really irritates me is errant grass that jumps out of its appointed section and moves into flowerbeds and into the spaces between paving stones. Grass, in my opinion, is far more insidious than weeds when it's in a place you don't want it to be, which it often is.

Invasive plants in general are a pet peeve, but I tend to wax and wane on what's invasive. Some self-sowers are welcome. Foxgloves, for example, distribute themselves here and there artfully and mercifully in limited numbers. But others, and right now I'm looking at a forest of *Verbena bonariensis*, just don't know when enough is enough.

At the other end of the spectrum are those relatively rare and expensive plants you order that, once planted, decide to become even rarer by disappearing. I get the feeling that they have decided my garden is too plebian for them to stay.

And while I'm griping about plants, I have to say I can't abide plants that flop, since I find staking a particularly tedious job and never can seem to get it right. By the time I remember to stake a plant, it's grown so much that I create a mangled mess that resembles an Alexander Calder sculpture, which is OK if you're dealing with metal but is decidedly unnatural in plant material.

Then there are the plants that appear to be in glowing health on top but begin to get brown and shriveled leaves at their base. You know what I mean if you have certain clematis. I really think a plant should have the decency to either live or die, but not drive you crazy with this in-between state.

In the nonorganic category, there's no contest. Sprinklers are at the top of my gripe list. We may have put a man on the moon and invented the wonder bra, but our technology apparently has not come up with an oscillating sprinkler that works for more than

Persicaria bistorta, *invasive, but oh, so sweet.*

one season, if that. I have tried the cheap ones and the expensive ones, and it's all the same. In no time at all, they forget the meaning of rotation.

Close behind come the famous kinking hoses that throw more elbows than Tonya Harding in one of her boxing matches. Hoses seem to come in two models—those that kink and those that don't, and price doesn't seem to dictate which is which.

I abhor power devices, any noisy devices, that go off at 5:30 on Saturday evening just when you are settling in for a barbecue with friends. Such devices should come with switches that do not allow them to operate at certain hours.

I am also annoyed to buy a new garden book and find it's one that I bought 10 or so years ago. If publishers are going to repackage a book in soft cover—or a new hard cover—they ought to have the decency to say it's a reprint.

So there, I feel better getting all that out. But what I really, really, really hate is being laid up so that I can't garden. Fortunately this is temporary, and I should be in a better mood next week.

AUGUST 5, 2004

THEME PARKS
Names ground gardens in tradition

EUROPEAN GARDENERS HAVE A PENCHANT FOR naming parts of their gardens: the Dell, the Italian Garden (only if you're in England), the Lime Walk, the White Garden, the Tea Pavilion, the Secret Garden, the Meditation Terrace, the Grotto, the Long Border and so on.

Whether this is affectation or simply affection is, I guess, in the eyes of the beholder.

Lately, I notice that Doug the Wonder Boy and I have fallen into a pattern of referring to parts of the garden by name. For example, there's a little area in front of the back shed where nothing used to grow because of shade from two Japanese maples. We paved it, planted ferns and woodsy things, and threw in a little stone basin, and now we refer to it as the Zen Garden.

My friend Denise was over the other day and asked if we'd gotten anything new, and I mentioned a little metal sculpture in the Zen Garden. What's that, she asked, and I had to admit I didn't know. The name Zen had just come about haphazardly because somehow it was a peaceful place with a slightly Asian air that I associated with the word Zen.

Now that I am forced to look it up, it turns out that Zen is an ancient Buddhist movement that, at its most basic, emphasizes enlightenment through meditation. I can't say I've ever stopped to meditate in this space, and I'm afraid that the only enlightenment I've received there is that one of the Japanese maples is dying. But still, Zen Garden is a nicer name than the more descriptive Dying Tree Garden.

Is it because we Americans lack romance or a sense of fantasy that we don't name parts of our gardens? Perhaps we're too practical. Somehow the Soft Drink Garden or Martini Place doesn't have the ring of Tea Garden. Dog Poop Alley, the Slug Walk and the Weedery lack a certain charm, realistic though they be.

Doug and I do have other little names that have stuck. A boggy area is known as the Minor Lakes. There's another place with bad soil that we've filled with container plants and now refer to as the Pot Garden. That, of course, could lead to a serious misunderstanding, so perhaps we should rename it.

The worst part of my garden is an area of deep and dry shade under some huge and messy water-slurping trees. Nothing really does well there. A couple of years ago, I stuck a bunch of blue pottery mushrooms throughout the area and took to calling it the Blue Mushroom Wood. I even, Lord help me, fell for a little gnome and put him there.

Unfortunately, the new name did not make the place any more interesting, so now I am thinking of just calling it the Dead Zone. On the other hand, we've also taken to calling Doug's vegetable garden the French Vegetable Garden since it is overrun by nasturtiums, and that seems to give some justification for its condition.

Sometimes a name can indeed work some magic. There's a fabulous garden outside Portland that, as you meander into the woods, has an area overrun by ferns. Instead of trying to clear it, the owners just refer to it as the Fernery.

Similarly, in England, I visited a garden that had a section called the Equisetum Glade. Equisetum, or horsetail, is an obnoxious weed that is very difficult to eradicate, but is, in a fernlike way, pretty. So simply

> *Simply naming these spaces what they are seems to make peace with nature.*

naming these spaces what they are seems to make peace with nature.

Of course, a name doesn't always work the appropriate magic. I knew someone who let his front lawn just grow and took to referring to it as the Meadow. This didn't work, at least with the neighbors.

AUGUST 12, 2004

❧

REMEMBERING HECTOR
The garden feels empty without our little dog

IT IS HARD TO WRITE ABOUT A HOLE. WE HAVE a hole in our hearts. We have a hole in our home, and we have a hole in our garden.

Our little dog Hector is gone. He was just short of 13 years old. We'd gotten him from the Humane Society when he was 2. They described him as a "special needs" dog, and indeed he was. He needed a lot of love and reassurance, and we were happy to supply both.

His death was not unexpected. He'd been diagnosed with bladder cancer in late winter, and we were told there was nothing we could do. We watched him closely so we could enjoy him as long as possible. But there was the inevitable morning when he awakened whimpering in pain and had to be put to sleep.

What I wasn't prepared for are all the holes he left behind. Wherever I went in the garden, he'd be there following me. When

Hector, holding court in the "bus stop."

we came home, he'd go wild with ecstasy at our reappearance, whether we'd been gone half an hour or two weeks.

For 11 years, he barked at the mailman, so we always knew when the mail arrived. I never knew him to snap or growl, but he'd sit at our front gate and bark whenever anyone passed by or entered our premises. Once they were in, he'd quiet down.

No one took him seriously. Neighbors would walk by with dogs the size of horses, and little Hector would bark ferociously—on the other side of the gate, mind you. The neighbors would roll their eyes in amusement and say, "Oh Hector," and the big dogs would roll their eyes in what I could only presume was disdain.

> *Hector was the perfect garden dog.*

Hector was the perfect garden dog. He never did his business on the lawn. He didn't trample plants, and he didn't lie in mud. But he did love to run in circles on the lawn and to chase "the boys" (cats Wilbur and Orville) back and forth across the lawn.

It may be all the rage these days to say get rid of your lawn, but I'm not in that camp. While big lawns may be out, I do believe you need a bit of flat green play area if you have young children or dogs. Cats can do just fine with a jungle of a garden, but dogs and kids need open space to dash about and play catch and, should they have tails, chase them in circles.

We will, in due time, get another dog or, as I sometimes mention, a pair of dogs. With that, my husband looks nervous, and I explain how they'd keep each other company the way Orville and Wilbur do. He's not convinced and has laid down some requirements:

A new dog must be small, so as not to intimidate the cats; short-haired; laid-back enough for a couple of old geezers (no Frisbee dogs for us); not yappy; and reasonably adoring.

At this point, I don't care if the dog does you-know-what on the lawn, tramples plants or lies in the mud. It's even OK if he plops his front feet in the water dish and then walks all over the just-mopped kitchen. I won't mind his snoring in my ear either, but I prefer a dog that is not an escape artist, because it is tiresome trying to find and plug up all the openings under our fences.

He, she or they (if I get my way) will be characters in their own right, not simply replacements for Hector. Hector was special. I considered getting a dog rose (*Rosa canina*) in his honor, but it turns out this is a sprawling and undistinguished rose; Hector deserved better. So his ashes now repose under a lovely dogwood (*Cornus controversa* 'Variegata') at the northeast corner of the house. It seems appropriate; the mailman has to pass that tree.

JUNE 26, 2008

IN A CHILD'S EYE
Forget 'gardening'—frogs, fairies and secret places draw kids in

IF YOU WANT TO ENTERTAIN KIDS IN YOUR garden, you need two things—frogs and fairies. Little boys are fascinated by the frogs, and little girls look for fairies.

I love to have kids visit my garden. They look at it from a different perspective than

Where fairies play . . .

adults. And, they always end up gathered around the pond, probably the least kid-friendly part of my garden. I sit there tensely watching them crouch over the water and worry they'll tumble in.

Meanwhile, their parents seem to have blissfully tuned this all out. I expect it's their survival mechanism. So far, no one's fallen in, although visiting dogs do like to jump in. That's one of the first things that Flora, Doug the Wonder Guy's dog, did. Last weekend, Ebby, a part black Lab, took the plunge. So far, Ernie, the world's most adorable dog according to my unbiased view, hasn't shown any tendency to be a swimmer. But I digress.

> *I may be jaded, but I still believe in fairies that dance in the moonlight.*

This is about kids. They ask different questions than adults. They don't want to know what a particular plant is, unless it has really big leaves. Here are the top five questions I get from them: *How did the frogs get there? Why do you have so many plants? What is the plant with big leaves? What is your favorite plant? Do you have fairies?*

Whereas adults want to see a beautiful garden, kids prefer an "interesting" garden, or one that is interesting to them. They like arbors, or anything they can duck under or crawl through. They like a bit of lawn to run around on. They want a jungly area with big leaves and possibly (this from the boys) hidden dinosaurs. They adore secret places and discoveries.

I don't really know where the frogs come from. They just seem to appear every spring. Unfortunately, most are bullfrogs, which eat the baby fish and the little tree frogs. By summer's end, the bullfrogs will have disappeared, and I suspect that Orville and Wilbur have had a hand, or paw, in that. I don't like to think too deeply about this.

As for the fairies, I tell the little girls in their flowered dresses (they are the ones who ask about the fairies) that they only come out at night to dance in the moonlight. That seems to be as satisfactory an answer as any.

Most young children like being in the garden but are not yet interested in gardening. They see it as a chore, although there are exceptions. They like plants that grow quickly since immediate satisfaction is high on their lists. This is why sunflowers are favorites, and so too are pumpkins that they can carve their names on and watch grow into their very own Halloween jack-o'-lanterns.

But as for the chores, like weeding, well, you can't fool them. I don't know about boys, but all it takes is accidentally touching one giant earthworm to put a child, especially a child who wears flowered dresses, off gardening for years.

I know this for a fact, because I was one of those children with a worm-adverse disposition. I remember running in the house and washing my hands a zillion times to get the Mr. Worm slime off me. How odd that I should grow up to be so cavalier about snipping and stomping slugs and not particularly shocked upon finding the desiccated body of a bullfrog on the Oriental rug in the living room.

I may be jaded, but I still believe in fairies that dance in the moonlight.

JUNE 24, 2010

LUST-FREE FLORA
With a jampacked garden, I avoid plants with unwanted traits

OCCASIONALLY SOMEONE ASKS IF THERE ARE any plants that I don't like. Well, yes.

I don't like those old-fashioned yuccas that the Victorians planted in giant clumps on their lawns. But maybe that's because years ago our good-hearted cleaning lady brought us a huge container of the feathery flowers for our living room. We didn't want to hurt her feelings, so we lived with the dusty things for years while they kept shedding worse than our Himalayan cat Yeti, the one who never comes downstairs.

But essentially I like most plants, although for various reasons there are some that I avoid. My list below is not meant to dissuade you from trying these plants. But when your garden is as stuffed as mine, a person has to draw some lines.

So here is my list of undesirable categories. Remember, there are many cultivars of these basic plants that don't have problems. I even have an adorable variegated baby yucca in a pot now.

Lazy, floppy plants: I don't grow asters and daisies because they flop just as they are about to bloom, and it's hard to stake bushy plants. I'm having second thoughts about autumn sedum for that very reason.

Plants that die ungracefully: Some plants

The editing process demands that each plant justify its place in the garden.

bloom stunningly but fleetingly, and then you're left with the dying flower. Red-hot pokers (*Kniphofia*) are like that. One moment brilliant lemon or coral bloom, then the next you've got an ugly browning poker. The jury is still out on *Phlomis*, which has wonderful whorls of yellow around its stalks. Alas, they soon turn to dried brown ruffles.

Plants that need backbone: You know how there are some jobs you just hate, sometimes quite illogically? I hate staking. So no tall delphiniums. But I make an exception for tall lilies.

Blink-and-the-bloom-is-over plants: I went away for a week once just as some irises were about to bloom. By the time I came back, the bloom was over. I still love and have irises, but now choose varieties with longer bloom such as Japanese iris. Also, I will tolerate (doesn't that sound imperious?) short bloomers if they also have great foliage.

Plants that really insist on good drainage: Touchy, touchy. There is just so much effort you want to put into clay soil, and apparently I didn't do enough when I first dug my flowerbeds. I suspect that most of the plants I lost over the years were due to poor drainage, not winter temperatures. Were I 10 years younger, I might address this problem. But now I've gotten lazy and have the attitude that enough things grow here despite my inferior soil.

Plants that get the vapors: I have roses aplenty but only one hybrid tea, and she

> *When your garden is as stuffed as mine, a person has to draw some lines.*

('Julia Child') alas has black spot. But it's not just tea roses. My favorite English rose, 'Graham Thomas,' had to go. I also have an old clematis that may be dispatched, despite its prolific bloom, since it gets mildew every summer. And the lupine is long gone, since it is the world's greatest aphid magnet.

Plants with bad attitudes: Now I know that everyone west of the Cascades can grow beardtongue (*Penstemon*) with impunity. Still I try them every year. It's a war of wills.

Plants that cats eat: Never have been able to grow catmint (*Nepeta*). It's chewed to the nub before it's even out of the pot. Worse yet are some ornamental grasses that end up in a foamy puddle on my Oriental rug.

Plants that just plain dumped me: These are the heartbreakers. They wowed me for a season or two or three and then disappeared without even texting a "breakup" note. How could you, geum, crambe, foxgloves, and so many others that did so well in my younger days? I suspect they got swamped as more aggressive plants took over, and now they've run off to younger gardens. Who can blame them?

AUGUST 12, 2010

❧

OPEN TO ANXIETY
Anticipating guests is a mixed bag of fear, uncertainty . . . and chocolate

MY GARDEN WAS ONE OF SEVERAL GARDENS open for a recent fundraiser for our

The late lamented banana.

shows. I imagine that, at the moment of the Big Bang, cymbals clang, rockets burst and slugs dance 'round the maypole.

Unfortunately, I am always asleep when it happens.

But as the day drew near, it became obvious that, gasp, bare ground would still show its vulgar self. So off I dashed to nurseries to find plants to fill gaps. What this means is that when you bring them home, you plant them way too close so that later they will have to be moved, and you will wander about looking for a place to put the errant spreading plant. Intellectually, I understand that cramming in plants does not make for good garden design. Emotionally, I can't help myself.

I was not alone. Two Saturdays before the Big Event, my neighbor Rosemary, whose garden also was on the tour, called and whispered the desperate words "I need to go to a nursery." I understood perfectly, so off we went.

local school. I hope I can now get back to normal, because I spent the three or so weeks before the open garden in a demented state.

If you want to know, opening your garden is like being a stage actor. It doesn't matter how often you've played the role, you still get stage fright.

In the preceding month, I kept waiting for the Big Bang, that moment when all the plants bang together so that no bare ground

Cymbals clang, rockets burst and slugs dance 'round the maypole.

As the event neared, I became more obsessed. I had Doug the Wonder Boy haul out the potted plants from the greenhouse so that I could see what survived and what I had to fill in. I managed to plant and repot on a drippy Sunday, spilling potting soil and dead leaves all over the terrace that he had just power-washed the week before.

I became more unnerved. I bought a whirligig at a nursery that, at the moment, I thought quite charming. But then I wondered, after I got home, if it was Too Much. I tried to remember where I stored the great ornament a friend had given me for Christmas.

I cursed the rhododendrons across the back fence that, in the early May sunshine, had the effrontery to bloom too early so that the flowers would be brown and dying by the Great Day. I saw that the *Philadelphus* and *Styrax japonicus* were beginning to open their buds and the iris was starting to bloom, and fervently lectured them to hold off. I looked around the yard for a place to plant a conifer that I bought last fall, thinking it cute and fuzzy, only to read that it would grow 80 feet.

I lay in bed at night thinking about what I still needed to do in the garden. I made lists of plants I needed and went off to nurseries and bought plants that weren't on the list. I wrote down everything that needed to be done (tie up vines, stake lilies, wash pots, etc.), then wasted time on other projects that were more fun, such as buying new chairs for around the fire pit.

I ordered a new banana plant because mine had died a tragic death at the first hint of a temperature dip, but it didn't arrive in time. I put the by now very large angel's trumpet (*Brugmansia*) back on the terrace even though it looked as dead as the banana because, in the past, it has managed to rise like Lazarus.

As the event loomed, I could see no hint of life in the angel's trumpet, which perhaps had finally joined the angels. I bought a vine to twine itself about the plant and hide the dead branches. But the soil in the pot was too compacted to squeeze the vine in. I even threatened, to Doug's horror, to spray-paint the twiggy monstrosity blue.

During this time I discovered and became addicted to a new antidote to stress—chocolate-covered coffee ice cream bars. If our local grocery store doesn't run out of those treats, I can probably manage to open my garden again.

MAY 25, 2006

❧

THE WRECKING CREW
Critters in the garden force us to make trade-offs

ERNIE HAS A GIRLFRIEND. This has repercussions for our garden. Ernie, who weighs all of 12 pounds, is in love with Flora, a big girl of about 65 pounds. She's Doug the Wonder Guy's yellow Lab, and she loves little Ernie back with all her doggy heart.

This is basically platonic love in the sense that both have had their discreet surgeries. Flora and Ernie spend hours running in circles over the back lawn, cutting through flowerbeds and tussling and slobbering all over each other.

As a result, our back lawn, put in new just last year, is a mess. There are bare muddy spots throughout, and the grass is thin. It should come back with spring, but not if two dogs continue to trample it. Also, now that flowers are poking up, there's the danger that plants will get mauled too.

Doug offered to keep Flora in the car when he comes over. But I can't bear the idea of crushing the doggy joy. So this is not the year of the "perfect" garden, an elusive goal I have never attained even without the doggy issue. At least this year I will have an excuse.

Critters and gardens have always forced us to make trade-offs. Some people can't stand cats in their gardens, and I can understand why. But for me, the companionship from my furry pals Orville and Wilbur as I dabble in my garden trumps everything. Each spring, a pair of ducks land in our pond to conduct their courtship.

After a few weeks, they fly away. Meantime, they do foul the pond and probably gulp some of our fish, and I'm always threatening to chase them away. But so far I haven't had the heart to break up the romance.

I can't even consider an electrified fence around the pond to keep raccoons away for fear of hurting an animal. So, instead of gorgeous koi, I have plain old goldfish. The pet store calls them "feeder" fish for a reason.

Most of us like to attract certain creatures to our gardens, especially birds, but that also involves choices. We used to put seed in bird feeders but stopped when our cats brought in a couple of presents. We've made a choice not to lure them to our garden for their own protection.

There are squirrels aplenty, and we delight in their antics. The cats show little interest in squirrels, although last year Wilbur did waddle into the house with a mole. He also dispatched a bullfrog. I'm not sure this is a bad thing. I prefer to think of it as nature taking its course, although I do not want to witness the event.

Lately, I am meeting more gardeners who are keeping chickens so they can have eggs. Part of it is the desire to grow one's own food and have fresh eggs, although before long the chickens get names and become pets. Of course, anyone thinking about chickens should check local ordinances to be clear about how many you can have.

Chickens, unlike romping dogs, can make a commendable contribution to the garden: They eat slugs.

It's all about trade-offs.

MARCH 5, 2009

SCARED SILLY
Halloween flamingos? To some folks, a faux flock is a treat

HALLOWEEN WAS PRETTY SCARY AT OUR house, thanks to reader Linda Mann. She left us two black flamingos with their skeletons showing.

I kid you not. If florid pink gets to you, a skeletonized flamingo should really curdle your good-taste buds. I have certainly enjoyed reader response to my flamingo flock. The stories have been fabulous.

One garden visitor, who comes from the South, told me that the local fire department has a flamingo mascot near its door, but this one is painted white with black dots.

> *I happen to believe that silliness is good for the soul.*

Another reader recalled a couple who lived in a posh neighborhood, who got a note in the mail. The note opined that the couple's pair of flamingos was not "respectful" of the taste and elegance of the neighborhood. Within the week, every house up and down the street sported a pair of flamingos. Except one house. Hoo hah.

One reader wrote that as she aged, she took to heart that little essay about wearing purple.

So she painted all her flamingos purple. She says the weight of the paint keeps them from flying south, although she believes they are molting since the pink now shows through.

Linda Mann's Halloween flamingos.

When I mentioned my little flock was flying south to winter in Las Vegas, some thought they wouldn't be back and even offered to adopt them. I had to explain that Las Vegas is where flamingos go to feel at home in winter. That's because florid pink or florid anything is like camouflage there. They'll be back when they run out of money.

One reader wrote of driving past a "chorus line" of flamingos encircling a house. The line seemed to grow each time she drove by. Inevitably the neighbors must have complained, because one winter's day our reader drove past and was startled to see the flamingos gone. In their place was a line of skating penguins, lit from within, by the way. Now there's the perfect squelch.

The sorriest tales, and there are many, are of flamingo kidnappings. One lady had flamingos peeking out through the openings in her picket fence. One day they disappeared. Some taste arbiters seem to think it's OK to steal flamingos.

Do we flamingo herders go around stealing moose heads, velvet paintings of Elvis, or toilet bowl planters? Of course not. We are honorable people who just want to enjoy the occasional and harmless silliness.

I happen to believe that silliness is good for the soul. Some seem to think a garden should have stone statues of gods and goddesses as in those revered English gardens. But who knows what frolics those creatures are getting up to in the night. Haven't you ever wondered why, in the morning, those little stone milkmaids won't look you in the eye?

At least my friends don't harass me. They simply do not speak of this fling I am having with flamingos. They may purse their lips, and I do believe I've seen a little eye rolling, but that's about it.

Well, that's not quite true. At least one friend wants to throttle me because her husband, Mike, feels that my having acquired flamingos gives him license to get some of his own.

All I can say is, go Mike!

NOVEMBER 5, 2009

TIME REPAINTS THE GARDEN
The view evolves with yearly applications of love and dedication

I FELL ASLEEP ONE DAY AND, LIKE RIP VAN Winkle, awoke to a brand-new world. I seemed to be in someone else's garden. My old-fashioned English cottage garden full of flowers had disappeared. I wouldn't even remember what it looked like if I didn't have a painting I commissioned by local artist Sharon Engel nearly 20 years ago.

Hydrangea, a favorite.

It's a lovely picture, and I recommend that everyone memorialize their early garden with a photograph or painting. It's a lot of fun to look back and see how the garden has been transformed over time. There I am, in a purple flowered dress with something that hasn't been seen in years—a, gasp, waistline. I wonder if I really had one or if the artist was being kind.

The painting shows a long flowerbed full of color with yellow yarrow, blue delphiniums and tall red somethings. I can't quite tell because the painting is in an Impressionist style, although taken as a whole, it accurately captures that early garden.

But that was not the garden I saw when I awoke. No, this new garden had few flowers. It was an explosion of shrubs, some huge and lush like my beloved mock orange (*Philadelphus*), smoke tree (*Cotinus*), elderberry (*Sambucus*), euonymus, and silvery willow (*Salix*). Others were diminutive but bright spots—barberry (*Berberis*), weigela, daphne, spirea—all quite common. And, of course, hydrangeas everywhere. They do seem to be the perfect plant for the Northwest.

What this new garden lacked in color, it has made up for in lushness. I do admit to intentionally inserting more shrubs and small trees after seeing the stunning borders in England. But I do not remember inviting a shrubbery takeover.

There's an ongoing joke in our house, only it didn't start out as a joke. I'll ask my husband if he's seen my glasses or the book I was reading or my car keys. He'll respond, "Well, where did you put them?" I'd answer in an exasperated voice, "If I knew, I wouldn't be asking you, would I?"

This scene replays itself as Doug the Wonder Guy and I gaze at an empty patch of ground or an exceedingly dead shrub. I'll ask DTWG what it was, and sometimes he has an answer and sometimes neither of us does. These days when we see a barren spot, we just insert a shrub. We've also taken to putting small trees and shrubs and even perennials in pots and moving them around as the season calls out for color spots.

You'd be surprised at how many flowers do quite well potted. This year DTWG made a garden of clustered pots on the front terrace. The banana trees set the tone. It is truly over the top with Chinese lanterns, exotic plants and lots of big leaves. But after this winter, a bit of the tropics does one's heart good.

I'm afraid Northwest gardeners have a new motto. It used to be, "You should have been here last week." Now it's "At least it's not raining."

JUNE 4, 2011

ENERGY SAVER

A grand discovery: the nap

AT MY AGE, NOT EVERY CHORE MAKES MY list.

The Perp isn't the only one who is growing old. In a few weeks I will turn 65, which isn't the big deal it once was. They say 65 is the new 50.

Still, the other day I was ruing the fact that I didn't start gardening at a much younger age so that I would have had several more years of "bendability." I just can't keep up with weeds and the irritating clumps of grass in the paths. I can bend down just so many times before my body rebels and screams, "Go directly to the kitchen and eat some ice cream."

Then there's the energy level. The front bed hasn't been satisfactory, and I think it's because the soil isn't good. Everything really needs to be lifted out so that I can dig in more compost. I did that years ago when the plants in the back bed weren't robust. Refreshing the soil worked wonders.

But, alas, I simply don't have the energy anymore, or the muscles. This became very apparent when, on a recent weekend, my husband and I took turns sprawling flat on our stomachs reaching down a hole to dig out the master turnoff knobs for the sprinkling system.

I won't even talk about how long it took to lurch up from that prone position, and lurch is appropriately descriptive. Ever since that adventure, I have had a sore shoulder and he has had sore knees. We managed to uncover one of the knobs, but we had to leave the other to Doug the Wonder Boy.

But even he isn't getting younger. He reminded me the other day that he is just two years from 40. I told him that once he hits 40, I will have to start calling him Doug the Wonder Man. He said he'd prefer the Wonder Guy. Sometimes people ask if he minds my nickname for him. All I can say is, he is a man of easy temperament. Also, I notice that he has taken to referring to his new dog as Flora the Wonder Dog. So I think that says something about his sense of humor.

There is something about autumn that increases my awareness of aging. Perhaps it's simply because the year is aging. But autumn also reminds me of the good things about an aging garden. With age, the garden has become abundant, bountiful, profuse.

Haul a light basket for collecting weeds and other debris.

The Perp.

Of course, the gardener also has become more abundant, and that ice cream sitting in the refrigerator—the cure-all for all stresses—may have something to do with that. This may also account for the gardener's lack of "bendability."

Nevertheless, there are some benefits to aging. The competitive urge is gone. I'm quite happy to have a somewhat messy garden, and don't feel I have to scramble and roll up the hoses if someone comes by. I have become much more pragmatic. If I don't have the energy to dig up the front border, then I'll just focus on plants that dig their toes into clay soil and make the best of it. I don't feel I must have every new plant that comes along. (Oh, did I really say that, and do I really mean that? Next spring will be the test.)

These days the garden benches are actually getting some use. I never used to stop and just sit in the garden. I always had to spring up and pull a weed or stake up something. Now I am content to let it go.

Oh, and I've discovered an exotic new luxury: Napping. Napping is an especially fine experience in the garden. During good weather, I sprawl on some pillows in my little "bus stop" bench shelter. It gets a little crowded with Hector and the cats, but it's deliciously comfortable.

The air smells so fresh. The sounds of the neighborhood—children playing somewhere, geese squawking as they fly south, squirrels chattering—make for a lovely lullaby. Napping in a garden is a very sensuous experience, with the scents and sounds and touch of breeze. If I didn't have my bus stop, I'd definitely invest in a hammock.

It is also interesting to note how one's idea of "sensuous" changes. Now it is a nap in the open air. It used to be an evening with Harrison Ford.

OCTOBER 5, 2006

GARDENS OF THE HEART
A single golden afternoon can blossom into a lifelong dream

I MUST WARN YOU. WHAT YOU ARE ABOUT TO read is sentimental drivel, and if that sort of thing puts you off, then proceed no further.

But I suspect that many of you, like me, have two gardens, an actual garden and the garden of your heart. The garden of our heart is some ideal we hold in our dreams and imagine as we fall pleasantly asleep after an active day.

It may have been inspired by a half-remembered garden from our childhood, a garden we visited in an English village, or even a picture in a storybook or magazine. Autumn always reminds me of my dream garden, because it is the season when I realized I had such a dream.

It happened on a lovely sunny autumn day nearly 50 years ago when I was in college. One Saturday afternoon, my boyfriend (now my husband) and his roommate along with me and my roommate decided to go out for a drive. My husband's roommate had an aunt and uncle who lived somewhere in the country around Eugene.

We traveled through dazzling autumn foliage and tawny fields dotted with pumpkins and arrived in late afternoon at an old but nicely maintained farmhouse set among lovely golden trees. Late summer flowers nestled against a picket fence. A mist was rising from the ground, giving everything a soft, blurry quality. I felt as if I'd tumbled into Brigadoon, the mythical Scottish village that wakes up once a century.

As we sat in the kitchen sipping cider, I knew I wanted to live in a place like this, and for years I've recalled that golden afternoon.

> *It was as if I had slipped into a magical time and place.*

There are also villages of the heart, places filled with those clichéd rose-covered cottages. One imagines they are places where Miss Marple might have traded cuttings with her neighbors when she wasn't tackling grisly murders. In fact, I am devoted to the English television series *Midsomer Murders*, despite the always improbable and often incomprehensible plots. But the series redeems itself because it is set in those perfect English villages with gardens galore.

Sometimes, however, these dream places are right under our noses.

I thought of this when I was invited to speak to the St. Paul Garden Club a couple of years ago. As soon as I turned off the high-way, it was as if I had slipped into a magical time and place. I drove through golden fields and bits of woods. It was sublimely lovely and peaceful.

My hostess, Marian Kuch, took me to some nurseries, but the highlight was a visit to one of her friends, who she said had the prettiest garden in St. Paul. As we drove up to a white farmhouse with a generous front porch and green shutters, I knew I had found another garden of my heart.

We sat and sipped iced tea and ate yummy chocolate treats out back in a little garden house full of recycled windows overlooking fields and hills in the distance.

That night, 30 people showed up to the garden club, a remarkable attendance when you realize that in 2000, according to the census, St. Paul had a population of 354, or just 123 households, and I haven't heard of a major population boom since then. Earlier this spring, 26 people showed up when the garden club called for volunteers to spread mulch and prune around the community hall. Big-city garden clubs would be hard-pressed to muster such a work party.

Dreaming about these enchanting gardens and villages like St. Paul will help me get through the coming gray months. I will cling to the thought that our drippy climate is the stuff that dream gardens are made of. I will dream of my pleasant afternoon in St. Paul and hope the gardeners there don't stumble on as many dead bodies as Miss Marple.

NOVEMBER 6, 2008

CALL IT GOOD

A day for thanks pushes me to focus on the positive

FOR MOST OF MY LIFE, I'VE TAKEN THANKS-giving for granted. It's been a day of family, friends and feasting. But finally I am gaining a bit of appreciation for the whole idea of Thanksgiving, a day to be grateful, to be positive and to be optimistic. What a great idea.

From a gardening perspective, I am thankful for many things. I am thankful:

For our seasons, including winter. Otherwise, I wouldn't appreciate spring so much.

For furry garden companions, even though they lack a certain (read: all) discipline. Ernie the dog has turned out to be a digger, and I've had to replant the tulips twice. Wilbur the cat has taken to jumping on visitors' shoulders, and his brother, Orville, petitions guests to carry him around.

For a husband who never asks, "How much did that cost?" or "Where will you put it?" or "Do we really need that?" Need? When has need ever figured into things?

For Doug the Wonder Guy and Jimmy the Handy Guy, both of whom help keep this old house and garden together, but most of all because they have begun to view it as their garden as well and take real pride in it. It's like having sons that I don't have to pay college tuition for.

For readers who write, "Dulcy, can I call you that? I feel like I know you." Hey, if you said "Mrs. Mahar," I'd look around to see if my mother-in-law had come back to life.

For those plants that grow despite lousy soil, too much or too little water, imperfect light and general neglect. Let's hear it for those maligned daylilies.

For those people who open their gardens. Whether it's at a grand estate or a tiny cottage, I never fail to feel inspired.

For our rain; yes, even that. It creates the lush world we Northwesterners thrive in, plus it gives us something to complain about. There are few things more satisfying than a good whine.

For a climate that allows such great plant diversity. That way you won't notice the lack of penstemons and other failures in my garden. You'll just think I didn't have room for them.

For an education from the nuns despite their rigidity. Where else would I have been forced to take four years of Latin, and who would have known it would turn out to be useful?

For all the young and new gardeners coming on the scene, bringing excitement, pizazz and amazing inventiveness to garden design and, dare I say that overworked word, sustainability.

For my gardening friends, because it means that I can have multiple vicarious gardens, ranging from my neighbor Rosemary's old-fashioned cottage garden to my friend Carol's grand country garden with its two-acre pond.

For the greatest cure for insomnia, which

is to fall asleep thinking about what next to do in the garden.

For the thrill I still get out of my garden. These days, rather than new-plant lust, the thrill is most likely to come from editing something out and suddenly seeing a wonderful new space.

For the fact that slugs aren't the size of cats and don't have cute fur.

NOVEMBER 26, 2009

A time and place for reflecting on the good in your life.

Q & A

Q: *Everything is blooming a month early. What can I plant now (late July) that will give me some interest if we have a warm fall?*

A: There's still time to plant annuals. This late in the year, the temptation is to pick the biggest plants, which is fine if they're compact and bushy. But avoid plants that have just gotten tall and straggly in their trays. They'll stay that way when transplanted into the garden. Ornamental grasses are another choice for late-season interest. Many grasses flower in August and September. Even those that don't flower have a muted, hazy look that's ideal for the late summer and autumn garden.

Q: *How can I keep my vine vegetables from rotting?*

A: Keep them off the ground. If cucumber, squash, and tomato vines have gotten too heavy to train on supports, put pieces of wood, pavers, or some other nonmetal, waterproof material under the ripening fruit.

Q: *Because of the ban on watering lawns, I have shut down my sprinklers and am now hand-watering my flowers. How can I tell when I have enough water?*

A: The day after watering, scratch the soil, which may be dry on top. Dig your finger two inches down. If your soil is moist at that depth, you have watered adequately.

Q: *I have heard that trees need water to survive the drought. How do I water my street trees without watering the strip of lawn between the street and sidewalk?*

A: Girdle the tree with a drip hose, rather than using a sprinkler. Established trees should have deep roots and will need a deep soaking only once or twice during this season. If soil is compacted around the tree, drill holes in the ground to aid water penetration.

Q: *How often should I fertilize chrysanthemums?*

A: Fertilize them every two weeks with a di-luted-strength fertilizer; then hold off on more fertilizer once the buds show color.

Q: *What's the difference between a clone and a hybrid?*

A: A cloned plant is produced from one parent and will have identical genetic characteristics. For example, if you take root cuttings from one plant, you are cloning. A hybrid is a cross between two genetically distinct plants. It may resemble its parents, but will have unique characteristics of its own. Put a simpler way, with a clone, you are duplicating a plant. With a hybrid, you are creating a new plant.

Q: *The flowers on my lavender plant are dried. Is it safe to cut them back?*

A: You can do more than cut the flowers off. The entire lavender plant can be sheared back several inches with clippers once it has bloomed. This will keep it full and compact. Otherwise, lavender can get leggy with bare woody stems. If sheared early enough, lavender will bloom again, although not as abundantly.

Q: *I have heard that you can change the color of hydrangea blossoms. True?*

A: Despite popular belief, not all hydrangeas can be made to change flower colors with soil additives. The common hydrangea (*H. macrophylla*) will change from pink to blue and back, depending on the soil. Aluminum sulfate added to the soil before bloom will produce blue flowers. Because aluminum is better absorbed in acid soil like ours, hydrangeas in this area generally are blue. The addition of lime, which changes acid soil to neutral or alkaline soil, will produce pink flowers.

Q: *Why is it necessary to rotate vegetable crops?*

A: Vegetables have different nutritional needs and are susceptible to different diseases and pests. When you plant the same vegetables year after year in the same spot, they leach all the nutrients out of the soil. By rotating crops, you give the nutrients an opportunity to replenish. Also, in the absence of the same crop, the pests and diseases present in the soil will taper off.

Q: *My honeysuckle and clematis have gotten sort of brown. Is it OK to cut them back now?*

A: Yes, but do it right now, in August. If you wait until autumn, cut back only growth that is clearly dead. Don't cut back anything green just before frost or you will trigger new growth and delay dormancy. This will make the plant more vulnerable to cold damage. If you have green growth in autumn that needs pruning or cutting back, wait until spring.

Q: *What can I do with a large tree stump? It would be too costly to remove.*

A: Either hide it or play it up. To hide it, make it the support for a colorful but dense vine such as honeysuckle, a small-flowered clematis or the beautiful *Actinidia kolomikta*. The last, a member of the kiwi family, has heart-shaped leaves tinged with pink. To play up the stump, stick a pretty flat bowl on top to serve as a birdbath or use the stump as a platform for a potted plant or a piece of garden sculpture.

Q: *When should I stop cutting roses?*

A: Stop cutting roses in October. This will allow them to form hips, a process that will trigger the plants to go dormant so that they can better withstand the coming frost.

Q: *I am going to need to divide my hostas this fall. Anything special I should know?*

A: Hostas are tough and very easy to divide. Dig up the clump, leaving as much soil around roots as possible. Take a sharp knife and cut vertically through the roots in one or more sections. Replant hostas in a semi-shady area in soil that has been worked with organic matter. Wait until the heat subsides, but don't wait too long in the season to divide hostas. Their leaves die back entirely, and you may not be able to find them.

Q: *Should I cut back the dead hydrangea flowers now, in September?*

A: Unless they really bother you, it is healthier for the plant to leave the dried flowers on until next spring. Some hydrangeas bloom on old wood, so just cut back the dead blossoms in spring, leaving the new buds. Generally, hydrangeas don't need pruning unless they have gotten very twiggy. If that's the case, in spring cut out some of the old wood rather than shearing the plant back.

Q: *How far should I prune my roses in fall?*

A: Prune roses enough to prevent wind damage now. Hybrid teas, which are shallow-rooted, need special attention. If they get too tall, the wind will rock them back and forth, which could uproot them. Save hard pruning for late February or early March.

Q: *I see pictures in decorating magazines of potted foxgloves and other flowers in pots. Can I grow flowering garden plants indoors during the winter?*

A: Unless you use special lighting on timers, you won't be able to bring most outdoor flowers to bloom indoors. The plants depend on the length of daylight as much as temperatures for bloom. If, however, you find already-blooming plants in pots, they may last quite a while outdoors.

Q: *How long can a cut Christmas tree stay indoors safely?*

A: A tree becomes a fire hazard when its needles lose their springy feeling, start dropping heavily or there are signs of browning. Keep the tree fresh longer by making a new cut at the base when you bring it home and keeping the trunk in water at least an inch above the bottom. This way a tree should stay fresh a month, unless it is directly in front of a heat source. But remember, even a fresh tree is unsafe when there are frayed electric lighting cords or candles on the tree.

Q: *Is it time to bring in my houseplants that have been outdoors?*

A: Indoor plants should be brought indoors by mid-November, and earlier if the weather service indicates very low night temperatures. Be sure to wash off the plants before bringing them inside, or you also will be inviting a community of bugs into your house.

Q: *When can I put in bare root plants?*

A: Bare root plants can be put in when the garden is dormant, generally from late December to mid-February. Don't plant when the ground is frozen or waterlogged. When you do plant, put in plenty of organic material to ensure good drainage. Reputable nurseries will not offer bare root plants for sale unless it is safe to plant them.

Q: *With tiny bulbs, is there a trick to get them to sit upright when you plant them?*

A: The flat base of a bulb is the bottom, and the pointed end that sends up leaves is the top. Ideally, bulbs should sit in the soil in that position. But most will grow no matter how they sit. The shoot end will send out leaves that curve around and go up to the top if the bulb is upside down. When making mass plantings with tiny bulbs, don't worry too much how they lie. The majority will do just fine.

Q: *How can I make hardwood cuttings of shrubs?*

A: Take about a half-foot of a branch and dip the cut end in a rooting hormone sold commercially for this purpose. Insert the ends in moist sand or a seedling soil mix and don't let it dry out. Bottom heat through coils sold by greenhouse suppliers will help speed root development.

Q: *Is there a quick, inexpensive way to add extra insulation to my greenhouse?*

A: Tape clear plastic sheeting to the inside of your greenhouse. The sheeting should be slightly loose to allow air space for insulation. But the edges should be taped securely to minimize heat loss. This is not a substitute for thermal panes, but it will help.

Q: *My Christmas cactus bloomed profusely last year when I got it but now shows no signs of blooming this year. What's wrong?*

A: Christmas cactus needs a rest period to bloom again. Normally, the plant blooms November-January. In February and March, it should be kept in a cool but not freezing place, with almost no water. In April, bring the cactus back into a warmer, lighter atmosphere and water when the soil is dry. Put the plant outdoors in summer to set buds; then bring indoors in the fall.

Q: *Is it safe to prune in winter?*

A: It's safe to prune in winter because trees and shrubs are dormant. Fall is the riskiest time because it's still warm enough that new growth may start, then freeze back. Winter is an especially good time to prune deciduous trees and shrubs because you can see the branch patterns best.

Q: *Will last summer's drought cause problems in the coming winter?*

A: The drought created substantial stress, so that less hardy plants may be more vulnerable to cold than usual. The long, hot summer also sustained longer bloom periods, and some flowers may have exhausted themselves. It will be interesting to see how the long-blooming lavatera holds up. Lawns were not in the healthiest state going into winter and may emerge in spring with more thin spots and more susceptibility to weeds.

Q: *I overdosed my lawn on fertilizer and burned it badly, causing huge yellow patches. Do I need to put in a new lawn in those areas?*

A: If you're willing to be patient, you don't need to put in new lawn. Eventually, the lawn will come back. You can hasten the process by raking out thatch (which will make it look even worse for a while) and keeping the lawn well watered.

Q: *I don't like hot colors. Are there any soft pastel flowers that I could plant this late that would still bloom this year?*

A: Yes, Japanese anemones come in pale pink

and white. They are perennials, and if you get big enough starts, they should bloom this year. Other perennials include veronica, blooming now, and the asters that will bloom in late summer. They come in white, pinks, mauves and purples. Among the annuals, good choices are cosmos (lavender or white) and white nicotiana for soft effects.

Q: *How do I keep raccoons from eating the fish in my pond?*

A: This is an increasing problem as more people install ponds and find that raccoons aren't limited to a few woodsy parts of the city. A net especially made to keep raccoons and herons out of ponds is sold at some garden and fish-supply centers. It must be well anchored on the edges, because raccoons are extremely adept at removing obstacles. Another help is to have a deep spot (about 3 feet) near the center of the pool that is partially hidden by a flat rock shelf. Raccoons are waders, but they don't like to swim. This will give the fish a place to hide from marauders.

Q: *I'm planning an herb garden, but I understand some herbs will take over. Which ones should I watch out for?*

A: Anything in the mint family is invasive, including some members of the family that aren't labeled mints, such as lemon balm. It's best to plant these in tubs where their roots can be contained. Other invasive herbs can't be contained in tubs because they spread by seeds, not roots. Examples are purple fennel and borage. Fennel is a beautiful plant, but it is invasive and has a deep taproot that makes it hard to get out. At least borage pulls out easily. Herbs that are used for ground covers, such as sweet woodruff, also spread.

Q: *I bought a beautiful bleeding heart this spring, but now it seems to be dying. What happened?*

A: Some perennials die back after flowering, while others remain green until frost. It is normal for bleeding hearts and Oriental poppies to die completely back. They will return and bloom next spring. Like bulbs, they should be planted toward the middle or back of a border where other plants will cover their dead foliage.

Q: *When a book says a plant requires full sun, how much sunlight does that really mean?*

A: For sun-lovers, such as roses, it means at least six hours of sun a day. Many sun plants also can grow in high dappled shade where some sunlight filters through. The best growing conditions are in beds that get the morning sun (called the growing sun) and some shade against the strong afternoon sun.

Q: *I see hollyhocks growing in cracks in sidewalks, but I can't get them to grow in my garden. What am I doing wrong?*

A: You may be killing your hollyhocks with kindness. Some plants don't like rich soil. (This is also true of nasturtiums.) Hollyhocks are highly susceptible to a fungus called rust. They don't do well in a mixed border. Instead, plant them where they get plenty of air circulation to prevent rust.

Q: *Several plant diseases seem to come from fungus. What is it?*

A: Fungi are plants that have no chlorophyll, therefore no green color. That means they can't produce their own food, so they are parasites that live on other plants or decaying material. Reproductive spores are carried on the wind. Some fungi are beneficial; for example, they break down organic material in compost piles. But others carry or make plants susceptible to diseases such as the common rust, black spot, blight, and mildew. The parts of plants affected with these diseases should be cut off, placed in a plastic bag and put in the garbage, not the compost pile.

Q: *I have several dahlias. Do I have to dig them up each fall and replant every spring?*

A: No. The lower elevations of the Willamette Valley are usually warm enough so that dahlias can survive winters in the ground. Many even survived last winter. However, they are not guaranteed winter-hardy like perennials. So if you have a particularly prized or hard-to-get dahlia, dig it up to be on the safe side.

DULCY'S FAVORITE GARDEN READS

Books are the next best thing to planting

These guides to garden spaces open to the public don't have the drop-dead-gorgeous photos of Carolyn Starner's *Emerald Journey*, but they offer far more places of interest:

Green Afternoons, by Amy Houchen (Oregon State University Press)

Garden Touring in the Pacific Northwest, by Jan Kowalczewski Whitner (Alaska Northwest Books)

Public and Private Gardens of the Northwest, by Myrna Oakley (Beautiful America Publishing)

SEPTEMBER 23, 2004

If you are a garden reader/researcher, here are my recommendations for a solid all-around reference library—not for the professional, but for, let us say, the earnest gardener.

The Plant Locator Western Region, compiled by Susan Hill and Susan Narizny (Timber Press). This handy reference lists more than 50,000 plants by botanical name and provides a key to nurseries where they can be found throughout the Western states. I find I use it as much for the comprehensive list of nurseries in the back.

Flora: A Gardener's Encyclopedia, with Sean Hogan listed as chief consultant (Timber Press). This book has become an overnight "must have" in the garden world despite its hefty two-volume size and $100 price tag. More than 20,000 plants are listed.

Sunset Western Garden Book, edited by Kathleen Norris Brenzel (Sunset Publishing). This is the Dick and Jane of gardening books that young gardeners grow up on. It has a wealth of information about climate zones in the West and what plants will do best in our specific conditions—not just cold hardiness, but also summer temperatures, precipitation patterns and more.

The Pacific Northwest Gardener's Book of Lists, compiled by Ray and Jan McNeilan (Taylor Publishing). This book has 200 lists that answer questions specific to the Northwest. The authors are prominent in Northwest garden circles, and Ray McNeilan coordinated Oregon's master gardener program for two decades.

The Oxford Companion to Gardens, edited by Geoffrey and Susan Jellicoe (Oxford University Press). This is a garden dictionary, not a plant dictionary. Among its alphabetical listings are famous gardens, famous gardeners, schools of design and much more.. It's a good read even if you're not a plants person.

Dictionary of Plant Names, compiled by Allen J. Coombes (Timber Press). It's a spelling and pronunciation guide that also includes common names of plants. I should use it more.

Botany for Gardeners, by Brian Capon (Timber Press). Here's the book for those of you who, like me, slept through their college botany class. If you're a science-minded sort or pollinator or propagator, this gives you the basic facts of life about plants.

Taylor's Dictionary for Gardeners, edited by Frances Tenenbaum (Houghton Mifflin). This dictionary is useful for the everyday gardener who wants to know what all those terms one sees in gardening books mean.

The Story of Gardening, by Penelope Hobhouse (DK Publishing). Hobhouse explores how different cultures have approached and influenced gardening.

NOVEMBER 18, 2004

My favorite book purchases of the past year:

The Jewel Box Garden, by Thomas Hobbs (Timber Press). Hands down, for me this is the most exciting garden book published in the past year. With so many garden books on the shelves, it's a joyous event to find one that is "original." This swoon-worthy book is that rarity that combines great writing and great pictures.

Gardening with Clematis, by Linda Beutler (Timber Press). Who doesn't love clematis? Almost no one, to judge by the number of people dancing away from spring plant sales with little vines on a stick.

Cass Turnbull's Guide to Pruning, by Cass Turnbull (Sasquatch Books). Turnbull's style is humorous and conversational, and she really takes the mystery out of pruning, whether it's guiding a new plant or rehabilitating an older one.

Annuals and Tender Plants for North American Gardens, by Wayne Winterrowd (Random House). What makes this book great are the "up close and personal" plant profiles complete with etymologies, histories, lore and design tips.

Emerald Journey: A Walk through Northwest Gardens, by Carolyn Starner (Greenstem Press). This book put me over the top. Starner, an interior designer who lives in Washington, presents 34 Northwest gardens open to the public.

The Collector's Garden, by Ken Druse (Timber Press). Technically, this is not a new book.

But it is newly published in paperback this year, and since I am writing this, I can make up the rules. It may be my all-time favorite garden book, and the American Horticultural Society named it Book of the Year in 1997.

NOVEMBER 25, 2004

The Year in Bloom by Ann Lovejoy (Sasquatch Books) proved transformative with its series of lyrical essays. Lovejoy didn't so much preach plant diversity as lure us into it with her rhapsodizing descriptions. Here was someone who lived in the Northwest and knew what we were up against.

DECEMBER 11, 2008

One of my new books is Valerie Easton's *The New Low-Maintenance Garden* (Timber Press). I haven't yet read it, but it has gotten good reviews. I'd come to appreciate Easton's work after reading a collection of her garden columns for the *Seattle Times*' "Pacific Northwest Magazine."

Anything written by Beverley Nichols will do. Other great bedtime reads include *Green Thoughts* by Eleanor Perenyi, *The Gardener's Year* by Karel Capek and—my very favorite—*Old Herbaceous* by Reginald Arkell. These are just scratching the surface.

JANUARY 14, 2010

DEAR DULCY

A sampling of letters from friends and fans

It's hard to know where to start to express what an inspiration your wit, humor and sound advice have meant to us. . . . We retired to a Portland condo in 2000. To fulfill our gardening needs we joined a Community Garden and became official "dead-headers" in the Washington Park International Rose Test Garden. But after six years in the condo, with 50 or more pots, including eight large trees on our decks, we realized that we needed to get back to a place with a garden. Hence our move to Vancouver in 2006.

The former owners were not gardeners, with cloth and bark everywhere, grass and just a tree or two—plus thorny shrubs outside the front windows to discourage robbers. It was ugly.

You inspired and informed us as we pulled out all the lawn and bark, ripped up the ground cloth and began our great adventure of developing our lovely gardens. Your columns have brought much beauty into our lives, and your legacy is great in the world of gardeners.

—Marilynn Gordon, Vancouver, Wash.

Just want you to know that I, though less than an avid gardener, would not miss reading your column. You have not only helped me overcome a guilt trip for being far from a high achiever in the garden, but to not be afraid to move or toss something that was not working.

—Virginia J. McBride, Beavercreek, Ore.

What I write is unbelievable, but very true. I want to share it, as it pertains to Dulcy. At least, that is what I accept as fact. A few weeks ago, a pink flamingo showed up in my backyard, which is fenced with locked gates. I forgot to mention that the bird was placed by my pool. Where did it come from? How did it get into my backyard? I believe it has something to do with Dulcy. Therefore, I have named my surprise gift in honor for this special woman who wrote with such wit and charm.

—Donna Keltz, Portland, Ore.

I'm from central Minnesota. My sister, also a gardener, lives in Portland. She mails Dulcy's columns to me, and I glean what I can for my Zone 3 garden. I love her sense of humor and have adopted her "plant lust" phrase.

—Margaret Grefe, Ottertail, Minn.

This woman is a rare jewel and absolutely one-of-a-kind. What do I love about Dulcy Mahar? Let me count the ways, in no particular order. Perhaps her humor grabbed me first, many, many years ago. Dulcy describes situations (including "dear husband") we gardeners understand and laugh at. Doug the Wonder Boy/Guy—we all wanted him. She is so lucky to have him, but she knows that. The goldfish story a few years back; the outdoor pond with neighbor Rosemary and the goldfish doctor. I still laugh to think of it. I cannot be alone in keeping so many Dulcy columns on my gardening bookshelf. Lucky am I to have a friend who clips and mails me each of Dulcy's columns. It is the highlight of my week.

—Barbara B. Stickler, gardening up the Coos River at the Elliot State Forest, Ore.

I am a 95-year-old widow (three years after 70 years married to the same man), and this is my first and probably last fan letter. I wanted you to know I have enjoyed your column for many years. I love your humor and attitude—and your advice. At this point in my life, and in in the same house for 49 years, I don't antici-pate any changes in the yard. Now it's a matter of maintenance, weeding and trimming. I am fortunate in having had the same good man do my yard work for 11 years. After he finishes work, we sit at the kitchen table, and he has a beer, and we have a good visit. He is probably like your Doug.

> —*Irene Buchanan*, Lebanon, Ore.

I am 76 years old. I have been reading your column for 20 years. I don't know the name of any other garden writer. I like that you believe in digging up lawn. And I'm glad to know there are "easy" plants that fail for you. I have quoted you to friends, but less about your advice than your unpretentious humor. When I saw the pic-ture of you and Wilbur "at work" (saved it), I knew I love you.

> —*Sandra Hoyt*, Salem, Ore.

As I anticipated Dulcy's column, you might think I am a gardener. Wrong. I don't know a peony from marigold. (They're not really the same, are they?) No, I read Dulcy for her sense of humor, her writing pizzazz, because she is a great cat-lover, and because I always wished I could be in her suitcase when she jetted off to Luau Land. Two of her passions are also mine (cats, Hawaii), and I have enjoyed her burning passion with every blade of my grass. My thoughts and prayers are with Dulcy, Ted, and their four-legged children.

> —*Carol Paul*, Portland, Ore.

I am so sorry to hear of Dulcy's passing. I will miss her writing, as I have missed yours, Ted. Dulcy contributed greatly to the culture of our state.

> —*Ginger Johnston*,
> retired *Oregonian* editor,
> Portland, Ore.

INDEX

LISTING OF COLUMNS BY DATE